Multicultural America

Volume V
The Jewish Americans

Multicultural America

Volume V
The Jewish Americans

Rodney P. Carlisle
GENERAL EDITOR

Facts On File
An imprint of Infobase Publishing

Multicultural America: Volume V: The Jewish Americans
Copyright © 2011 by Infobase Publishing

Facts On File, Inc.
An Imprint of Infobase Publishing
132 West 31st Street
New York, NY 10001

Library of Congress Cataloging-in-Publication Data
Multicultural America / Rodney P. Carlisle, general editor.
   v. cm.
   Includes bibliographical references and index.
   Contents: v. 1. The Hispanic Americans — v. 2. The Arab Americans —
v. 3. The African Americans — v. 4. The Asian Americans — v. 5. The
Jewish Americans — v. 6. The European Americans — v. 7. The Native
Americans.
   ISBN 978-0-8160-7811-0 (v. 1 : hardcover : alk. paper) — ISBN
978-0-8160-7812-7 (v. 2 : hardcover : alk. paper) — ISBN
978-0-8160-7813-4 (v. 3 : hardcover : alk. paper) — ISBN
978-0-8160-7814-1 (v. 4 : hardcover : alk. paper) — ISBN
978-0-8160-7815-8 (v. 5 : hardcover : alk. paper) — ISBN
978-0-8160-7816-5 (v. 6 : hardcover : alk. paper) — ISBN
978-0-8160-7817-2 (v. 7 : hardcover : alk. paper) 1.
Minorities—United States—History—Juvenile literature. 2.
Ethnology—United States—History—Juvenile literature. 3. Cultural
pluralism—United States—History—Juvenile literature. 4. United
States—Ethnic relations—Juvenile literature. I. Carlisle, Rodney P.
   E184.A1M814 2011
   305.800973—dc22   2010012694

Text design and composition by Golson Media
Cover printed by Art Print, Taylor, PA
Book printed and bound by Maple Press, York, PA
Date Printed: March 2011
Printed in the United States of America

11 10 9 8 7 6 5 4 3 2 1

This book is printed on acid-free paper.

CONTENTS

Volume V

The Jewish Americans

PREFACE

AMERICANS HAVE HAD a sense that they were a unique people, even before the American Revolution. In the 18th century, the settlers in the 13 colonies that became the United States of America began to call themselves Americans, recognizing that they were not simply British colonists living in North America. In addition to the English, other cultures and peoples had already begun to contribute to the rich tapestry that would become the American people.

Swedes and Finns in the Delaware River valley, Dutch in New York, Scots-Irish, and Welsh had all brought their different ways of life, dress, diet, housing, and religions, adding them to the mix of Puritan and Anglican Englishmen. Lower Rhine German groups of dissenting Amish and Mennonites, attracted by the religious toleration of Pennsylvania, settled in Germantown, Pennsylvania, as early as 1685. Located on the western edge of Philadelphia, the settlers and later German immigrants moved to the counties just further west in what would become Pennsylvania Dutch country.

The policies of other colonies tended to favor and encourage such group settlement to varying extents. In some cases, as in New Jersey, the fact that each community could decide what church would be supported by local taxes tended to attract coreligionists to specific communities. Thus, in the colonial period, the counties of southern New Jersey (known in colonial times as West Jersey) tended to be dominated by Quakers. Townships in New Jersey closer to New York City were dominated by Lutheran, Dutch Reformed, and Anglican churches and settlers.

Ethnicity and religion divided the peoples of America, yet the official tolerance of religious diversity spawned a degree of mutual acceptance by one ethnic group of another. While crossreligious marriages were frowned upon, they were not prohibited, with individual families deciding which parents' church should be attended, if any. Modern descendants tracing their ancestry are sometimes astounded at the various strands of culture and religion that they find woven together.

To the south, Florida already had a rich Hispanic heritage, some of it filtered through Cuba. Smaller groups of immigrants from France and other countries in Europe were supplemented during the American Revolution by enthusiastic supporters of the idea of a republican experiment in the New World.

All of the 13 colonies had the institution of African slavery, and people of African ancestry, both slave and free, constituted as much as 40 percent of the population of colonies like Georgia and South Carolina. In a wave of acts of emancipation, slaves living in the New England colonies were freed in the years directly following the Revolution, soon joined by those in Pennsylvania, New York, and New Jersey. Although some African Americans in the south were free by birth or manumission, emancipation for 90 percent of those living south of Pennsylvania would have to wait until the Civil War, 1861–65. Forcibly captured and transported under terrible conditions overland and across the ocean, Africans came from dozens of different linguistic stocks. Despite the disruptions of the middle passage, African Americans retained elements of their separate cultures, including some language and language patterns, and aspects of diet, religion, family, and music.

Native Americans, like African Americans, found themselves excluded from most of the rights of citizenship in the new Republic. In the Ohio and Mississippi Valley, many Native Americans resisted the advance of the European-descended settlers. In Florida, Creeks and Seminoles provided haven to escaped slaves, and together, they fought the encroachment of settlers. Some of the African Americans living with the Seminoles and other tribes moved west with them on the Trail of Tears to Indian Territory in what later became the state of Oklahoma. Other groups, like the Lumbees of North Carolina, stayed put, gradually adjusting to the new society around them. Throughout scattered rural communities, clusters of biracial and triracial descendents could trace their roots to Native-American and African ancestors, as well as to the English and Scotch-Irish.

The Louisiana Purchase brought the vast Mississippi Valley into the United States, along with the cosmopolitan city of New Orleans, where French exiles from Canada had already established a strong Creole culture. With the annexation of Texas, and following the Mexican-American War (1846–48), the United States incorporated as citizens hundreds of thousands of people of Hispanic ancestry. Individuals and communities in Texas and New Mexico preserve not only their religion, but also their language, cuisine, customs, and architecture.

As the United States expanded to the west, with vast opportunities for settlement, waves of European immigrants contributed to the growth of the country, with liberal naturalization laws allowing immigrants to establish themselves as citizens. Following the revolutions of 1848 in Europe, and famines in Ireland, new floods of immigrants from Central Europe, Ireland, and Scandinavia all settled in pockets.

By the late 19th century, America had become a refuge for political and economic refugees, as well as enterprising families and individuals from many countries. More geographic-ethnic centers emerged, as new immigrants sought out friends and families who had already arrived, and settled near them. Neighborhoods and whole states took on some aspects of the ethnic cultures that the immigrants brought with them, with the Italians settling in New York City, San Francisco, and New Jersey; Azoreans and continental Portuguese in Rhode Island and southern Massachusetts; Scandinavians in Wisconsin and Minnesota; Germans in Missouri; and Chinese and Japanese in a number of West Coast cities and towns. San Francisco and Boston became known for their Irish settlers, and Italians joined Franco-Hispanic Catholics of New Orleans. In some other scattered communities, such as the fishing port of Monterey, California, later Portuguese and Italian arrivals were also absorbed into the local Hispanic community, partly through the natural affinity of the shared Catholic faith.

As waves of immigrants continued to flow into the United States from the 1880s to World War I, the issue of immigration became even more politicized. On the one hand, older well-established ethnic communities sometimes resented the growing influence and political power of the new immigrants. Political machines in the larger cities made it a practice to incorporate the new settlers, providing them with some access to the politics and employment of city hall, also expecting their votes and loyalty during election. The intricate interplay of ethnicity and politics through the late 19th century has been a rich field of historical research.

During the Progressive Era, American-born citizens of a liberal or progressive political inclination often had mixed feelings about immigrants. Those with a more elite set of values believed that crime, alcoholism, and a variety of vices running from drug abuse through prostitution, gambling, and underground sports such as cockfighting, all could be traced to the new immigrants. The solution, they believed, would be immigration reform: setting quotas that would restrict immigrants from all but Great Britain and northern Europe.

Other reformers took the position that the problems faced by new immigrants could be best dealt with through education, assistance, and social work. Still others approached the questions of poverty and adjustment of immigrants as part of the labor struggle, and believed that organizing through labor unions could bring pressure for better wages and working conditions. Meanwhile, immigrants continued to work through their churches, community organizations, and the complexities of American politics for recognition and rights.

Ultimately, two approaches emerged regarding how different ethnic groups would be viewed and how they would view themselves in America. For some, the idea of a melting pot had always held attraction. Under this way of thinking, all Americans would merge, with ethnic distinctions diminishing and the various cultures blending together to create a new American culture. Such a process of assimilation or integration appealed to many, both among American-born and immigrant groups. Others argued strongly that ethnic or racial identity should be preserved, with a sense of pride in heritage, so that America would continue to reflect its diversity, and so that particular groups would not forget their origins, traditions, and culture.

Whether an individual ethnic group should become homogenized, integrated, and assimilated into the total culture, or whether it should strive to maintain its own separate cultural identity, was often hotly debated. For some, like the Chinese, Native Americans, and African Americans, armed power of the state, law, and social discrimination tended to create and enforce separate communities and locales. For others, self-segregation and discrimination by other ethnic groups, and the natural process of settling near relatives and coreligionists led to definable ethnic regions and neighborhoods. Among such diverse groups as African Americans, Asians, Hispanics, Italians, Arab Americans, and Native Americans, leaders and spokesmen have debated the degree to which cultural identity should be sacrificed in the name of assimilation. In the 21st century, the debates have continued, sometimes with great controversy, at other times, the dialogues went on almost unnoticed by the rest of the country.

Armed conflict, race-wars, reservation policy, segregation, exclusion, and detention camps in time of war have shown the harsh and ugly side of enforced separation. Even though the multiethnic and multicultural heritage of the United States has been fraught with crisis and controversy, it has also been a source of strength.

With roots in so many cultures and with the many struggles to establish and maintain social justice, America has also represented some of the best aspirations of humanity to live in peace with one another. The search for social equity has been difficult, but the fact that the effort has continued for more than two centuries is in itself an achievement.

In this series on Multicultural America, each volume is dedicated to the history of one ethnocultural group, tracing through time the struggles against discrimination and for fair play, as well as the effort to preserve and cherish an independent cultural heritage.

THE JEWISH AMERICANS

The history of the American Jewish community is unlike that of other ethnic groups in the United States in that Judaism is both an ethnicity and a religion. It is possible to convert to Judaism, and many people of Jewish ancestry have converted to Christianity or to an entirely secular view of life, so most histories of Jews in America focus on the history of various Jewish ethnic lines of ancestry rather than simply on adherents to the faith. However, the fact that almost all people of Jewish ancestry who came to the United States practiced the religion has shaped the experience of this minority in unique ways.

Jewish Americans, like several other minorities in the United States, have faced spoken and unspoken discrimination, relying on the strengths of their cultural heritage to successfully adapt to the American environment. In the colonial period, the colonies worked out systems of religious tolerance, a rather unique practice for countries in Western civilization in the 17th and 18th century. Although some of the British colonies had a dominant sect of Christian religion by 1750, all allowed a variety of sects and religions to flourish side-by-side. In this environment, Jews (and Muslims) were able to establish non-Christian congregations and places of worship that formed community centers as a basis for mutual support, political action, and a method or vehicle for preserving and passing on culture, religious values, and ideas. Such communities developed not only in New York and Philadelphia, but in cities in the south, such as Charleston.

Traditionally, Jews in Europe had been prevented from owning land, so Jews tended to find occupations other than agriculture, pursuing trades, crafts, or enterprises, largely in urban environments. Although a product of anti-Semitic laws in Europe, this aspect of the heritage became a strength in the American setting as time went on. From the colonial period into the early national period in the United States, the American legal and political system favored wealthy landholders. But as the country urbanized and industrialized, the power and influence in the United States shifted from land to business and commerce.

Through the 19th century, most Jewish immigrants gravitated to the cities, and often found occupations at the bottom of the employment scale—such as rag dealers, garment workers, scrap-dealers, and push-cart vendors. A few Jewish settlers in the South acquiried not only land, but also plantations and slaves. But for the majority, the tradition of moving to urban centers and finding a socio-economic niche there persisted. In the 19th century, as cities grew and as the importance of trade and commerce began to outweigh the importance and power of the agricultural interests, business opportunities in urban centers increased.

Another aspect of the Jewish heritage, passed through families, was respect for intellectual and creative achievement. By the early 20th century, enrollment of young Jewish men and women in institutions of higher learning began to rise, and increasingly, graduates found their way into professions such as medicine, law, higher education, journalism, and the arts. Throughout this volume, the achievements of individuals in all of these fields and more serve as a benchmark of successful adaptation to the freedoms and opportunities that could be found in the expanding economy of the United States. Even as more and more people of Jewish ancestry found their way into the middle class and the professional classes, anti-Semitism persisted, and prestigious hotels and restaurants often made a point of excluding Jews and African Americans well into the 20th century. One consequence of the fight against such outright discrimination was a working alliance between Jewish and African-American political leaders demanding equality before the law and the outlawing of discrimination in housing, public accommodation, and elsewhere.

Other factors contributed to make the history of Jews in America complex. For one thing, waves of immigration continued to bring new generations to American shores, a process that continued from the colonial period well into the late 20th and early 21st centuries. Sephardic (Spanish and north African) and Ashkenazic (German and north European) Jews often found they had little in common, but the American setting and majority culture sometimes tended to treat both ancestral lines much the same. In the middle and late 19th century, many Jewish immigrants came to the United States from politically radical backgrounds. Influenced by Marx and anarchist leaders, several prominent radical leaders in the first decades of the 20th century were Jewish, including Emma Goldman, a leading anarchist; and David Dubinsky, a leader of the International Ladies Garment Workers' Union.

Intermarriage of Jews and non-Jews continued to make identifying "Jewishness" a difficult matter. The rise of a Reform Judaism challenged the dominance of traditional or Orthodox Judaism in the late 19th century. As noted earlier, the establishment of the independent state of Israel in 1948 tended to bring support from Jewish voters for politicians who gave vigorous support to the continued security of that nation against efforts to destroy it. The fact that the modern state of Israel automatically grants dual citizenship to Jews around the world, including those who hold American citizenship, has tended to make the tie to Israel even stronger than the tie felt by second- and third-generation descendants to other nations of ancestry.

This volume spells out the many factors that have shaped the unique experience of Jewish Americans, clarifying the intricate interplay of ethnicity, religion, economics, politics, and culture against the backdrop of the larger changes in American society through the decades from colonial times to the present.

RODNEY CARLISLE
GENERAL EDITOR

CHAPTER 1

The Colonial Era and the American Revolution: Beginnings to 1783

THE HISTORY OF Jews in America begins in Spain. In the 14th century, the Catholic Church had become increasingly powerful in Spain and persecuted the Jewish population, giving Jews the ultimatum: convert to Christianity or die. Some Jews left Spain; others converted publicly, but practiced Judaism in private. These Jews came to be known derogatively as Marranos and were persecuted along with others in 1478 by a court known as the Spanish Inquisition. The court tortured those it suspected were unfaithful to the Catholic Church, considering them to be heretics, and often forced them to confess, after which they might be punished in a variety of ways ranging from fines to death.

In the same year that King Ferdinand and Queen Isabella of Spain gave Columbus permission to seek a new passage to the Indies, they also expelled more than 150,000 Jews from Spain at the demand of the Inquisition. These Jews went to various places, including Italy, France, Turkey, Greece, and Portugal. Those who went to Portugal were soon forced out by the spread of the Inquisition and made their way to Holland. These people were among the first Jewish settlers in America, but their time in Holland is important for understanding both the nature of the rights they would later demand, and their ability to gain those rights.

By the 1650s, Jews in Holland were able to run for and hold public office, own their own land, and worship publicly (they built a synagogue in Amsterdam).

The Marranos of Spanish New Mexico

In the 14th and 15th centuries, laws targeting practicing Jews and the Spanish Inquisition resulted in the conversion of thousands of Jews to Roman Catholicism in the Iberian countries of Spain and Portugal. Some Jews who converted to remain in the country fully embraced their new religion. These people became known as *conversos*. Others outwardly converted, but secretly maintained Judaic customs, traditions, and/or religious practices. These people became known as *Marranos* or Crypto-Jews. Common theories of the origin of the term *Marrano* include the outward practice of eating pork, which is against Jewish dietary laws, as a sign of conversion and the idea that they were not of clean blood because of their lack of a line of descent from Christians. All converted Jews remaining in Spain and Portugal faced the constant threat of suspicion that they were Marranos.

Many Jews, including Marranos, migrated to the Hispanic colonies in the New World as a means to escape the atmosphere of religious persecution, find economic opportunities unavailable to many in Europe, and advance socially in a land where their ancestry was less known. Even New World religious intolerance and a periodic Spanish ban on New World immigrants of Jewish and Muslim origin did not stop the flow of migration. Jews of Iberian decent are known as Sephardic Jews. Some Marranos traveled to Spanish-controlled regions of the future United States, including southwestern areas like New Mexico. Many of these Marrano immigrants maintained contact with each other as well as with Jews who remained in Europe. Many Marranos sought to secretly preserve their Jewish identity in some form. Some secretly maintained the Jewish faith, laws, and customs, while others maintained only certain Jewish cultural practices.

Fear of persecution or discrimination led many Marrano families to maintain the secrecy surrounding their Jewish heritage and practices for generations. Marrano communities of colonial Hispanic descent remain in New Mexico and other areas of the U.S. southwest, with some openly claiming a Jewish identity. Some scholars have debated the accuracy of their claims to have maintained a continuous practice of Judaic religious or cultural practices since the colonial period due to the circumstantial evidence used to prove these claims. Such evidence includes a family history of anticlericalism, gravestone markers such as the Star of David, Hebraic family names, and the ongoing practice of Jewish dietary practices or customs such as lighting Friday night candles to mark the beginning of Shabbat. This self-identification has linked New Mexico's modern Marrano communities with similar emerging movements in other areas, such as Mexico, Brazil, Spain, and Portugal.

Holland, like many countries at this time, was attempting to develop trade through colonization. In Holland, this goal was carried out by the Dutch West India Company, in which the Jewish community had invested heavily.

The Dutch West India Company established a colony in Brazil in the 1630s after gaining control of Brazil from Portugal, and hundreds of Jewish settlers helped colonize northeast Brazil under Dutch rule. They settled mainly in Recife, establishing Jewish schools and synagogues. The Recife Jewish community was the first legally recognized Jewish community in the New World, but it didn't last long. In 1654, Portugal recaptured Brazil from Holland, and Jews were again given a choice: convert to Christianity or leave. Most of the Jews in Recife returned to Holland, but some found their way to New Amsterdam (later known as New York).

The Recife Jews were followed to New Amsterdam by Jews from Holland, Spain, Portugal, Germany, and England. In addition to New Amsterdam, Jews established communities in four other North American cities, including: Newport, Rhode Island; Charleston, South Carolina; Savannah, Georgia; and Philadelphia, Pennsylvania. While Jews lived in other places during the colonial era, including cities in Maryland, North Carolina, and Virginia, these five port cities contained the largest numbers of Jewish people during the colonial era.

NEW AMSTERDAM AND NEW YORK

The 23 Jews from Recife who came to New Amsterdam left on a ship from Brazil. Some believe that the ship was captured by Spanish pirates. After being rescued by a French vessel, the Jews were taken to New Amsterdam on the *Ste. Catherine*. In 1654, New Amsterdam was Dutch, like Brazil, but the environment for Jews was very different in New Amsterdam. New Amsterdam, a part of the Dutch colony of New Netherland, was under the leadership of Governor Peter Stuyvesant, and settlement efforts in Holland sought to attract Calvinists to the colony. The 1640 charter for New Netherland affirmed that only Reformed Orthodoxy could be practiced publicly in the colony. The charter did not prohibit Jews and others from settling in New Netherland, though. The result was an environment hostile to Jews and others, such as Lutherans, Catholics, Puritans, and Quakers. The leaders viewed these groups as a threat to the colony, and Stuyvesant used many methods, including imprisonment and beating, to try to force them to leave.

Stuyvesant wrote to the leaders of the Dutch West India Company within weeks of the Recife refugees' arrival, asking for permission to expel the 23 immigrants from the colony. He argued in a letter to the company "that the deceitful race,—such hateful enemies and blasphemers of the name of Christ,—be not allowed further to infect and trouble this new colony, to the detraction of your worships and the dissatisfaction of your worships' most affectionate subjects." Stuyvesant also argued in his letter that the Jewish ref-

This print shows the Dutch Governor Peter Stuyvesant and his soldiers being forced to leave New Amsterdam after losing the colony to the English in 1664.

ugees, generally poverty-stricken after their hardships, would place a hardship on the colony.

Stuyvesant was denied, but his rejection was due, in part, to Jewish leaders in Holland. Jewish leaders in Holland wrote to the Dutch West India Company, stressing that the expulsion of Jews from the colony would be detrimental to both the Jewish nation and the company, reminding the company of Jews' role in financing the company and in supporting the Brazilian colonies.

The Jewish leaders were successful in their request. The Dutch West India Company ordered Stuyvesant to allow the Jews to remain in the colony: "after many deliberations we have finally decided and resolved to apostille [endorse or approve] upon a certain petition presented by said Portuguese Jews that these people may travel and trade to and in New Netherland and live and remain there, provided the poor among them shall not become a burden to the company or to the community, but be supported by their own nation. You will now govern yourself accordingly."

The company's letter didn't indicate that Jews could worship publicly or own land, or even designate where they could "travel and trade" within the colony—the letter only guaranteed that Jews could remain in New Netherland. They would have to fight for rights and privileges, and they did so, defending

A Letter from the Jews of Amsterdam

The following excerpts are taken from the letter written by Jewish leaders in Holland to the directors of the Dutch West India Company in January 1655. These leaders successfully argued for allowing Brazilian Portuguese Jews to live in New Amsterdam in defiance of Governor Peter Stuyvesant's attempts to bar them from the colony.

The merchants of the Portuguese nation residing in this City respectfully remonstrate to your Honors that it has come to their knowledge that your Honors raise obstacles to the giving of permits or passports to the Portuguese Jews to travel and to go to reside in New Netherland, which if persisted in will result to the great disadvantage of the Jewish nation. It also can be of no advantage to the general Company but rather damaging.

[M]any of the nation . . . have lost their possessions at Pernambuco and have arrived from there in great poverty, and part of them have been dispersed here and there . . . And as they cannot go to Spain or Portugal because of the Inquisition, a great part of the aforesaid people must . . . be obliged to depart for other territories . . .

It is well known to your Honors that the Jewish nation in Brazil have at all times been faithful and have striven to guard and maintain that place, risking for that purpose their possessions and their blood.

Yonder land is extensive and spacious. The more loyal people that go to live there, the better it is in regard . . . to the payment of various excises and taxes which may be imposed there, and in regard to the increase of trade, and also to the importation of all the necessaries that may be sent there . . .

Your Honors should also please consider that many of the Jewish nation are principal shareholders in the Company. They having always striven their best for the Company, and many of their nation have lost immense and great capital in its shares and obligations.

The Company has by a general resolution consented that those who wish to populate the Colony shall enjoy certain districts of land gratis. Why should now certain subjects of this State not be allowed to travel thither and live there? The French consent that the Portuguese Jews may traffic and live in . . . their territories . . . The English also consent . . . [that the] Jewish nation may go from London and settle at Barbados, whither also some have gone.

As foreign nations consent that the Jewish nation may go to live and trade in their territories, how can your Honors forbid the same and refuse transportation to this Portuguese nation who reside here and have been settled here . . . ?

Therefore the petitioners request . . . that your Honors be pleased not to exclude but to grant the Jewish nation passage to and residence in that country; otherwise this would result in a great prejudice to their reputation. Also that . . . the Jewish nation be permitted . . . to travel, live, and traffic there, and with them enjoy liberty on condition of contributing like others.

themselves against anti-Semitic policies at every turn and seeking help from powerful Jews in Holland when needed.

Although the story of the 23 refugees' journey to New Amsterdam is well known, they were not the only Jews who arrived in the 1650s. Other Jews traveled from Holland to New Amsterdam, including the merchants Asser Levy and Jacob Bar Simon. Jews with roots in the Iberian Peninsula are called Sephardim, from the Hebrew word for Spain. Ashkenazic (from the Hebrew word for Germany) Jews, or Jews from central and eastern Europe, were also in the colony as traders.

Asser Levy, Jacob Bar Simon, and others were vocal in their battle for rights. With the help of Jews in Holland, they were successful in securing many rights. Stuyvesant was ordered to use rights that Jews had gained in Holland as a guide for rights that they should be allowed in the colony. He was repeatedly reprimanded for trying to deny Jews rights that they had in Holland, but, by 1658, Jews could own land, trade inside and outside New Amsterdam, become burghers, and had earned the right to participate in the militia.

The Dutch rule of New Amsterdam soon came to an end. In 1664, the Dutch lost New Amsterdam after leaders surrendered to a British fleet, and it was renamed New York. Jews in New York had to regain the rights from the British that they had held under the Dutch—no easy task since Jews in England had not yet attained the same level of rights as Jews in Holland.

What followed was a tumultuous time during which Jews received freedoms in the 1667 Treaty of Breda (which granted rights to trade, own property, and worship to settlers in New York), had them taken away under the Charter of Liberties (in effect from 1683 to 1685), received freedoms again due to policies of religious freedom promoted by Kings Charles II and James II, and lost freedoms after the English overthrow of James II in the Glorious Revolution of 1688. In 1689, Jews were in familiar territory as Jacob Leisler, who, after the overthrow of the king, led the colony in rebellion against the king's agents in New York, and wanted all residents to swear Protestantism was the one true religion. Leisler's government was never recognized by the British, and he was soon executed and replaced by Governor Henry Sloughter.

After arriving in 1692, Sloughter returned rights and freedoms to the Jews, but the Jews of New York were once again helped by Jews in Europe: the new English king William III needed Jewish financial support as he fought France's Louis XIV.

JEWISH LIFE IN EARLY NEW YORK

By 1695, Jews could practice Judaism publicly in New York, and Shearith Israel (Remnant of Israel), the first synagogue in New York, was established on Mill Street (today called William Street) in 1730. Shearith Israel's practices were Sephardic in nature (Portuguese prayer rituals were used, and minutes were written in Portuguese), but the Jewish community in New

York was comprised of both Sephardic and Ashkenazic Jews. The synagogue did not have a *hacham* (or rabbi), and the officers and elders of the synagogue led it. Few churches had professionally trained leaders at this time. The synagogue was responsible for performing religious services, for providing unleavened bread for Passover, and supporting Jewish community members in need.

The officers of the synagogue held great status within the synagogue and the community. Religious custom of the time, whether Jewish or Christian, generally required obedience to the officers of the congregation. Some Jews would have found disagreeing or challenging leadership dangerous to themselves and their idea of community.

Entering a new century in 1700, Jews had attained some degree of acceptance and even influence. Jews and non-Jews established and maintained business partnerships, socialized, shared the responsibility and burdens of civil duties, and inter-married, although some Jewish leaders were unhappy with the latter.

The congregation of Shearith Israel, New York City's first synagogue, established this Jewish cemetery in lower Manhattan in 1683. It is the oldest remaining Jewish cemetery in the United States and is listed on the U.S. National Register of Historic Places.

Many Jews were shopkeepers or merchants of some sort. For example, there were few butchers in New York at this time, and butchers had to take an oath of office. Asser Levy was granted permission to open a slaughterhouse, and Garret Janson Rose, a Christian, became became his business partner.

Business relationships were not just between individuals, though. Jews were active in the larger business community. In 1733, for instance, merchants, both Jewish and Christian, were concerned with fair trade practices related to the export of flour, and two Jews were among the 27 New York merchants who petitioned to ensure that only flour of a certain quality left New York.

In 1740, some business endeavors became easier with the 1740 Naturalization Act, which created new conditions for obtaining citizenship. Under the act, residents who were born in a British colony or who had resided in one for seven years could apply for citizenship. Even more importantly for Jews, the act eliminated the need to take a Christian oath.

Jews also engaged with Christians socially. They joined Masonic lodges and held offices within them. Myer Myers, a prominent silversmith, and Moses Michael Hays, for instance, were both members of the lodge in New York. Myers would later help in fundraising efforts for the Newport synagogue and made the Rimonim (in Jewish ritual, the small, round finials that ornament the ends of the bars of the scroll for the Torah) for both the synagogue in Newport and for his own synagogue, Shearith Israel. Hays later moved the New York lodge during the American Revolution to Newport, and then to Boston. Jews also donated to gentile causes; several Jewish families, including the Levy and Gomez families, contributed funds to the building of the Anglican Trinity Church in 1711.

While Jews did not yet have equal political rights with Christians, they did engage in civil duties. Nathan Simson and Samuel Levy were elected constables of the North Ward in 1718, for instance. Like some prominent Christians, Simson and Levy paid deputies to take on their duties. And, like Christians, Jews could decline an office altogether by paying a fine, as Jacob Franks did when he was elected later.

Some Jews also married outside the faith and converted to Christianity. Marriage within the small Jewish community was problematic. Jews often remained unmarried; devout Jews who wanted to marry within their faith found it difficult to do so. The community was still small, and members didn't always find each other worthy. The situ-

This 17th-century Dutch Torah scroll uses a Spanish and Portuguese style of script, which was also used by Jewish scribes in early America.

ation grew worse in the decade before the American Revolution as the Jewish community in New York became increasingly divided, and factions developed within the synagogue.

By the time of the American Revolution, New York had one of the largest Jewish populations in the colonies: however, it never exceeded 200 people. Jews in New York had made significant strides toward political, economic, social, and cultural equality while trying, with varying degrees of success, to develop a cohesive community of their own—no mean feat with many Jews from different countries and with very different traditions. They had also established relationships with Jews in other colonial settlements through marriage and business partnerships, and maintained relationships with Jews in Europe.

NEWPORT, RHODE ISLAND

Roger Williams was granted a charter for Rhode Island in 1663. Governor Williams had left Massachusetts in order to establish a colony based on religious indifference, and he believed that others should be allowed to practice their religion without persecution. He did not believe that all religions were equal or valid; he simply believed that persuasion toward the true God and Church would be more effective than persecution.

Attracted by Williams's philosophy of tolerance, Jews were among the first settlers in Newport, and a Jewish community was established when 15 Sephardic families came there in 1658. These families may have been from Holland or perhaps Barbados, since members of the community retained both business and familial ties with the island.

While Jews and other groups might have been assured of religious tolerance, they had few other assurances, and were not given political or other rights. Jews continued to live in the colony, however, establishing themselves as merchants and tradesmen and developing business and social relationships with Christians—relationships that would become important in the years to follow. Both Jews and Christians achieved wealth and status through their shipping and trading activities in Newport's busy port, which attracted ships from around the world. Newport, like most other ports of the time, saw the import and/or export of candles, rum, sugar, and slaves.

Jacob Rodrigues Rivera was among the Jewish merchants who helped make Newport successful. Rodrigues Rivera was a merchant of spermaceti products (products made from whale glands), perhaps the most common of which was candles. Rodrigues Rivera actually introduced the manufacture of whale-based products to the colonies. Agreements relating to the manufacture and sale of spermaceti products were common between Jews and Christians in Newport and in other cities. More informal agreements were common as merchants, Jew and gentile alike, in different cities kept in close contact about the activities of British inspectors. What also helped make Newport successful was the

The Touro Synagogue in Newport, Rhode Island, was completed in 1763. It is the oldest synagogue in the United States, and is still in use today.

African slave trade, in which several prominent Newport Jews were involved. Aaron Lopez was perhaps the preeminent Jewish slave trader in Newport, but Jacob Rodrigues Rivera and Moses Levy also owned as least a portion of a ship involved in the slave trade, although importing only about 6 percent of Newport's slaves.

Unlike other colonies, the colony of Rhode Island promised obedience to the 1682 Acts of Trade and Navigation—these acts were part of a British attempt to tighten control over her colonies, and some chose to use them as an opportunity to persecute Jews. In 1684, Governor William Coddington argued that Jews in Rhode Island did not have the right to conduct trade and seized the goods of two prominent Jews. In 1685, Surveyor of Customs William Dyer argued that seven prominent Rhode Island Jews did not have the right to trade; Coddington, supporting Dyer, ordered the estates of these seven Jews to be seized. Ultimately, neither Coddington nor Dyer succeeded, and local authorities returned the Jews' properties.

Newport, like New York, also claimed a group of Masons that included Jews as members, and Jews were involved in other community activities. Moses Michael Hays, for instance, became the Deputy Inspector General of Masonry in 1768. Jews like Jacob Rodrigues Rivera, Abraham Hart, Moses Lopez, and Aaron Lopez donated funds and books to Newport's first library. Rodrigues Rivera and Aaron Lopez both donated lumber to Rhode Island College (today known as Brown University).

Jews also maintained personal relationships with Christians. Reverend Issac Touro (who later became the *hazzan*, or cantor, at Yeshuat Israel Synagogue) was friends with Dr. Ezra Stiles; Stiles, who later became the president of Yale University, frequently discussed the Bible with Touro and other Jews. While he likely hoped his discussions would lead to conversion to Christianity, his letters reveal how impressed he was with the learning of the Jewish community in Newport.

In addition to growing businesses and social relationships with Christians, Jews worked to develop their own community. As in New York (and the other colonies for that matter), the Newport Jewish community worked to acquire a burial ground, succeeding in 1677. Two poems were later written about the cemetery and became famous: Henry Wadsworth Longfellow's "The Jewish Cemetery at Newport" and Emma Lazarus's "In the Jewish Synagogue at Newport."

Until the early 1760s, the community worshiped in private, but in the late 1750s and early 1760s, a synagogue was built in Newport. Construction began in 1759 and was finished four years later: on December 2, 1763, Yeshuat Israel was consecrated. It was built with financial support from the New York Jewish community and from congregations in London, Jamaica, and Curaçao. This synagogue is known as Touro Synagogue, in memory of the congregation's first *hazzan* Issac Touro. In 1761, Newport Jews established what may have been the first Jewish social club in a British colony. The supper club was limited to Jews, had membership fees and a number of rules governing behavior.

The 1760s were tumultuous times as the country headed toward the Revolutionary War. As in other colonies, Newport residents, Jew and gentile alike, protested British actions, and they joined with other colonies' protests against the 1765 Stamp Acts. These acts required that all legal documents (wills, newspapers, contracts, and even playing cards) carry a special stamp; the effect was a direct tax on residents of the colonies. But Newport residents didn't join the other colonies in drafting non-importation agreements after the 1767 Townshend Acts, which required colonists to pay duties on various items imported from Britain, like paper and tea. While Newport Jews generally did not support the British Crown, they were often attacked as Tories (those loyal to the British Crown). While some of these Jews remained in Newport during the British occupation of the city after the onset of the American Revolution, most Jews left Newport at that time, the synagogue was closed, and its Torah and other religious objects were moved to New York and Philadelphia.

CHARLESTON, SOUTH CAROLINA

Carolina (divided in the early 1700s into the separate provinces of North and South Carolina) was initially settled as a way to guard against encroachment or invasion from Spanish Florida. The Charleston settlement is noteworthy because its constitution of 1669 welcomes Jews explicitly. This document is extraordinary for several reasons. It was written by Anthony Ashley Cooper, first earl of Shaftesbury, and his famous friend John Locke. It not only welcomes non-Christians, it also gives groups the right to form religious congregations. The notable exception in Charleston, as in most British colonies, was Roman Catholics. It also prohibits people from speaking negatively about

Jewish Americans in the American Revolution

There were approximately 2,000 Jewish Americans by the time of the American Revolution, and most of them supported the American patriot movement seeking independence from Great Britain. Jewish soldiers participated in many of the war's major battles, as well as the Continental Army's famous winter camps in the harsh weather at Valley Forge, Pennsylvania. Many of the soldiers fought with Henry rifles manufactured at Jewish-American Joseph Simon's Lancaster, Pennsylvania, forge. Jewish-American David Franks served as the aide-de-camp to General George Washington, leader of the Continental Army.

Several key Jewish Americans made significant contributions in finance and politics as well as military events, many at the expense of their personal fortunes. Polish immigrant Haym Salomon, also spelled Solomon or Solomons, supplied American troops in New York and provided interest-free loans to the Continental Congress. He also secretly encouraged Hessian mercenaries fighting with the British Army to desert. The British arrested Salomon several times as a spy. He lost his property and narrowly escaped death, and was left in bankruptcy in the postwar period. New England Jewish merchants such as Aaron Lopez outfitted their ships to serve as privateers attacking British ships, while Jewish arms traders and merchants on the Dutch island of St. Eustatius smuggled guns through the British blockade. Many were imprisoned and lost their homes and personal property when British Admiral Sir George Rodney destroyed the island's Jewish settlements.

Several notable southern Jewish Americans also played prominent roles in the American Revolution, including Francis Salvador, a well-educated London-born South Carolina planter and politician. Another southern Jewish American involved in the war was Colonel Mordecai Sheftall, the son of Orthodox Jews, who served as chairman of the Savannah, Georgia, Parochial Committee coordinating boycotts of British goods, among other goals. He served as commissary general to troops in Georgia as well as the Continental Army and as a colonel in the Continental line of the Georgia brigade, becoming the highest-ranking Jewish officer on the American side. Sheftall also participated in the 1778 Battle of Savannah, and was imprisoned on a British ship for two years before being freed in a 1780 prisoner exchange. Like Salomon, he had also lent large sums to the American cause, leaving him in a dire financial situation after the war. He returned to Savannah after British occupation ended and remained a leader in the city's small Jewish community.

other religions. While these provisions are laudable, they were not necessarily executable; the constitution's acceptance of Jews did not necessarily translate into the people of South Carolina's welcoming Jews, and Jews were blamed for the colony's troubles.

The original settlers of the Carolinas came primarily from the West Indies, especially Barbados, and it is possible that some Jews were included in those first waves of settlers. The first documented mention of a Jewish settler, however, relates to Governor Joseph Archdale's need for an interpreter in 1695; the unknown Jewish settler acted as an interpreter in Archdale's communications with Spanish-speaking Indians.

The British Navigation Acts of 1695 troubled both Jews and French Huguenot settlers in Carolina. They were worried that provisions of the acts would deny them the opportunity to trade, since early drafts of the law mentioned that trade would be limited to native Englishmen. As in New York, the Carolina Jews relied upon influential Jews to help—London Jews argued for the colonists and were successful.

Dissent arose over religion in the early 1700s. Many wanted to establish an Anglican state church in Carolina. The British Crown resumed control of Carolina, and the colonies became royal colonies in 1729. After this, the Jews' political rights

The Hebrew Orphan Society of Charleston, South Carolina, the oldest incorporated Jewish charitable organization in the city, built this building for use as an orphanage soon after the end of the American Revolution.

Francis Salvador

The Salvador family was a prominent Sephardic Jewish family in London, and Francis Salvador's grandfather Joseph Salvador was a leading businessman in London who had extensive assets in America. In the 1750s, the family lost much of its wealth as a result of the failure of the Dutch East India Company, and Francis Salvador, leaving his wife and four children behind, moved to South Carolina in 1773 to regain the family's fortune.

Salvador quickly established himself as a planter in South Carolina and as a supporter of American independence. He was the 96th District's largest landowner, with 7,000 acres, and was friends with many Christians.

At a time when Jews in South Carolina could not be elected to office or even to vote, Salvador did that which was prohibited: he was elected to South Carolina's General Assembly in 1774 and as a delegate to South Carolina's First and Second Provincial Congresses for the 96th District. As a member of the congresses, he was on several committees, including committees charged with working with Tories in South Carolina to ensure they would not aid the Crown, and perhaps to convert them to the cause of American independence.

In 1776, Tories were inciting Indians to violence against American rebels. Salvador accompanied Major Andrew Williamson and the militia in a defense of South Carolinian settlements. The group was ambushed on August 1, 1776, and Salvador was shot and scalped in the battle with the Tory-led Indians.

Salvador's last words were recorded by Major Williamson in a letter to John Rutledge, the president of South Carolina. Williamson wrote, "He died, about half after two o'clock in the morning; forty-five minutes after he received the wounds, sensible to the last. When I came up to him, after dislodging the enemy, and speaking to him, he asked, whether I had beat the enemy? I told him yes. He said he was glad of it, and shook me by the hand—and bade me farewell—and said, he would die in a few minutes."

The American rebels won the battle, but Salvador became the first Jew to die for American independence.

became increasingly limited. The General Assembly limited the right to vote to Christians several times.

As in New York and Newport, and as in Savannah and Philadelphia, most Jews in Charleston were merchants or traders (in part why the Navigation Acts were so worrisome to Jews). Jews traded with Indians, for instance, as they did with most of the other colonies.

Francis Salvador, then, is noteworthy as an exception to this rule: he became a well-respected plantation owner in South Carolina, with as many as

30 slaves. He also was the first South Carolina Jew to be elected to office: he became his district's representative in the state's Provincial Congress. While performing duties as a district representative, he was killed by American Indians under the direction of British Tories, thereby becoming the first Jew to die in the American Revolution. Salvador wasn't the only Jew to hold a prominent office, however. Moses Lindo was the inspector and appraiser of indigo, drugs, and dyes. South Carolina's largest export at this time was indigo, so Lindo's role was important.

As in New York and Newport, Jews developed various relationships with Christians. Jews were members of the Masonic lodge in Charleston, and the first Jew to become a member was Isaac DaCosta, in 1753.

The population of Jews in Charleston grew steadily from 1740 to 1775, as some Jews left Georgia and settled in Charleston, and others arrived from the West Indies, England, and Germany. Jews worked to establish both a cemetery and a synagogue in Charleston, as they had elsewhere. One prominent family—the DaCosta family—purchased land for a cemetery and eventually turned it over to the synagogue in 1762. The congregation Kahal Kadosh Beth Elohim (Holy Congregation and House of the Lord) was established in 1749.

SAVANNAH, GEORGIA

The colony of Savannah, Georgia, was founded in 1733 by Governor James Oglethorpe, and the first Jewish settlers arrived in that year. Prominent and wealthy Sephardic Jews in London raised funds to help Jews travel to Georgia, and 41 Jewish settlers, both Sephardim and Ashkenazim, arrived in Savannah in July 1733. This move did not have approval from many of Georgia's trustees, who attempted to exclude Jews from the Georgia colony. Savannah, like South Carolina, was intended to serve as a deterrent to Spanish invasion.

The trustees of the colony weren't particularly pleased with the influx of Jews. Oglethorpe, however, allowed Jews to settle in Georgia, perhaps because Dr. Samuel Nunes Ribeiro, one of the Jewish settlers from London, helped stop an epidemic. Then again, Oglethorpe may have simply realized that the colony was in danger of failing with many settlers sick, and few new settlers willing to come to Georgia. When Oglethorpe began assigning land to newcomers, Jews received land alongside Christians.

There were several policies related to this land that affected the growth of the colony. There were limitations on land ownership (settlers received 50 acres that could not be sold), and settlers in Georgia were originally not allowed to own slaves. Both policies limited the growth of the colony, and soon settlers wanted to know if they could lease other lands. Policies changed in 1759, and private ownership of land and ownership of slaves were both approved.

The original Jewish settlers from London did not stay long; in response to the policies on land ownership, the fears of Spanish invasion, or the anti-

The Minis Family of Savannah, Georgia

The Minis family became one of the first Jewish families to settle in Savannah in July 1733. Abraham Minis, with his wife Abigail, daughters Leah and Ester, and brother Simeon, came from England. The Minis family, like others, received a parcel of land in December that first year. The family quickly began raising food, and, by 1740, they were raising Indian corn both for their own use and for sale and trade. The family also began cattle ranching and opened a store in town. They imported food and other goods from New York.

Abraham died in 1757, leaving his wife with nine children to raise. Many families of the era would have been economically devastated by a father's death, but Abigail took up the reins of the family's various businesses and even established new ones. Abigail continued to run the ranches and farms that the family operated, adding acreage to what the family already owned. She owned at least 15 slaves. She also operated a tavern and shop out of her home in the city of Savannah. The tavern saw both elegant entertainments for officials and daily use in the form of renting beds to travelers. In the 18th century, guests generally rented a bed, or part of a bed, rather than a room, and beds could be set up anywhere in the house. Abigail's family helped her run these various endeavors. Her son Philip, the first male white child born in the colony on July 11, 1734, was a successful merchant in Savannah and later became the *parnas* (president) of the Mickva Israel Synagogue. He was also known for his support of American independence, advancing funds for the payment of Revolutionary troops.

Abigail and her family supported the American Revolution: she even provided troops with food. Like other Jews, she left Savannah in late 1778 when it was occupied by British troops.

This Savannah, Georgia, house was built by members of the Minis family in 1822.

Semitic attitudes of the leadership after Oglethorpe left the colony, most Jews left Savannah by the beginning of 1741. Many went to other prosperous port cities, such as New York and Charleston. Only two families remained—the Minis and the Sheftall families—until around 1750, when some families returned to Savannah.

PROMINENT JEWISH FAMILIES OF SAVANNAH

In Savannah, Jews once again became merchants and traders, but also farmers, which was unusual for Jews in the colonies. One of the most notable of these Savannah Jewish families was one that became all three—and a few other things besides. The Minis family was one of the first Jewish families to settle in Savannah. Abraham Minis with his wife Abigail and their two children came from England in 1733. The Minis family received a parcel of land that first year. They farmed the land, but also raised cattle and opened a shop and tavern.

The Sheftall family was prominent in Savannah. Benjamin Sheftall brought his family to Savannah in 1733, and his son Mordecai was a landowner and merchant. Mordecai was also involved in the timber industry and sometimes acted as an interpreter. Mordecai married a woman from Charleston named Frances Hart; marriages during colonial times often brought together families in different colonies, forging or extending business partnerships along with familial ones. And, like Jews elsewhere, Mordecai served in a civil capacity when permitted to do so—he served in the state legislature and as the state's commissary general—and had other connections with Christians. Both Benjamin and Mordecai belonged to the Masonic lodge, and Mordecai served as a master of the lodge in 1758.

The usual move of obtaining a burial ground became a political battle in Savannah when Anglican clergyman Samuel Frink convinced local leaders to deny the Jews' petition regarding their burial ground. Eventually, Mordecai Sheftall solved the problem by donating part of his private family burial ground to the Jewish community. This wasn't his only service to the Jewish community—he also hosted services in his home before Savannah Jews built a synagogue.

Most Jews in Savannah supported the American Revolution, but many Jews left Savannah either before or in December 1778 as British troops conquered Georgia. After the treaty between Great Britain and the United States, Jews began to return to Savannah.

PHILADELPHIA, PENNSYLVANIA

In 1681, William Penn was granted a charter for the Pennsylvania colony, but it is likely that Jews were already in the area as traders. Jews were certainly in the area by the early 1700s, as several appear in city records. It wasn't until the 1730s and 1740s, however, that a Jewish community began to grow as individual Jews steadily arrived and set themselves up as merchants and traders.

Brothers Nathan and Issac Levy (New York merchant Moses Levy's sons) arrived in the 1730s and became well-known and respected merchants and ship owners in Philadelphia. In 1740, they were followed by brothers David and Moses Franks (the children of New York merchant Jacob Franks and his wife Abigail Levy Franks). David Franks imported the Liberty Bell on one of his ships.

Brothers Barnard and Michael Gratz arrived in the mid and late 1750s. Prominent merchants in Philadelphia, they played a key role in western expansion by making trade agreements with Shawnee and Delaware Indians for fur pelts. The Gratz brothers also engaged in business partnerships with Christians and Jews in other colonies, their marriages to Jewish women helping them with the latter.

As in other colonies, Jews engaged in civil and social activities with Christians. Issac Miranda, for instance, was the first Jew to earn a judicial position in the British colonies in 1727. Miranda was the first Jew known to arrive in Philadelphia around 1710, but he did not stay in the city and later converted to Christianity. Jews were also members of the Masonic lodge, the Franklin Library Company, and a Philadelphia dancing assembly.

The Jews obtained a burial ground in 1740 after Nathan Levy requested land for burying his family, and the congregation named Kahal Kadosh Mickvé Israel began about five years later. The congregation met in a small house in Philadelphia.

Jews also supported Great Britain in its Great War for the Empire (more commonly known as the French and Indian War in the United States), a battle over American colonies. Moses Franks and three gentile merchants were responsible for providing provisions like food and clothes to British troops in the colony.

As in other colonies, Jews and Christians in Philadelphia protested the 1765 Stamp Act and the 1767 Townshend Acts. The non-consumption and non-importation movements grew steadily in the late 1760s. Merchants in Boston encouraged others to join in boycotting British goods with the goal of forcing a repeal of the Townshend Acts. Importantly, Jews were among the merchants who signed the non-importation agreements, and, in fact, Mathias Bush was the first to sign the October 25, 1765, agreement that demanded the repeal of the Stamp Act. Other Jews who signed the acts included Moses Mordecai, brothers Michael and Barnard Gratz, Benjamin Levy, and David Franks. They were successful, and the movement died briefly in the early 1770s when Britain repealed the acts, but was reborn a few years later when the British passed the Coercive Acts in 1774.

War was soon to come, however. After Great Britain passed the Coercive Acts (or Intolerable Acts) in 1774, colonists organized resistance to the new acts. Jews could be found both as supporters of the American cause and as supporters of the British Crown. Several Philadelphia Jews served with distinction in the war, donated money to the cause, or helped in other ways (for example, the Gratz brothers supplied gunpower and weapons to the Revolutionaries).

CONCLUSION

By the time of the American Revolution in 1776, 2,500 Jews were in America—the population had grown slowly, but steadily since the first group of Jews arrived in New Amsterdam. These Jews came from diverse origins and had varied traditions. This diversity led to some disagreement within Jewish communities, but while Jews dealt both with these disagreements and with stereotypes and other forms of anti-Semitism in the New World, Jews did not experience the pogroms and violence that they had faced elsewhere.

In each of the colonies discussed here, Jews established congregations and, in some cases, built synagogues, some of which still survive today, although only Touro survives in its original form. Through these congregations, Jews attempted to maintain their distinctively Jewish traditions that included educating and caring for their own people. Jews also, though, adapted to the frontier lands and American culture. They learned English, adopted clothing and decorating styles that had more do to with their class than their religion, and joined and supported gentile organizations.

By 1776, Jews had made considerable strides within the colonies when it came to political, economic, social, and cultural rights. Jews could settle in any of the 13 colonies and, in some colonies, could vote and be elected to office. Jews also formed business partnerships with both Jews and Christians, and often moved or sent family members (usually sons) to other colonies. Some of these moves, in turn, led to additional business partnerships. While some Jews did not marry or married outside the faith, some Jews married within the faith, and familial relationships often led to new business connections. Through initiative and these business connections, Jews made important economic contributions to the growth of the colonies and later to the cause of American independence.

SUMMER LEIBENSPERGER
UNIVERSITY OF HOUSTON-VICTORIA

Further Reading

Archdeacon, Thomas J. *New York City, 1664–1710: Conquest and Change.* Ithaca, NY: Cornell University Press, 1976.

Dimont, Max I. *The Jews in America: The Roots, History, and Destiny of American Jews.* New York: Simon and Schuster, 1978.

Doroshkin, Milton. *Yiddish in America: Social and Cultural Foundations.* Rutherford, NJ: Fairleigh Dickinson University Press, 1969.

Glazer, Nathan. *American Judaism.* Chicago, IL: University of North Chicago Press, 1957.

Karp, Abraham J., ed. *The Jewish Experience in America: Selected Studies from the Publications of the American Jewish Historical Society.* New York: KTAV Publishing House, 1969.

Marcus, Jacob R. *The Colonial American Jew 1492–1776.* Detroit, MI: Wayne State University Press, 1970.

———. *Early American Jewry: The Jews of New York, New England, and Canada, 1649–1794.* New York: KTAV Publishing House, 1975.

Pencak, William. *Jews and Gentiles in Early America 1654–1800.* Ann Arbor, MI: University of Michigan Press, 2005.

Sarna, Jonathan D., ed. *The American Jewish Experience.* New York: Holmes & Meier Publishers, 1986.

———. *American Judaism: A History.* New Haven, CT: Yale University Press, 2004.

Schappes, Morris U., ed. *A Documentary History of the Jews in the United States: 1654–1875.* New York: Schocken Books, 1971.

CHAPTER 2

The Early National Period and Expansion: 1783 to 1859

THE PERIOD BETWEEN 1783 and 1859 saw vast changes in the composition of Jewish-American life in the newly declared democracy. Beginning with the end of the Revolutionary War and ending at the dawn of the Civil War, 1783–1859 was a time of relative peace and prosperity in the United States, and Jews benefited greatly from the ensuing stability. The major changes that came to pass during these years were lasting and would have a tremendous impact on the composition and structure of the Jewish-American community for years to come.

This era can be broken down into two distinct periods, each with defining problems and characteristics. The federal period (1783–1819) was a time of internal growth, democratization, and institution building for American Jews. It was also a period of hard-won battles for civic equality in virtually every state in the Union. American Jews in colonial America were highly conscious of their relative freedom in comparison to their brethren across the Atlantic. By the end of the federal period, Jews in the United States were able to own land, hold office, trade freely, become artisans, and vote of their own voli-tion—all rights that were denied to most Jews in other countries. Many of these, such as the right to vote and the right to hold office, were acquired on a state-by-state basis. The Revolution and the subsequent establishment of American democracy created the necessary preconditions that allowed the emerging Jewish-American community to develop, change, and flourish in this era. The progress made during the first years after the Revolution was the initial step toward Jews becoming fully accepted in the New World.

The second period, spanning 1820–59, was an era that saw tremendous demographic growth, the development of new religious and social institutions, and the acquisition of true civic equality for Jews in America. This period also witnessed the beginnings of Reform Judaism in America with the founding of Isaac Harby's Reformed Society of Israelites on January 16, 1825. The Jewish-American population also increased tenfold during this period. In 1790, Jews made up 0.04 percent of the overall American population (reported at anywhere from 1,300 to 2,000 Jews out of nearly 4 million Americans). By 1840, Jews had become 0.09 percent of the population (15,000 Jews out of an American population of just over 17 million). Any increase in the Jewish population during these years can be attributed to the immigration of Jews from central Europe beginning in the 1820s. Jews in this period were able to acquire complete religious and political equality in all but five of the 26 states by 1840. These gains in civic equality, combined with the increase of the Jewish population, enabled American Jews to assimilate into American society and culture, while simultaneously building and maintaining their own institutions.

1783–1819: AMERICAN JEWS IN THE FEDERAL PERIOD

Tremendous institutional growth occurred for the young American Jewish community 1783–1820. In the aftermath of the Revolutionary War, American Jews reestablished their prewar synagogues; created many more in the rapidly expanding postwar Jewish communities of Baltimore, Savannah, and Philadelphia; and began to found the organizations and institutions that would define Jewish life in America for the next century and beyond. Important Jewish-American figures during this period included Judah Touro (1775–1854), a Newport merchant and philanthropist and the son of the namesake of the Touro Synagogue; and Mordechai Manuel Noah (1785–1851), politician, journalist, and playwright.

The Revolutionary War ended on February 4, 1783, when England officially declared an end to hostilities in America. A few months later, the United States and Britain signed the Treaty of Paris. The treaty was ratified by the newly inaugurated U.S. Congress on January 14, 1784. Congress soon voted for a census count to be completed every 10 years. The first census in American history began in August 1790 and lasted for nine months. The census, submitted to Congress by President George Washington counted a total of 3,929,000 persons in the United States and its territories. Though Jews were not tallied as a separate group in the 1790 census, contemporary scholars estimate, based on the last names of householders in the census taken together with other corroborating evidence (including congregational

Assimilation in the Early United States

Many American Jews had mixed feelings about their rapid acculturation in America. A young Jewish woman named Rebecca Samuel describes the situation in her diary in 1791:

Anyone can do what he wants. There is no rabbi in all of America to excommunicate anyone. This is a blessing here.

Yet a few pages later, Samuel adds:

Here they cannot became anything else [but gentile], Jewishness is pushed aside here . . . We have a shochet [ritual slaughterer] here who goes to market and buys terefah [non-kosher meat] . . . We have no Torah scrolls and no talit [prayer shawls] and no synagogue. We do not know what the Sabbath and the holidays are. On the Sabbath all the Jewish stores are open.

Like Rebecca Samuel, American Jews continued to feel a tremendous ambivalence about their rapid assimilation into American society for decades to come.

membership lists, tombstone inscriptions in Jewish cemeteries, marriage and death certificates, and wills and other public documents), that there were between 1,300 and 1,500 Jews in the United States at the time of the first census.

Jews thus made up less than one-tenth of one percent of the American population during the federal period. However, despite their small numbers, Jewish Americans were instrumental and highly influential in the founding of the new nation and the gradual development of religious equality and tolerance. In September 1787, Jonas Phillips (1736–1803), a prominent Jewish leader who had served in the Philadelphia militia under Colonel William Bradford during the war, sent a letter to the Federal Constitutional Convention outlining Jewish loyalty to the soon-to-be Republic and advocating for freedom of religious expression:

It is well known among all the Citizen of the 13 united states [sic] that the Jews have been true and faithful whigs, & during the late Contest with England they have been foremost in aiding and assisting the states with their lifes [sic] and fortunes, they have supported the cause, they have bravely fought and bled for liberty which they can not Enjoy . . . the Israelites will think themself happy to live under a government where all Religious societies are on an equal footing—I solicit this favour for myself my children and posterity, & for the benefit of all the Israelites through the 13 united states of America.

As Phillips's letter indicates, most Jews had sided against the British during the War for Independence. On July 4, 1788, Jews were full participants in the Grand Federal Procession celebrating the ratification of the Constitution that took place in Philadelphia. Jewish leaders, including Rabbi Jacob Raphael of Congregation Mikveh Israel, paraded side-by-side with Protestant ministers and major American political figures.

At the end of the parade, Jews were provided with their own table of kosher food. American Jews saw this parade, and the kosher banquet that followed, as symbolizing both the right of Jews to full equality and the importance of Jews continuing to observe their own distinctive traditions. Jews also played a major role in the 1789 presidential inauguration procession, marching alongside Christian clergymen and taking part in the formal celebratory proceedings.

JEWISH LIFE DURING THE FEDERAL PERIOD

Jewish life in the early years of the United States was concentrated in six major cities: Philadelphia, New York, Richmond, Baltimore, Charleston, and Savannah. About 90 percent of American Jews lived in urban environments during this period. Cities were the centers of Jewish-American life and culture. Though Newport and Lancaster had been major centers of Jewish life prior to the Revolution, both declined in importance during the federal period. The destruction of Newport's port during the Revolution left few economic opportunities for aspiring merchants, and Jews relocated southward to other towns like Philadelphia and Charleston. By 1790, there were approximately 76 Jews remaining in Newport. Philadelphia, in contrast, developed a thriving Jewish community during the same period. It is estimated that as much as 40 percent of the entire Jewish population of America lived in Philadelphia during the Revolution, as many Jews fled to Philadelphia from British-occupied cities to the north, and south. In 1790, New York counted 242 Jews within its boundaries. Baltimore boasted approximately 50 Jews, while Richmond and Charleston had about 200 each. Further south, Savannah had about 100 Jews who were active members of its Congregation Mikve Israel. The New England states, in contrast, had a Jewish population of approximately 150, due to a series of restrictive settlement policies and a distinct lack of synagogues and Jewish organizations in major New England cities. Boston, for example, did not have any synagogues until 1840.

Jews were highly mobile during the first years of the Republic. The Revolutionary War had caused massive dislocation, and Jews in the postwar period relocated frequently in search of better economic opportunities and greater stability. This increase in economic and geographical mobility also

The ark inside the Lloyd Street Synagogue in Baltimore, Maryland, as it looked around 1860. Dutch and West Indian Jews built the Greek Revival–style synagogue, which was Maryland's first, in 1845.

led many Jews to abandon their distinctive religious rituals, such as observing the Jewish Sabbath, keeping kosher, and attending synagogue services in their quest for financial success and American acceptance. In addition, these wartime and postwar migrations had a tremendous effect on Jewish visibility in the United States. Americans who had never met Jews before encountered them for the first time, while Jews from one part of the country encountered other Jews and created strong communal connections outside the framework of the city community. Despite these major shifts in Jewish settlement patterns, Jews in early America continued to hold fast to their

This 1858 newspaper illustration depicts workers in a New York City kosher bakery preparing matzoh for Passover under a rabbi's supervision.

identity as Jews and to be active members in their local Jewish communities.

The Jewish population of the United States was relatively stable during this period. Between 1790 and 1820, the Jewish population of the United States grew from about 1,500 to 2,700. In contrast, the overall population of the United States grew from 3.9 to 9.6 million during the same period, due primarily to western European immigration. There was very little Jewish immigration to the United States prior to 1820, which changed when German immigrants began to arrive en masse.

Jewish Americans in the early years of the Republic were generally on good terms with their non-Jewish neighbors. They mingled freely with neighboring Christian communities, and intermarriage was very common. More men than women inhabited the early Jewish-American community, and the population was largely made up of young people. About one-half of the population was under age 20, while less than one-fifth of the population was over 40. Census data also reveals that most American Jews during this period were merchants by profession. Many made their living as owners of small commodity stores. A few very wealthy Jews were involved in the trade that brought African slaves to the Americas; however, those Jews were in the minority.

JEWS IN EARLY AMERICAN LITERATURE AND LETTERS

The literature of the early Republic was full of imagery linking the young nation to ancient Israel and yoking together American and Jewish fates. Americans, as imagined by Jews and non-Jews alike, were the spiritual descendants of the ancient Hebrews.

Samuel Langdon (1723–97), a former president of Harvard College in the years leading up to the Revolution and a prominent New Hampshire clergyman, was well known throughout the nation for his mythologizing sermons connecting the United States with ancient Israel. In one famous sermon, "The Republic of the Israelites as an Example to the American States" delivered on June 5, 1788, in Concord, New Hampshire, Langdon lauded the development of Jewish law in ancient Israel and drew parallels between the Israelite freedom from Egyptian bondage and the new American freedom from British rule and oppression. This overt linking of Jewish and American fates was by no means limited to the clergy. President George Washington made similar connections in his address to the Hebrew Congregation of Savannah written in May of 1789:

May the same wonder-working Deity, who long since delivering the Hebrews from their Egyptian Oppressors planted them in the promised land—whose providential agency has lately been conspicuous in establishing these United States as an independent nation—still continue to water them with the dews of heaven and to make the inhabitants of every denomination participate in the temporal and spiritual blessings of that people whose God is Jehovah.

Jews in the early Republic described America with a fervent passion in sermons, essays, and private correspondence. America was the New Jerusalem, a land of milk and honey in which Jews could thrive and flourish. In 1798, the great orator Hazzan Gershom Mendes Seixas preached that God had purposefully brought the Jews to America "where we possess every advantage that other citizens of these states enjoy." Myer Moses of Charleston wrote in an 1806 essay, "To us, my brethren, should particularly belong a sacred love to this our country." Jacob De La Motta, a Savannah doctor, wrote in 1820, "On what spot in this habitable Globe does an Israelite enjoy more blessings, more privileges, or is more elevated in the sphere of preferment, and more conspicuously dignified in respectable stations?"

GEORGE WASHINGTON AND THE NEWPORT COMMUNITY

Perhaps the most famous expression of Jewish loyalty to the young American nation was the 1790 letter written by the Jewish community of Newport, Rhode Island, congratulating President Washington on his recent inauguration. In August 1790, Jewish leader Moses Seixas met Washington as he toured the nation and handed him a letter written on behalf of all American Jews congratulating Washington on the presidency and wishing him many years of good luck and happiness. President Washington's response to the Newport Jewish community, guaranteeing the safety and security of American Jews, became iconic for generations to come as a symbol of Jewish acceptance in America.

With this statement, George Washington became the first American president to acknowledge the Jewish right to both civic equality and religious tolerance. The correspondence between the Newport Jewish community and the newly inaugurated President Washington illustrates both the loyalty of the Jewish-American population to the new government and the American government's first guarantees of religious inclusion and civic equality that were extended specifically to Jews.

However, despite Washington's assurances and the stipulations of the Bill of Rights, these guarantees were not yet law in every state in the Union. Following the wide dissemination of Washington's letter throughout the Jewish

George Washington's Response to the Jews of Newport, Rhode Island

August 1790
To the Hebrew Congregation in Newport Rhode Island

Gentlemen,

While I receive, with much satisfaction, your Address replete with expressions of affection and esteem, I rejoice in the opportunity of assuring you, that I shall always retain a grateful remembrance of the cordial welcome I experienced in my visit to Newport, from all classes of Citizens . . .

The Citizens of the United States of America have a right to applaud themselves for having given to mankind examples of an enlarged and liberal policy: a policy worthy of imitation. All possess alike liberty of conscience and immunities of citizenship. It is now no more that toleration is spoken of, as it was by the indulgence of one class of people, that another enjoyed the exercise of their inherent natural rights. For happily the Government of the United States, which gives to bigotry no sanction, to persecution no assistance, requires only that they who live under its protection should demean themselves as good citizens, in giving it on all occasions their effectual support.

It would be inconsistent with the frankness of my character not to avow that I am pleased with your favorable opinion of my administration, and fervent wishes for my felicity. May the Children of the Stock of Abraham, who dwell in this land, continue to merit and enjoy the good will of the other Inhabitants; while every one shall sit in safety under his own vine and figtree, and there shall be none to make him afraid. May the father of all mercies scatter light and not darkness in our paths, and make us all in our several vocations useful here, and in his own due time and way everlastingly happy.

George Washington

press, Jewish communities began to marshal their resources to fight for equal political and religious rights in every state.

COMING OF AGE: THE FIGHT FOR EQUALITY

Inspired by Washington's promise, Jews began to demand full civic equality from their government, with mixed results. On the one hand, Jews were officially awarded the rights and responsibilities of full citizenship upon the passage of the Bill of Rights, which was ratified with the Constitution in 1789. As historian Eli Faber wrote:

Early American Jews were also among the first to experiment with citizenship for Jews in the modern world . . . The Jewish experience in early America verified that this was a land in which the outsider could become an insider, where the stranger in the land and the wanderer in history could find sanctuary and serenity.

However, American Jews had to fight hard before they were awarded full civic equality. The Bill of Rights may have technically guaranteed religious freedom, but individual states granted true civic equality at their own pace. In the immediate postwar period, Jews believed that they deserved the equal rights of all citizens for their exemplary service during the Revolutionary War. "Having passed the test—having shed blood for God and country—they considered themselves due full equality," historian Jeffrey Gurock writes of the Jewish mindset during this period: "They felt that America owed them a debt, and they demanded full repayment." At the Constitutional Convention of 1787, American Jews made their needs known to the new political leaders of the United States.

STATE LAWS

Individual states adopted their own constitutions following the conclusion of the national convention. Some extended full civic liberty to the Jewish-American community, while others explicitly withheld it. New Hampshire, the first state to ratify its constitution, ignored the topic of religious freedom altogether. South Carolina's constitution contained a provision that required all officeholders and voters to be Protestant. Virginia provided for freedom of religion, but denied Jews the right to vote until Thomas Jefferson fought for a bill to overturn that discriminatory provision in 1779. Delaware, Pennsylvania, and Maryland all required a religious test as a prerequisite for anyone seeking office. New York was virtually the only state whose constitution initially imposed no restrictions on Jews. The Northwest Ordinance, which governed the territories northwest of the Ohio River, provided full religious and political rights for all people, regardless of their religion. In 1785, Thomas Jefferson's Act for Religious Freedom became law in the state of Virginia, propelling many of the surrounding states to adopt similar laws. By 1830, virtually every state had given Jews complete equal rights. New Hampshire was the very last to grant full equality in 1877.

In the early years of the 19th century, Jewish Americans continued to publicly voice their disapproval of laws that permitted states to discriminate against Jews on the basis of religion. In 1809, North Carolina politician Jacob Henry was elected to the state legislature, but his election was challenged by local authorities when he refused to swear an oath affirming the divine origins of the New Testament. Backed by the Jewish-American community, Henry sued the state for illegal discrimination and won his case. In 1816, a

Charleston resident named Isaac Harby wrote a moving letter to secretary of state and future president James Monroe arguing against the constitutionality of discriminatory laws that made Jews ineligible for public office in many states. Though Harby's letter did not achieve the desired effect, it was significant for the fact that Harby brought the matter to Monroe's attention. These examples are just a few representative occurrences that demonstrate the Jewish commitment to attaining full civic equality during this period.

Perhaps the most famous conflict in the nationwide fight for Jewish equal rights was the debate over Maryland's "Jew Bill" that galvanized the state from 1818 to 1826. Maryland's initial constitution prohibited Jews from holding municipal and state office. Candidates for civil office in Maryland were required to swear an oath upon the New Testament. Beginning in 1818, Maryland Jews fought for a bill that would allow Jews to take the oath of office on the Pentateuch instead. After a long and bitter battle, Maryland politicians finally passed the Jew Bill in 1826, permitting Jews to hold office, practice law, and become officers in the Maryland state militia.

CREATING JEWISH INSTITUTIONS

While Jews slowly acquired religious and political freedom, Jewish-American society was engaged in yet another major transformation: the shift from transient and informal Jewish communities into organized Jewish communal institutions. The most important site where these developments took place was the synagogue.

Exhilarated by the founding of the new nation and the adoption of the Constitution, Jewish congregations began to write their own constitutions, redefining the traditional synagogue community by incorporating the principles of American democracy. These constitutions used the language and terminology popularized during the revolutionary period to define the function of the synagogue and the standards of membership. As synagogue constitutions became increasingly common, American Jews began to conceptualize the role of the synagogue in different terms.

Throughout the United States, American Jews began to choose their leaders through an annual democratic election. Before the Revolution, congregation officials were usually selected by an executive board; after the Revolution, leaders were chosen in a congregation-wide election. However, the democratization of the synagogue also led to the influx of Christian influences in synagogue life. A synagogue constructed in Charleston in 1792 was built to look like a church and featured a spire on its roof. In 1820, the dedication ceremony for a new synagogue in Savannah prominently featured organ music. In addition, congregations began to incorporate the English language and American customs into synagogue life. Many congregations switched from the Hebrew calendar to the Western calendar for internal records and event planning after the Revolution.

Cultural assimilation proceeded rapidly during this period in both synagogue and family life, aided by the high rates of intermarriage among Jews and non-Jews in early America. One survey of 699 American marriages between 1790 and 1840 involving Jews showed that 201 married outside the Jewish community. Conversion of the non-Jewish spouse was rare in most circumstances. American Jews adopted the clothing, hairstyles, architecture, music, and cultural norms of the surrounding Christian population. At the same time, American society accepted Jews virtually as equals in a wide variety of social, political, and cultural organizations. In 1791, the New York Stock Exchange was founded, with three Jews among the primary founders: Benjamin Mendes Seixas, Ephraim Hart, and Alexander Zuntz. At the turn of the 18th century, Georgia elected America's first Jewish governor, Daniel Emanuel. Harvard began accepting Jewish students in 1800, and Jews were admitted to Yale and West Point

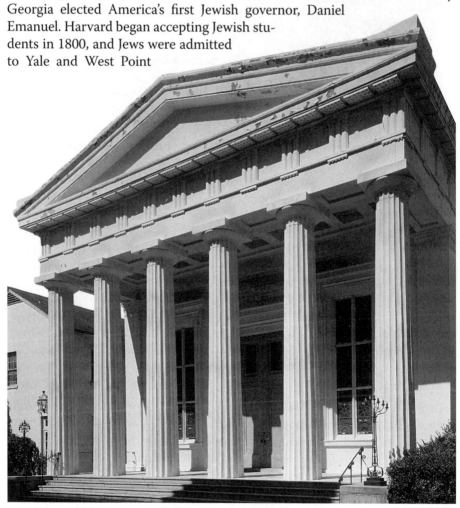

In 1843, the Jewish community of Charleston, South Carolina, replaced the previous synagogue, which had been built in the style of a church with a spire, with the Kahal Kadosh Beth Elohim Synagogue, shown above. It is now the second-oldest synagogue in the United States.

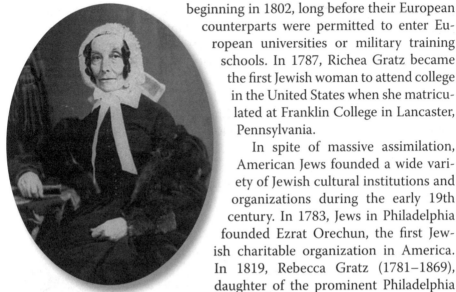

Rebecca Gratz in a photograph
from the mid-19th century.

beginning in 1802, long before their European counterparts were permitted to enter European universities or military training schools. In 1787, Richea Gratz became the first Jewish woman to attend college in the United States when she matriculated at Franklin College in Lancaster, Pennsylvania.

In spite of massive assimilation, American Jews founded a wide variety of Jewish cultural institutions and organizations during the early 19th century. In 1783, Jews in Philadelphia founded Ezrat Orechun, the first Jewish charitable organization in America. In 1819, Rebecca Gratz (1781–1869), daughter of the prominent Philadelphia Gratz family, organized the Female Hebrew Benevolent Society (FHBS) together with a group of women at her synagogue. The FHBS, the first Jewish agency in the United States that was not a synagogue, sought to provide for impoverished Jewish women in need throughout the city. Within a year, women's groups in other cities throughout the United States had begun to found their own versions of the Philadelphia FBHS. Jews also began to found publishing houses to produce their own religious and secular books. The first Hebrew book to be printed in the United States was published in 1814. A decade later, the first Hebrew journal was published.

Despite major gains in political equality, Jews were still not fully accepted as equals by all Americans. Anti-Semitism persisted in discriminatory laws, religious sermons, and popular culture. Sunday laws, which restricted commerce on Sundays (a non-religious day for Jews), remained common in many states and municipalities. Religious leaders were openly anti-Semitic in their sermons. Baptist minister Isaac Backus vehemently defended the Massachusetts law that prohibited Jews from holding office. Henry Melchior Muhlenberg, a Lutheran leader, supported a similar law in Pennsylvania. Anti-Semitic rhetoric was heard in the campaigns of leaders from both political parties. In addition, Jews were stereotyped in American popular novels and plays. Greedy and uncivilized Jews were major characters in novels such as *The Algerian Captive* (1797) and *Modern Chivalry* (1792–1815), and in plays such as *Slaves in Algiers* (1794) and *Trial Without Jury* (1815). In spite of continuing anti-Semitism, Jews in early America were not subject to economic sanctions and could feel secure in the federal protection of their civil rights.

1820–59: THE NEW WAVE

Prior to 1820, Jewish immigrants to the United States came mainly from London and Amsterdam. Most were Ashkenazic and Sephardic Jews, and nearly every congregation established in America before 1820 followed Sephardic religious customs. Beginning in 1820, however, a new wave of Jewish immigrants from central and eastern Europe redefined the contours of American Jewish communities, religious life, and culture. This fundamental shift in the demographics of the American Jewish population changed old institutions and led to the establishment of new synagogues, schools, social and political organizations, and geographical centers of Jewish life. Before 1820, most American Jews spoke English and had largely assimilated into gentile American society. The influx of new immigrants led to the immediate diversification of Jewish life in America. The German and central European Jewish migrations of the 1820s were only a prelude to the massive waves of immigration that would follow 60 years later. However, the "emigration fever" of the 1820s established the flexible and diverse Jewish community that would continue to attract large numbers of immigrants well into the 20th century.

What spurred the waves of immigration in the 1820s? In 1815, the Napoleonic Wars ended in Europe, providing central and eastern European Jews with the mobility to consider emigration as a viable option. New forms of transportation emerged during the 1820s that allowed potential immigrants to travel far from their homes with greater ease, safety, and comfort. However, Jews did not come to America for positive reasons alone. Many left their ancestral homelands fleeing unstable economics, revolutionary upheaval, restrictive laws, and rampant anti-Semitism. In 1819, violent anti-Semitic riots broke out in German cities and towns along the Rhine, spurring many German Jews to emigrate. This was the worst outbreak of anti-Jewish violence in central Europe since the Middle Ages, and German Jews feared that their situation would continue to decline. In 1832, a second wave of riots began, causing even more German Jews to try their luck in America.

Between 1780 and 1820, there were virtually no significant increases in the Jewish population of the new American nation. Very few Jews immigrated, and the total American Jewish population hovered consistently around 2,000–3,000 Jews. By 1820, the census recorded a total of 2,750 Jews, comprising approximately 0.03 of 1 percent of the overall American population. However, approximately 5 million European immigrants came to America between 1820 and 1861. About 250,000 of those immigrants were Jews, largely from the German states or from other German-speaking countries such as Austria, Hungary, Bohemia, and Moravia. Between 1830 and 1840 alone, America's Jewish population increased from 4,000 Jews to over 15,000.

Unlike early American Jews, the new German-speaking Jewish immigrants settled throughout the United States. By 1860, organized Jewish communities existed in over 50 cities. Instead of joining their Sephardic brethren in New

This 1866 photo of a San Francisco synagogue attests to the western movement of Jewish immigrants in the mid and late 19th century.

York, Philadelphia, and Charleston, many of the new Jewish immigrants migrated west to the rapidly growing cities of Rochester, Albany, Syracuse, Buffalo, Pittsburgh, Cleveland, Columbus, St. Louis, Minneapolis, Milwaukee, Louisville, Chicago, and Cincinnati. Jews also began to settle in the new cities farther west, such as Detroit, Denver, Los Angeles, and San Francisco. Over the next 60 years, German-Jewish immigrants continued to settle westward in search of new economic opportunities. Soon, Chicago and Cincinnati became major Jewish centers that could boast of their own synagogues, community centers, philanthropic institutions, and social organizations. Cincinnati became the host city for Hebrew Union College, the rabbinical seminary for the rapidly expanding Reform movement, and was also a major center for German-Jewish commercial trading networks, earning it the nickname of "Jerusalem on the Ohio." By 1880, there were over 20 congregations throughout the far west, including two in San Francisco.

GERMAN JEWISH IMMIGRANTS IN AMERICA

The German-Jewish immigrants brought about many firsts in the history of American Jewry. In 1825, German immigrants founded the first Ashkenazic synagogue in New York City. In 1838, Rebecca Gratz founded the first Sunday Hebrew school (modeled on the Protestant Sunday school) to educate the immigrant masses. The first Jewish fraternal organization, the B'nai Brith, was founded in 1843 to organize and unite American Jewry. In 1849, German-speaking Jewish immigrants founded the first Jewish weekly paper, *Israel's Herald*, edited by Isidor Busch, an Austrian refugee. Entrepreneurs, sensing the opportunity to make a profit, founded a variety of weekly papers soon after *Israel's Herald* went into circulation, including *The Jew* (1823), *Asmonean* (1849), *American Israelite* (1854), and *Jewish Messenger* (1857). In

The New Immigrants

The trip from Europe to American ports usually took about six weeks. When immigrants arrived, they often began working as petty traders and peddlers. Itinerant peddlers moved to the burgeoning small towns in the west where they would face less competition. Gradually, these new Jewish Americans found more established work as shopkeepers and small business owners in the growing towns and cities of the American west. German-Jewish immigrants also fundamentally changed the demographics of the Jewish-American community. By the 1830s and 1840s, young Jews far outnumbered their older brethren in many cities, and recent German-Jewish immigrants under the age of 30 began to take leadership roles in their communities. The most famous young Jewish leader during this period was Isaac Leeser, an immigrant from Westphalia

The influential religious leader and writer Isaac Leeser around 1868.

who took over the leadership of Philadelphia's Jewish community at the age of 24. Leeser soon became the most famous Jewish religious leader of his era. In addition to serving as the cantor of Congregation Mikveh Israel in Philadelphia, Leeser was a prolific writer who published scores of texts dedicated to combating the efforts of Christian missionaries seeking to convert newly arrived Jewish immigrants.

1852, the first eastern European congregation, Beth Hamidrash, was founded in New York. Jews also made major gains in becoming an accepted part of American society and culture. In the 1850s, Jews began to hold elective office in significant numbers. In 1850, Morris Goodman, a Bavarian immigrant, was elected to the city council of Los Angeles. Two years later, San Francisco voters elected Elcan Heydenfeldt to the California State Assembly. Mar Strouse was elected chief of police in Virginia City, Nevada, in 1863, and Bernard Goldsmith was elected mayor of Portland, Oregon, in 1869. Between 1820 and 1880, 20 Jews were elected to the U.S. Congress. In 1845, David Levy Yulee of Florida became the first Jew elected to the Senate.

Jews in America during this period wrote freely and often to the presidents and former presidents of the United States, following the lead of the congregations that had corresponded with Washington during the early years of the new nation. In April 1818, Mordechai Manual Noah gave a speech at the dedication of the second Mill Street Synagogue about the importance of American opportunities and American values for Jews. He mailed copies of his speech to former presidents John Adams, Thomas Jefferson, and James Madison, and he received a lengthy reply from each. Others followed Noah's example. On one memorable occasion, Joseph Marx of Richmond sent Jefferson a copy of the proceedings of Napoleon's Sanhedrin in France; Jefferson, in turn, replied with a letter expressing his support for the Jews. These exchanges reflect the extent to which Jews had become comfortable with American customs, politics, and culture.

German-Jewish immigrants to the United States brought the radical ideas and tenets of the new Reform movement (a modernization movement within the Jewish religion) with them. Jews in Charleston were the first who sought to alter the nature of Jewish observance and synagogue life. In 1824, a group of young Charleston Jews rebelled against their Congregation Beth Elohim, asking for a shorter service, prayers in English, and other reforms to relax the standards of observance. When they did not get the changes, the group left to form an alternative congregation. They later returned to Beth Elohim and their changes were adopted. This led to the secession of the traditionalists By 1843, Beth Elohim had incorporated all of these reforms and more, including the installation of an organ to be played at every service. Two years later, a group of German immigrants founded Congregation Emanu-El in New York. Emanu-El featured prayers in German, organ music during services, family pews, and the elimination of prayer shawls, phylacteries, and the second-day observance of holidays like Rosh Hashanah and Passover. In 1846, another Reform congregation, Beth-El, was established in Albany by Isaac Mayer Wise, who abolished separate seating for women, counted women in the prayer quorum, and gave his sermons in English. The founding of these synagogues signified the rapid growth of the Reform movement in the United States following the arrival of the German-Jewish immigrants. Before 1840, Beth Elohim in Charleston

New York City's Temple Emanu-El in 1868. It was built by a Reform congregation made up of descendants of German Jews.

was the only Reform congregation in America. After 1840, however, Reform synagogues gradually became a normative part of American Jewish life. By 1880, over 90 percent of American Jewish congregations would be reformed.

This period also saw the immigration of the first rabbis to the United States. Prior to the waves of immigration, early American Jewish communities relied on European rabbis for their essential Jewish needs, such as, Torah scrolls, prayer books, and rabbinical decisions. American Jews wrote to established rabbis in Amsterdam and London, requesting books and materials as well as *halakhic* (according to Jewish law) decisions in matters of concern to the community. In 1840, Bavarian immigrant Abraham Rice became the first ordained rabbi to lead an American congregation. Other prominent immigrant rabbis during this period included Isaac Mayer Wise, Max Lilienthal, and David Einhorn.

In 1840, an international incident occurred that brought American Jews of all political and religious stripes together to advocate for their persecuted brethren abroad. After the mysterious disappearance of a Catholic monk in Syria, anti-Semites accused Jews of committing the murder in order to eat the monk's blood in their Passover *matzah*. This centuries-old blood libel, though crude, proved effective, and several Jews were arrested and tortured for their alleged participation in what soon became known as the Damascus Affair. American Jews were shocked by the malicious use of the blood libel (false accusations that Jews used blood in ceremonies) to attack Syrian Jewry. They gathered together in public meetings across the country and sent a series of petitions to President Martin Van Buren, encouraging him to denounce the affair as a fraud and to demand a fair trial for the Jews who had been falsely accused. Their petitions were ultimately successful and Van Buren issued a highly influential statement that encouraged authorities to resolve the Damascus Affair without any further violence and to denounce the anti-Semitic blood libel. The American Jewish response to the Damascus Affair was significant not only for its effectiveness, but also because it represented the first time that American Jews organized themselves in response to Jewish suffering elsewhere in the world. The response to the Damascus Affair thus signified the convergence of a diverse population into a united community with a distinctly American Jewish identity.

CONCLUSION

Between 1783 and 1859, virtually everything about American Jewish religion, life, and culture was fundamentally altered. At the beginning of this period, American Jews were mostly Sephardic and highly assimilated, with few of their own organizations and institutions. Their communities were centered in a few major cities, all on the East Coast, and few lived in states that supported full civil rights for Jews. By 1820, American Jews had founded communal organizations and synagogues in every city in which they had settled and had acquired political equality in most states. The American Jewish community had an established infrastructure that would serve as the basis of communal organizations and interaction for years to come. During the second half of this period (1820–59), the Jewish population grew tremendously as German and central European immigrants entered the United States in large numbers. These immigrants brought with them Reform Judaism, a new language, and the critical mass necessary to establish a commercially successful Jewish publishing industry. By mid-century, the Jews of America were distributed throughout the country and had established thriving communities and communal organizations that adapted to the changing conditions and desires of the immigrant population. This period established the preconditions for Jewish growth and development that would come to be increasingly necessary as a new wave of Jewish immigrants from eastern Europe began to arrive on the shores of Manhattan.

DEBRA CAPLAN
HARVARD UNIVERSITY

Further Reading

Diner, Hasia R. *A New Promised Land: A History of Jews in America*. Oxford: Oxford University Press, 2000.

———. *The Jews of the United States, 1654 to 2000*. Berkeley, CA: University of California Press, 2004.

Faber, Eli. *A Time for Planting: The First Migration, 1654–1820*. Baltimore, MD: Johns Hopkins University Press, 1992.

Finkelstein, Norman H. *American Jewish History: JPS Guide*. Philadelphia, PA: Jewish Publication Society, 2007.

Gurock, Jeffrey S., ed. *American Jewish History: The Colonial and Early National Periods, 1654–1840*. New York: Routledge, 1998.

Norwood, Stephen H. and Eunice G. Pollack, eds. *Encyclopedia of American Jewish History*. Santa Barbara, CA: ABC-CLIO, 2008.

Raphael, Marc Lee, ed. *The Columbia History of Jews and Judaism in America*. New York: Columbia University Press, 2008.

Reiss, Oscar. *The Jews in Colonial America*. Jefferson, NC: McFarland & Co., 2004.

Rosenwaike, Ira. *On the Edge of Greatness: A Portrait of American Jewry in the Early National Period*. Cincinnati, OH: American Jewish Archives, 1985.

Schappes, Morris U., ed. *A Documentary History of the Jews in the United States, 1654–1875*. New York: Citadel Press, 1950.

CHAPTER 3

The Civil War to the Gilded Age: 1859 to 1900

THE PERIOD FROM the Civil War until the turn of the 20th century witnessed an enormous change in the Jewish-American community. American Jews, like other Americans, struggled with the violence and the moral issues that the Civil War presented. But the Jewish-American community also changed in ways that differed from many other communities. While many American Jews had previously concentrated on fitting in as Americans, the later decades of the 19th century marked a time when many American Jews began to focus on their Jewishness and involvement in the Jewish community. They also had to deal with a rise in anti-Semitism, especially in American social life. Furthermore because of immigration from Europe, Russia, and many other locations, the size and diversity of the Jewish-American community grew dramatically.

THE CIVIL WAR

When the Civil War began in 1861, Jews lived all over the United States. Although American Jews are most commonly associated with northern cities like New York and Philadelphia, many Jews also lived throughout the south. While some lived in established Jewish communities in urban centers like Richmond or New Orleans, others lived in rural areas where a single Jewish family might run the local country store.

This geographic distribution—the majority (about 125,000 individuals) in the north, but a sizeable minority (about 25,000 individuals) in the south—meant that the Jewish community would not be unified in its opinions about slavery or the union of the states. Like other Americans, most Jews tended to be loyal to the geographic region in which they lived. The Solomon family of New Orleans serves as a typical example of southern Jewish families. Sixteen-year-old Clara Solomon gives a personal account in her diary of the first years of the Civil War: her family owned a domestic slave named Lucy, her father supplied equipment and clothing to Confederate troops, and a prominent family friend, Eugenia Levy Phillips, was imprisoned by Union forces for speaking out against the union.

Northern Jews collected or made clothing and food like the women of the Philadelphia organization Ladies Hebrew Association for the Relief of Sick and Wounded soldiers. Others wrote political poetry, like a young Emma Lazarus. Jews' Hospital in New York, funded mainly by the local Jewish community, opened its doors to care for sick and injured Union soldiers. American Jews on both sides also participated in less tangible ways, as when they prayed for the success and safety of their loved ones fighting on the front lines.

SLAVERY

There were quite a few exceptions to the generalizations that equated antislavery, pro-union stances with the north and proslavery stances with the south. For instance, New York Rabbi Morris Raphall was an early and outspoken defender of slavery on the basis of a particular literal reading of the Bible, however, Rabbi David Einhorn was forced out of his Baltimore pulpit because of his arguments against slavery.

Because of these diverse opinions, national Jewish groups rarely aligned themselves with one side or the other. Even members of individual families had to employ this strategy of quiet discretion in order to keep loving ties across ideological lines. For instance, an aging Rebecca Gratz emphasized the commonalities remaining among her northern and southern relatives, rather than discussing political issues in her letters. Because of resettling, especially for education and business reasons, many Jewish families had members in both the north and the south. Like Gratz, the prominent rabbis Isaac Mayer Wise and Isaac Leeser both advocated neutral positions and declared that peace and harmony were more important than decisively resolving the slavery issue. Unlike many Christian denominations that split into separate bodies during the war, Jewish religious communities were not officially divided. Most held that each individual was entitled to hold an opinion independently leaders and rabbis.

This did not stop most leaders from articulating their opinions publicly in an effort to convince others. Women's rights activist and socialist Ernestine Rose announced, "The question which now distracts the country is no longer

Emma Lazarus

Emma Lazarus, a Jewish-American poet, wrote many poems about the Jewish community in the United States and around the world. Her family had lived in the United States since colonial times, having come from Portugal. Although she was not an immigrant, she was carefully attuned to the plight and persecution of Jews as a reason for their immigration. In her poem "1492," Lazarus refers to two simultaneous events, both of which she sees as crucial events for Jews. First, the monarchs Ferdinand and Isabella issued an edict expelling all Jews from Spain. But in the same year, they provided support for Christopher Columbus to sail toward what they would call "the new world." Lazarus sees the expulsion as the violent closing of a door for Jews, but the exploration of the Americas as a hopeful opening of doors. The poem begins with these lines:

Thou two-faced year, Mother of Change and Fate,
Didst weep when Spain cast forth with flaming sword,
The children of the prophets of the Lord,
Prince, priest, and people, spurned by zealot hate.
Hounded from sea to sea, from state to state,
The West refused them, and the East abhorred...

Emma Lazarus is probably most famous for another poem Americans associate with immigration: the poem that appears on the pedestal of the Statue of Liberty. Emma Lazarus wrote the sonnet in response to a fundraising call for the construction of the pedestal, and it was read at the exhibit's opening. It was inscribed onto the pedestal in 1903. The poem reads:

The New Colossus

Not like the brazen giant of Greek fame,
With conquering limbs astride from land to land;
Here at our sea-washed, sunset gates shall stand
A mighty woman with a torch, whose flame
Is the imprisoned lightning, and her name
Mother of Exiles. From her beacon-hand
Glows world-wide welcome; her mild eyes command
The air-bridged harbor that twin cities frame.
"Keep, ancient lands, your storied pomp!" cries she
With silent lips. "Give me your tired, your poor,
Your huddled masses yearning to breathe free,
The wretched refuse of your teeming shore.
Send these, the homeless, tempest-tost to me,
I lift my lamp beside the golden door!"

one of color—it is freedom or slavery, the life or death of the North—it is whether a vile mob, headed by corrupted and treacherous politicians, who would dissolve not only the Union but the universe to get themselves into office, shall be allowed to trample the dignity, the manhood, and the liberties of the North into the dirt." With equal venom, a Richmond rabbi asked that God punish the north: "Cause them to fall into a pit of destruction, which in the abomination of their evil intents they digged out for us."

THE BATTLEFIELDS OF THE CIVIL WAR

On both sides, Jewish men fought in uniform and Jewish women volunteered their time and skills, raised money, and cared for the sick and wounded. About 3,000 men fought for the Confederacy (south), while about 10,000 Jewish men fought for the Union (north). Most of the men who enlisted were immigrants, but they saw fighting for their ideals—whether Union or Confederate—as an honorable duty. Some Jews fought in regiments that were mostly Jewish, while others found themselves as one of a very few Jews in their units.

The exact number of women who worked for their causes is much more difficult to ascertain, because neither side kept comprehensive records of noncombatants. A few women disguised themselves as men in order to fight. Much larger numbers of women were instrumental as nurses, and they worked in field and military hospitals. Phoebe Yates Levy Pember, for instance, served as matron of the Chimborazo Hospital in Richmond, Virginia, where 76,000 patients were treated during the war. Even in those critically undersupplied and desperate conditions, she did everything from dressing wounds and assisting surgeons with operations to providing emotional support for dying patients.

In 1861, a controversy arose in the Union when Congress passed a law requiring that any military chaplain must be an ordained Christian minister. Michael Allen, a Jewish man who had been serving as chaplain to Jewish soldiers, was dismissed, and became a figurehead for those who opposed this new legislation. The Jewish community sent rabbi Arnold Fischel to Washington to lobby for a change in the law. Lincoln met with him and proposed the change to Congress, and it was accepted. Fischel himself never served as a chaplain, but several other rabbis did. A revised bill, a source of considerable debate, finally insisted that "some Christian denomination" actually meant "some religious denomination." To the relief of the Jewish community, the new interpretation allowed Jewish chaplains into the Union Army for the support of Jewish soldiers.

Although practicing Judaism while living in a camp and fighting a war could not have been easy, evidence suggests that many, if not most, Jews found ways to observe some traditions. In response to Abraham Lincoln's recommendation that all soldiers observe the Sabbath on Sunday, Bernhard Behrend wrote a letter detailing his soldier son's desire to observe the traditional Jewish Sab-

August Belmont

August Belmont was born on December 8 in Alzei, Germany, in either 1813 or 1816. He began his career as an apprentice for the Rothschild family, wealthy and influential European bankers. During the financial panic of 1837, he came to New York City for a brief visit that became a permanent stay. There he adopted the surname Belmont. He opened August Belmont and Company, his own Wall Street firm, with limited capital and used his strong work ethic, talent, and earlier connections to build it into one of the country's leading international finance firms. He gained his U.S. citizenship and married the socially prominent Caroline Slidell Perry, the daughter of Commodore Matthew Perry and niece of Oliver Hazard Perry, a hero of the War of 1812. His more colorful exploits included an 1841 duel with William Hayward that left him with a permanent limp.

August Belmont gained political prominence in the antebellum period, serving as Democratic Party chairman for 12 years. He also served various Democratic presidential administrations in a diplomatic capacity, including stints as the U.S. consul general for Austria from 1844 to 1850 and minister to the Netherlands from 1853 to 1857. Although Belmont opposed the institution of slavery, he did not support abolition. He backed the popular sovereignty policies of Stephen Douglas and opposed Abraham Lincoln, but remained loyal to the Union during the Civil War.

Belmont supported the Union through funding the first German regiment from New York City in the Union Army and through invaluable behind-the-scenes diplomacy in Europe to prevent various European nations and families, including the Rothschilds, from supporting the Confederacy. He visited London and Paris during the war and maintained correspondence with his European friends. He maintained an interest in politics after the war, attending state and national Democratic conventions.

August Belmont around the time of the Civil War.

Belmont's success continued to grow through the Gilded Age of the late 19th century. The Belmonts were among New York's social elite, renowned for their lavish entertainments, art collection, and involvement in thoroughbred racing. Belmont died of pneumonia on November 24, 1890.

Judah Benjamin, at far left, with the cabinet of the Confederacy in an illustration from the June 1, 1861, Harper's Weekly. *Benjamin served as attorney general under President Jefferson Davis.*

bath. "I gave my consent to my son, who is yet a minor, that he should enlist in the United States army; I thought it was his duty, and I gave him my advice to fulfill his duty as a good citizen, and he has done so. At the same time, I also taught him to observe the Sabbath on Saturday, when it would not hinder him from fulfilling his duty in the army." Other Jewish soldiers made certain that they could observe Passover with unleavened bread, kosher meat, and other traditional foods, even when it meant foraging. Soldiers on both sides found their Passover celebrations of 1862 so memorable that they wrote about them in letters and memoirs.

Other Jewish soldiers, however, did not participate in Jewish rituals; some even tried to conceal their Jewishness. Especially in regiments that primarily contained evangelical Christians, many Jewish men preferred to keep their religion and ethnicity to themselves as much as possible. Others simply found it very difficult to observe the Sabbath on Saturday, eat kosher food, or observe holidays while they were away from home fighting a war.

Both the Union and the Confederacy appointed Jewish officers and awarded commendations to Jewish soldiers. Seven Jews won the Medal of Honor, the highest Union award for bravery. Abraham Lincoln, realizing in 1862 that "we have not yet appointed a Hebrew" to a senior-level job placed C.M. Levy in a quartermaster post. The Confederacy listed at least 23 Jewish officers and also boasted the highest-ranking Jew of the Civil War. A lawyer and former planter, Judah Benjamin had sold his plantation and his slaves before the war to become

Judah Benjamin

Judah Benjamin was born in the British West Indies on August 6, 1811 but was raised in Charleston, South Carolina, and New Orleans, Louisiana. He attended Yale Law School, but did not complete his studies. Benjamin then began his career as a commercial lawyer and political lobbyist in New Orleans. He also co-organized the Illinois Central Railroad and owned a sugar plantation with approximately 140 slaves. He married Natalie Martin, but the couple lived apart after she moved to Paris with their daughter. He was elected to the Louisiana state legislature in 1842.

While Benjamin did not practice his religion, he did not deny his Jewish heritage either, and endured frequent attacks due to his heritage throughout his political career. He was elected to the U.S. Senate in 1852 as a Whig and in 1858 as a Democrat, becoming the first acknowledged Jew elected to the U.S. Senate. He gained an antebellum reputation as an eloquent orator in defense of southern interests.

Confederate President Jefferson Davis, who had developed a friendship with Benjamin during their Senate careers, appointed him to various posts within the Confederate government. Many historians have termed Benjamin the "brains of the Confederacy." He first served as attorney general, advocating the Confederacy follow the policy known as cotton diplomacy by emphasizing the importance of Confederate cotton to the European textile industry in an effort to gain European recognition and support for the Confederate cause.

Benjamin next became secretary of war despite his non-military background. He mainly served to implement President Davis's strategies but also strongly advocated for the implementation of a proposed policy of offering slaves freedom in exchange for military service. However, he received much criticism from the press as well as the generals in the field and was eventually forced to resign. Davis then appointed him secretary of state, a post he held until the end of the war.

Benjamin maintained a private life in the postwar period, writing little about the war and burning most of his personal papers. He achieved brief notoriety for his involvement in a Confederate spy ring located in Canada that became implicated in the plot to assassinate President Abraham Lincoln.

Benjamin then left the United States for England, where he became a successful international lawyer and authored a classic work on English commercial law, entitled *Treatise on the Law of Sale of Personal Property* and commonly known as "Benjamin on Sales." When Benjamin later moved to Paris, he was reunited with his wife and children. He died in Paris on May 6, 1884. He is remembered as one of the most powerful Jewish Americans in 19th-century U.S. politics.

a Louisiana senator. Although he no longer owned slaves, he firmly supported the Confederate cause. When Confederate President Jefferson Davis appointed him attorney general in 1861, Benjamin became the first Jew to hold a cabinet-level office in an American government. Later in the war, Benjamin served as the secretary of war and as secretary of state.

MIGRATION

In the years following the Civil War, the American Jewish community began to grow at unprecedented rates. Many Jews emigrated from central and eastern Europe and chose the United States as their new home. Some popular histories have painted a very simple picture of when and from where immigrants came: a small number of modern, mostly assimilated Jews came from Germany in the 1840s and 1850s, while a large number of traditional Jews came from eastern Europe after 1880. But while this picture may be a good starting point, it is too rudimentary to tell the whole story of Jewish immigration to the United States.

The first wave of immigrants (those who came between 1820 and 1880) included Jews from Germany, but also from Lithuania, western Russia, and Galicia. Even some of the "Germans" actually came from Polish provinces that were under German control. Many of these Jews spoke Yiddish, not German, and had religious and cultural traditions much like those of the second wave. The number of immigrants in the second wave (between 1880 and 1920) was certainly much higher than the first: roughly 250,000 before 1880, compared with about 2.5 million after 1880. But the differences in background, disposition, and attitude toward the United States were not nearly as dramatic as the difference in numbers.

The push factors for emigration—the reasons for leaving a country—were generally similar across the years. European Jewish life was in a state of upheaval: many countries emancipated Jews (gave them political rights), the population grew rapidly for many years, industrialization changed the way Jews made their livelihoods, and Jews left smaller towns for more urban environments. Many of these changes made various aspects of life difficult for Jews. Industrialization meant that the economy demanded fewer peddlers and small-town traders, which were heavily Jewish occupations. Emancipation was a mixed blessing; while some Jews could take advantage of new rights, most Jews who were poor found they were unable to benefit from them. Thus, emancipation deeply divided many Jewish communities into "winners" and "losers."

Population increase, coupled with legislation restricting the number of Jews in some places, presented one of the most prominent reasons for emigration. The eastern European Jewish population ballooned from 1.25 million in 1800 to 6.5 million in 1900. The number of jobs open to Jews did not grow at this pace, so many faced the decision of terrible poverty or emigration. In eastern Europe

This illustration depicting Jewish refugees from Russia arriving in New York appeared in the February 18, 1882, issue of Harper's Weekly.

during the end of the 19th century, pogroms (organized violence against Jews) provided another compelling reason to pick up and start life anew in another land. In many places, these actions to drive away Jews were conscious strategies for solving what had come to be called "the Jewish problem."

Jewish immigrants from across Europe and even from the Balkans, Turkey, and Greece also found appealing similar "pull" factors—reasons for choosing the destination of their migration. Technological advancements made railroad and steamship travel widely available and more affordable. The United States' growing economy offered many jobs for both skilled and unskilled laborers. It also offered a political climate that was very stable in comparison to points of origin for many immigrants. Although history indicates significant differences in Jewish life in different regions of the Old World, a simple early German-Jewish immigration wave and a later eastern European–Jewish immigration wave obscure the many similarities (and some of the differences) that different Jewish immigrants had over time.

Although each family had its own circumstances, many Jewish immigrants followed similar migration patterns. Often families did not have the money to send all members together. A male member of the family, usually an adult son or father, would be first to travel to the United States. If an unmarried son immigrated first, he would often return to his home province and search for a woman to marry him. Then she would leave her family to accompany him back to the United States. The two of them would often work hard to raise the money to bring other members of their families over. If a woman's husband immigrated first, she would usually stay with any children and elderly members of the family. They would continue to live and work at home,

Immigrants at Castle Garden, a precursor to Ellis Island, in a magazine illustration from 1880.

Rose Cohen

In 1892 Rose Cohen came to the United States with her aunt in order to join her father, who had come a year and a half earlier. The rest of her family would be able to come only after she and her father saved money from their work in the garment industry. In her autobiography *Out of the Shadows* she remembers her impressions as a 12-year-old upon being reunited with her father:

> *From Castle Garden we drove to our new home in a market wagon filled with immigrants' bedding. . . . As we drove along I looked in bewilderment. My thoughts were chasing each other. I felt a thrill: "Am I really in America at last?" But the next moment it would be checked and I felt a little disappointed, a little homesick. Father was so changed. I hardly expected to find him in his black long tailed coat in which he left home. But of course yet with his same full grown beard and earlocks. Now instead I saw a young man with a closely cut beard and no sign of earlocks. As I looked at him I could scarcely believe my eyes. Father had been the most pious Jew in our neighborhood. I wondered was it true then as Mindle said that "in America one at once became a libertine"?*
>
> *Father's face was radiantly happy. Every now and then he would look over his shoulder and smile. But he soon guessed what troubled me for after a while he began to talk in a quiet, reassuring manner. He told me he would take me to his own shop and teach me part of his own trade. He was a men's coat finisher. He made me understand that if we worked steadily and lived economically we should soon have money to send for those at home. "Next year at this time," he smiled, "you yourself may be on your way to Castle Garden to fetch mother and the children." So I too smiled at the happy prospect, wiped some tears away and resolved to work hard.*

while the man in the United States would save money from his earnings to send to them or to purchase tickets on a steamship. After several months, families might decide to send children—traveling one at a time, in pairs, or with other family members—to help earn money faster. Author Mary Antin's family provides a typical example: she and her family had lived in czarist Russia, where they were restricted to the Pale of Settlement (the region of Imperial Russia where Jews were allowed permanent residency). Because of economic and social difficulties, her family decided to make the journey to the United States. Her father emigrated from Russia in 1891, and he worked until he could buy tickets for the passage of Mary, her three siblings, and her mother in 1894. Mary and her two younger siblings went to public school, while her older sister worked in the garment industry as a seamstress.

During this period, immigrants from many different ethnic backgrounds— especially men, both married and unmarried—came to the United States to get jobs to earn money, and then they returned to their countries of origin. Jewish immigrants, however, tended to immigrate with the intention of bringing the whole family. In large part, once they came, they stayed to make the United States their new home. Even once they were financially stable, the vast majority of Jews who came remained. Less than 10 percent of Jewish immigrants went back to their countries of origin; other immigrant groups averaged more than 30 percent.

GENDER ROLES AMONG IMMIGRANTS

Since Jewish immigration was usually family immigration, women came to play an important part of both the immigration experience and of life in the United States. The Jewish immigrant community had the largest proportion of women among immigrant communities of the time. Traditional Judaism, with its highly differentiated gender roles, often had a place for women to work outside the home. In the ideal situation for pious families, a man was able to study Jewish texts, while a woman provided material support. In practice, many Jewish families, especially in war-torn and difficult economic times, needed income from adult men and women and sometimes even from older children. These gender roles meant that the idea of Jewish women working outside the home in the United States was not met with extreme resistance. In fact, Jewish women participated visibly in labor movements and economic boycotts.

But the American environment changed some other gender ideals: instead of studying Jewish texts, many Jewish men in the United States strived to achieve monetary success through work. Relative to other immigrants, Jews tended to come with skills that could easily translate into employment. This meant that Jewish women, although they often continued to manage the household's consumption patterns, often were able to stop working outside the home once they married. In many ways, then, Jewish immigrant communities embraced and often achieved middle-class American family ideals: one working male parent and one domestic female parent.

JEWISH IDENTITY

Although many historians mark the end of the 19th century as simply the eastern European migration, that was only one thread in a complex tapestry. The major cultural shift was not caused solely by immigration, although immigrants participated in many of these changes.

Many of the cultural changes concerned how American Jews viewed themselves and how they presented themselves to other Americans. At the time of the Civil War, most American Jews were very similar to their neighbors, and they were generally optimistic about their ability to fit into American life. But a simple survey of the national Jewish organizations founded in the last decade of the 19th century hints at this growing interest in Jewish culture and learning. This included the founding of the American Jewish Historical Society in 1892, Gratz College (the first Hebrew teacher's college to train women) in 1893, the Jewish Chautauqua Society in 1893, the National Council of Jewish Women in 1893. The plans for the Jewish Publications Society's *Jewish Encyclopedia* were also solidified in 1898. By 1900, a growing sense of Jewish particularity—in religion, culture, and ideology—had taken root in Jewish-American communities. Previously, they had primarily concerned themselves with becoming American, but

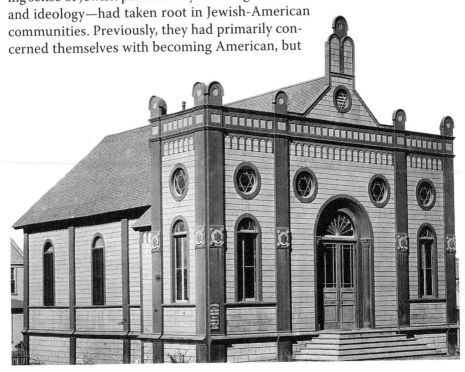

Built in 1889, the Temple Beth Israel in San Diego is now one of the oldest remaining synagogues in California.

The Young Men's Hebrew Association organized this large Hanukkah celebration in New York City in December 1879. Many new Jewish organizations arose in the late 19th century.

in the late 19th century, American Jews began to concentrate on being Jewish, although not at the expense of being American.

This turn from an outward to an inward orientation became a feature of many aspects of Jewish community life, but it was perhaps most apparent in the sphere of religious practice. In the earlier decades of the 19th century, the Reform movement of Judaism held much sway over the religious outlook and practices of American Jews. Reform had emphasized a tradition influenced by Enlightenment thought, and it often rejected what it saw as antiquated obedience to Jewish law in favor of adherence to ethical standards. For example, one of its most notorious moments was a Hebrew Union College banquet where shellfish was served—food prohibited by laws of *kashrut* (kosher laws). As the years wore on, however, more and more Jews who were aligned with the Reform movement wondered if they had too quickly jettisoned some meaningful traditional practices.

With many traditional practices gone or replaced, women became more responsible for the continuance of Jewish culture and learning. Both in the home and outside, they were becoming the teachers of Judaism, the leaders of agencies of social betterment. These included hundreds of local Ladies Hebrew Benevolent Societies and homes for orphans, and even the public faces of Judaism like the "lady preacher" Ray (Rachel) Frank, and the women who worked on the Jewish women's exhibit at the World's Columbian Exposition.

Especially in urban environments, women also formed groups to help new immigrants adjust to American life. Although this sometimes produced a dichotomy of haves and have-nots, it also paradoxically reinforced a Jewish solidarity across lines of class and geography. These new modes of women's involvement were just some of the ways that Jewish culture and religion were becoming more important in the lives of many Jewish men and women in the United States.

Immigrants also brought their own forms of spirituality and Jewish identity. Most were more traditional and lived according to Jewish laws and customs upon their arrival. Because most had lived almost exclusively among other Jews in their countries of origin, it was natural and easier to adhere to Jewish laws, and Jewish identity was effortless. In the United States, however, no legal restrictions identified Jews, and thus living according to Jewish customs was no longer the default position. Adding such large numbers of new immigrant Jews to the American mix reinforced such trends as the return to some forms of ritual observance. The result was a wide spectrum of religiosity and identification with Jewish culture. As these aspects of a Jewish "awakening" transpired, Reform rabbis gathered to address what they saw as a growing need to redefine what the Reform movement was, and although they had produced a document called the Pittsburgh Platform in 1885, the issues at hand remained in large part unresolved at the turn of the century. Some of the more traditionally minded Reform Jews would soon break off to form the Conservative movement.

Many American Jews, then, were confronted with choices about their own identities concerning adherence to religious rituals, educating their children in traditional Jewish subjects, participating in secular Jewish activities like social clubs and attending the theater, and keeping ties to the Jewish community. While some American Jews chose to abandon any attachment to Judaism, most negotiated the possibilities of spirituality and cultural involvement in the Jewish community. Jewish life in the United States had brought not only new dilemmas for living "Jewishly," but its freedoms also offered novel solutions.

ANTI-SEMITISM

One of the many contributing factors for the American Jewish community to "turn inward" and focus on Jewish particularity came from non-Jews in the United States. During this period, many non-Jews in Europe and the United States spoke out against Jews, calling them Christ-killers and dishonest businesspeople and characterizing Jews as physically and mentally strange people. The last decades of the 19th century marked a time of increasing nativism in general, but Jews were specifically and harshly targeted. One historian singles out the period of 1865 to 1900 as "The Emergence of an Anti-Semitic Society" in the United States.

The term *anti-Semitism* first appeared in the 1870s when German publisher Wilhelm Marr coined it to describe the anti-Jewish campaigns under way in central Europe at that time. He wanted to distinguish between a simple hatred of Jews and the modern, "scientific," political, and racial ideology repudiating the Jews. The term lent a rational, scientific air to the word describing the prejudice growing in Europe, but it did not make that hatred any more rational or any less real.

Social anti-Semitism, or discrimination against Jews in American social life, also became more pervasive in the last decades of the 19th century. Jewish immigrant women and men might have to contend with abuse in the streets at the hands of non-Jews, like young Rose Cohen who was physically abused and terrorized by a non-Jewish boy for weeks. Hotels, restaurants, and vacation spots began to exclude Jews. One sign outside a hotel, grouping Jews with sick people, read: "No Hebrews and Tubercular Guests received." Jewish women increasingly found themselves isolated from women's clubs in the 1880s. Even famous Jewish families were excluded from clubs and establishments. For example, in 1877, the wealthy banker Joseph Seligman and his family wanted to stay at the upscale Saratoga Hotel. The manager, Judge Henry Hilton, indicated that "Israelites" were no longer welcome at the hotel because their presence would repel Christian patrons. Newspapers across the nation picked up on the story, and Jews and non-Jews across the nation took sides. Several years later, attraction owner Austin Corbin insisted that Jews did not belong on the New York resort of Coney Island. One popular cruel song conveyed this contempt for Jews and their religious practices: "I had a piece of pork, I put it on a fork. And gave it to the curly-headed Jew. Pork, Pork, Pork, Jew, Jew, Jew."

Political anti-Semitism, although growing in popularity in Europe, did not take the same foothold in the United States. Small-scale discussion about disenfranchising Jews made little headway. However, American Jews did experience some economic prejudice. Jewish business owners were often suspected of practicing underhanded business. In 1866, seven insurance companies entered into a pact not to insure Jewish-owned busi-

The Jewish man in this July 1877 cartoon from Harper's Weekly asks a hotel clerk ". . . how voz it dot you knowed I vozn't a Ghristian?"

Anti-Semitism during the Civil War

The most overt act of anti-Semitism during the Civil War came from General Ulysses S. Grant of the Union. Because he felt that some financial problems were exclusively the fault of Jews, he ordered that all Jews be expelled from the area, regardless of age, sex, or loyalty. He issued the following order:

GENERAL ORDERS No. 11.
Holly Springs, Miss. December 17, 1862.
*　　The Jews, as a class violating every regulation of trade established by the Treasury Department and also department orders, are hereby expelled from the department within twenty-four hours from the receipt of this order.*
*　　Post commanders will see that all of this class of people be furnished passes and required to leave, and any one returning after such notification will be arrested and held in confinement until an opportunity occurs of sending them out as prisoners, unless furnished with permit from headquarters.*

Jewish communities throughout the occupied areas responded quickly to Grant's general orders. These orders had forced women and men to abandon their property and belongings and move far from their communities. Many penned their grievances directly to President Abraham Lincoln. One group from Kentucky wrote: "The undersigned, good and loyal citizens of the United States and residents of this town for many years, engaged in legitimate business as merchants, feel greatly insulted and outraged by this inhuman order, the carrying out of which would be the grossest violation of the Constitution and our rights as good citizens under it." Many other people called on Grant to see Jews as loyal Americans as well. On January 4, 1863, the general-in-chief of the War Department in Washington wrote to Grant and stated that his order, if genuine, had been immediately revoked.

A cartoon poking fun at Ulysses S. Grant's attempt to appease Jewish voters after the war.

nesses because, they claimed without evidence, Jews often set fire to their own buildings to collect money. Many Americans also harbored the conspiratorial idea that Jews somehow pulled the strings behind the world's finances, and they therefore found individual Jews both untrustworthy and blameworthy. Racial anti-Semitism, or the hating of Jews based on supposed physical and inborn social characteristics, also began to gain hold. Anti-Semitism was becoming a part of the American landscape, but the reasons for its emergence during this time are not clear. Perhaps the growing number of Jews because of immigration caused other Americans to express their dislike. The European rhetoric of scientific anti-Semitism may have mirrored and reinforced the American situation. American society also faced uncertainty about what was "normal" and "truly American," and it used anti-Semitism as a way to draw boundaries between "us" and "them."

CONCLUSION

At the start of the Civil War, the 150,000 Jews living in the United States were a relatively homogeneous minority. Most lived in cities and engaged in business or trades. Those who lived in small towns and farming communities made a living as shopkeepers or in other retail businesses. Even though a large proportion of pre-civil War Jewry had migrated from Germany during the 1840s, by 1861 most Jews had become relatively indistinguishable from their Christian neighbors.

From the 1880s through the early 1920s, a wave of 2.5 million Jewish immigrants from eastern and southern Europe landed on these shores. Speaking mostly Yiddish, often with manual rather than merchant skills, these newcomers tended to stay together in urban neighborhoods soon dubbed "ghettoes." Their presence stimulated domestic anti-Semitism, which engulfed both assimilated and newly arrived Jews alike. This challenge to Jewish inclusion would persist throughout the first half of the 20th century.

SARAH IMHOFF
UNIVERSITY OF CHICAGO

Further Reading

Ashton, Diane. "Expanding Jewish Life in America." In *Columbia History of Jews and Judaism in America*. Ed. by Marc Lee Raphael. New York: Columbia University Press, 2008.

Barish, Louis. *Rabbis in Uniform*. New York: J. David, 1962.

Bingham, Emily. *Mordecai, an Early American Family*. New York: Hill and Wang, 2003.

"Chapters in American Jewish History." American Jewish Historical Society. Available online, URL: http://www.ajhs.org/publications/chapters/. Accessed September 2008.

Diner, Hasia R. *A Time for Gathering: The Second Migration, 1820–1880*. Jewish People in America. Baltimore, MD: Johns Hopkins University Press, 1992.

Dinnerstein, Leonard. *Antisemitism in America*. New York: Oxford University Press, 1994.

Ettinger, Shmuel. "Migration—within and from Europe—as a Decisive Factor in Jewish Life." In *A History of the Jewish People*. Ed. by H.H. Ben-Sasson. Cambridge, MA: Harvard University Press, 1985.

"General Grant's Infamy." Jewish Virtual Library. Available online, URL: http://www.jewishvirtuallibrary.org/jsource/anti-semitism/grant.html. Accessed September 2008.

Glenn, Susan. *Daughters of the Shtetl: Life and Labor in the Immigrant Generation*. Ithaca, NY: Cornell University Press, 1990.

Goldstein, Eric. *The Price of Whiteness: Jews, Race, and American Identity*. Princeton, NJ: Princeton University Press, 2006.

Grubin, David. *The Jewish Americans*. PBS. (DVD) 2008.

Hyman, Paula. "Gender and the Immigrant Jewish Experience in the United States." In *Jewish Women in Historical Perspective*. Ed. by Judith Baskin. Detroit, MI: Wayne State University Press, 1991.

"Jews in the Civil War." Available online, URL: http://www.jewish-history.com/civilwar/. Accessed September 2008.

Klapper, Melissa. *Jewish Girls Coming of Age in America, 1860–1920*. New York: NYU Press, 2005.

Korn, Bertram Wallace. *American Jewry and the Civil War*. Philadelphia, PA: Jewish Publication Society of America, 1957.

Rosen, Robert N. *The Jewish Confederates*. Columbia, SC: University of South Carolina Press, 2000.

Silverstein, Alan. *Alternatives to Assimilation: The Response of Reform Judaism to American Culture 1840–1930*. Hanover, NH: University Press of New England, 1994.

Solomon, Clara and Elliott Ashkenazi. *The Civil War Diary of Clara Solomon: Growing Up in New Orleans, 1861–1862*. Baton Rouge, LA: Louisiana State University Press, 1995.

CHAPTER 4

The Progressive Era and World War I: 1900 to 1920

ALTHOUGH THERE WAS a Jewish presence in America from colonial times, most of these Jewish residents were Sephardic Jews whose presence was spread throughout the nation, although primarily in cities. The more dramatic increases in Jewish immigration came with the arrival of Ashkenazi Jews, primarily from Germany in the 1880s, soon creating a national Jewish population of over 250,000. In response to persecution in the Russian Empire, eastern Europe, and the Pale of Settlement, Jewish immigration rose steadily from the late 19th century to over 2 million by the 1920s, when immigration restrictions in the form of a quota system ended such movement. Jewish immigrants settled primarily in New York City and other urban areas. By the end of the era, America's Jewish population was the third largest in the world. Beside religion, the newly arrived Jews were linked by a Yiddish language and a culture that provided a common means of identity as they adjusted to the new land.

Industrialization had changed the American landscape, and this growth stimulated the need for a variety of jobs at all levels of the production process. Many of these recent eastern-European Jewish immigrants arrived poor, and they took work wherever they could—often within the booming industries that were transforming urban America.

The Progressive Era unfolded during a time of rapid U.S. population growth spurred by both immigration and internal migration from the countryside to cities. By the 1920 census, half the American population were classified as urban dwellers. In addition, the American population grew from 76 million in 1900 to over 106 million in 1920. Various European nations dominated immigrant numbers, and by the middle of the Progressive period, 15 percent of the American population was foreign born.

PROGRESSIVE ERA ANTI-SEMITISM

Among many Progressive concerns, the spectacular rise in total population through immigration represented to many reformers a key aspect of what was wrong with America as well as an issue needing a quick fix. Although Jews comprised only two to three percent of the total population, their concentration in urban areas raised widespread Progressive objections. Just as muckrakers uncovered other ills within society, the Jew was often portrayed as another ill that needed correction. The degree of this concern was reflected in Benton J. Hendrick's 1907 two-part investigation published in *McClure's* that examined the Jewish question, and actually speculated as to whether Jews could be successfully assimilated and Americanized.

Hendrick expressed an accepted nativist belief, backed by the popular eugenics of the time, that saw the Jew as a separate race with mental and physical deficiencies. Many assumed that the Jew was an inferior being compared to the Anglo-Saxon races. Of all immigrants during the Progressive Era, Jews often received the most vitriolic commentary and hatred. They were blamed for rises in crime and general unfair practices. Jews were seen as the source of a host of economic, religious, and social misfortunes. Questions were raised as to whether they could ever adapt enough to join the American mainstream. Although most Jews suffered poverty during the first decade after arrival, the economic rise of many Jews as business owners and in the professions provided further grievances, particularly for Irish Americans, who became the most visible and vocal anti-Jewish antagonists.

The issue was made worse by the popularity of Madison Grant's eugenics tract, *The Passing of the Great Race* (1916), which perpetuated anti-Semitic perspectives, and by the 42-volume 1911 Dillingham Immigration Commission reports that argued for tighter immigration controls. Jews were at the forefront of those to be restricted.

The Jewish community also lived within the Progressive tradition and responded to this situation by forming associations to protect Jewish and Jewish-immigrant interests from abuses. The American Jewish Committee was formed in 1906, and the Anti-Defamation League of B'nai B'rith was established in 1913. The American Jewish Committee was initially concerned with the rise in pogroms in Russia that represented systematic persecution and brutality directed against the Jewish population.

In America, the growing anti-immigrant, racially charged climate of the Progressive Era led many Jews to try to protect their civil and religious rights.

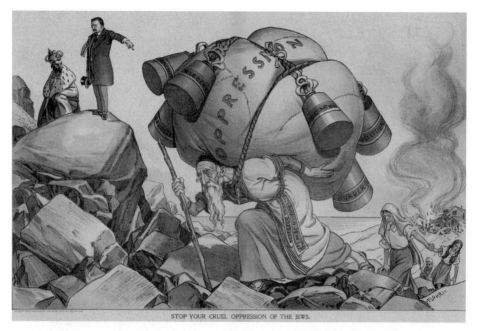

STOP YOUR CRUEL OPPRESSION OF THE JEWS.

This 1904 cartoon depicts President Theodore Roosevelt urging the Russian czar to "stop your cruel oppression of the Jews." The figure representing Russian Jews carries a burden with weights labeled "Murder, Assassination, Deception, Robbery, Cruelty, and Autocracy."

Louis B. Marshall (1856–1929) was committee president from 1912 to 1929 and directed the American Jewish Joint Distribution Committee formed in 1914 to help Jews affected by World War I. Marshall was an 1877 graduate of Columbia Law School who eventually became chairman of New York State's Commission of Immigration. From this position he campaigned against new immigration restrictions such as the introduction of literacy testing to exclude potential immigrants. To curb Russian restrictions on Jewish emigration, he also pressured the U.S. government to end American-Russian trade agreements and, in 1919, he extended his influence to the Paris Peace Commission, where he investigated minority rights issues.

Other groups such as the Anti-Defamation League, founded by Sigmund Livingston, a Chicago attorney, arose as a direct result of the disturbing Leo Frank affair in Georgia. The organization's main thrust was to protect the Jewish population against injustice and discrimination, particularly when Jews were denied legal due process and full citizenship rights.

JEWISH PROGRESSIVES
Beside the creation of associations that protected Jews from anti-Semitic forces, the Jewish-American community took up other Progressive Era causes such as organizations that raised funds for victims of the war in Europe. Many

The Leo Frank Case

Leo Frank (1884–1915) was born in Texas, the son of German-born Jewish parents, and raised in New York City. He graduated from Cornell University in 1906 and, after his marriage to Lucille Selig, he moved to Atlanta, where he worked as superintendent of Atlanta's National Pencil Company.

On April 26, 1913, Mary Phagan, a 13-year-old factory employee, came to the factory to collect $1.20 in wages from Frank. Early on April 27, her raped and brutalized body was found in the factory basement by the night watchman, Newt Lee. Police investigations uncovered several suspects and collected much dubious testimony, some of which came from intimidated witnesses, and included several contradictory statements from the African-American janitor, Jim Conley, who became the principal witness against Leo Frank.

Leo Frank in the early 1910s.

From this less-than-convincing evidence, Frank, on May 13, 1913, was indicted for the murder of Mary Phagan. His July trial was sensationalized in both the local and the national press, and was exploited by Georgia's populist politicians such as Tom Watson and by an emergent Ku Klux Klan. This atmosphere was hardly conducive to a fair trial, and Frank's "differentness" was used against him. He was presented by the prosecution as the stereotypical perverted exploiter of young women.

Frank was found guilty, but a series of appeals followed that raised serious questions regarding the validity of the conviction. This eventually led Georgia governor John Slaton on June 15, 1915, to commute Frank's death sentence. Slaton believed that the evidence was faulty and that Frank was denied due process. However, before he could attain a retrial, on August 17, 1915, a mob kidnapped Frank from a prison farm and took him to a field near Marietta, Georgia, where he was lynched by a gang of local men—many of them with Klan and other political connections. Without any sense of shame, crowds gathered and took souvenirs from Frank's nightshirt-clad body. As a response to this outrage, many of Georgia's Jews left the state.

In 1982, Alonzo Mann, a witness to the crime who was 13 years old at the time, and who, it was later discovered, had been threatened with death, came forward and signed an affidavit. In this document he declared that he saw Jim Conley dragging away the body of Mary Phagan. With this new information in hand, the state of Georgia in 1986 gave Leo Frank a posthumous pardon for the crime. Nevertheless, for many American Jews, the 1913 Leo Frank case symbolized what nativist rhetoric and prejudice could produce.

different groups within the Jewish community united to form the American Jewish Joint Distribution Committee, and eventually accumulated over $60 million in relief aid.

The association or federation idea was very much a product of Progressive thinking, in which organization, cooperation, efficiency, and philanthropy were combined to solve problems and to make community life better. Jewish institutions found this approach compatible with their own welfare and relief approaches such as the *kehillah* concept, a historic Jewish organizational apparatus that sometimes operated as an internal community governing body. Representatives of this type of federation could be found as early as the American Civil War in Chicago's United Hebrew Relief Association. By 1900, the Jewish Federation of Chicago was formed and operated much within this federation idea. This organization provided for many projects that aided and assisted the building of better neighborhoods.

WOMEN REFORMERS

As in the gentile community, the Progressive Era saw the rise of an army of Jewish women reformers who became activists and leading voices for change. They mainly came from the educated middle classes and from German backgrounds, and they willingly joined in the many campaigns for reform.

Hannah G. Solomon (1858–1942) founded the National Council of Jewish Women in 1893 in Chicago, which established schools and settlement

Young women protesting child labor, probably during a May 1, 1909 labor parade in New York City. Their banners read "Abolish Child Slavery" in Yiddish and English.

houses to aid newly arrived Jewish immigrants who needed assistance in the transition to American life. Her experience at the Maxwell Street Settlement helped her formulate social welfare—related programs that were expanded in the second decade of the Progressive Era. Solomon was supported by Sadie American (1862–1944), whose organizing and executive skills helped the council to prosper and develop branches throughout the United States.

In addition to reinforcing religious traditions and values, programs supported low-cost housing projects and slum clearance, building preschool facilities, combating truancy, and promoting various educational improvements. In 1912, the council also created the International Council of Jewish Women, largely in response to the increasing difficulties facing Jews in the decaying Russian Empire. Providing help remained the organization's main focus throughout these years. This aid enabled immigrant Jewish women to make the transition to the New World, equipping them with the skills to become a part of American life.

The Progressive Era overlapped with the growth of the Zionist movement, which promoted Jewish settlement in Palestine. Baltimore-born Henrietta Szold (1860–1945) saw the value in promoting Jewish women's organizations as a means to aid general educational projects, public health, and youth development in America and later in Palestine. In 1912, Szold founded Hadassah, the American Jewish Zionist Volunteer Women's Organization. She headed this group until 1926 and, although a committed Zionist whose destiny would end in Palestine, she wanted America's Jewish women to benefit from American freedoms.

By the end of the era in 1920, the vast numbers of eastern European Jewish immigrants replaced the previously German-dominated Jewish communities in America's urban areas. Many women from these newer immigrant areas worked to gain advancement in American life by becoming educated professionals. They also became active in reform, or even radical movements.

This 1917 poster used a symbolic figure standing in front of the New York City skyline to promote American help for Jews abroad.

Prominent in this drive for recognition and change were women such as Rose Schneiderman (1882–1972), a labor organizer and president of the National Women's Trade Union League of America, and Rose Pastor Stokes (1879–1933), a socialist writer and agitator who wrote for the *Yidishes tageblatt* (Jewish Daily News) in New York. They were joined by many others including such notables as Pauline Goldmark (1874–1962), a member of the New York branch of the National Consumers' League, and, most famously, by the significant radical anarchist Emma Goldman (1869–1940).

Labor organizer Rose Schneiderman in a photograph from before 1920.

Goldman gained national prominence during this era as a keen supporter of a variety of radical political causes including birth control. She also accepted revolutionary violence as a tool to secure change. Her lover, Alexander Berkman, gained fame through his failed assassination attempt on industrialist Henry Clay Frick. Her views on politics, feminism, birth control, suffrage, and many other topics found expression in her writings and through the anarchist journal, *Mother Earth,* which she founded in 1906.

Berkman and Goldman campaigned against U.S. participation in World War I, which brought her to the attention of the Justice Department as an undesirable alien. During the 1919 Red Scare, she was arrested and, along with Berkman, exiled to Russia. However, the couple left Russia in the 1920s after becoming disenchanted with the actions and direction of the Russian Revolution and eventually settled in Canada, where she died. Her body was returned to America after her death when permission was granted for her burial in Chicago.

RECREATION AND SPORTS

As a means to combat anti-Semitism and to foster the Progressive goals of assimilation and Americanization, sports increasingly came to play a part in Jewish lives during this era. There was also increased participation in a range of recreational activities that reflected community aspirations.

Earlier in the 19th century, prominent Jews such as August Belmont became involved in horseracing to mark their place in the New World. However, given

Abe Attell (right), the featherweight world champion boxer 1904–12, fighting Young Corbett in an outdoor bout early in the 20th century. Attell was sometimes referred to as the "Little Hebrew."

the size of mass immigration and the concentration of Jewish lives in urban areas, it became clear that more general participation was necessary. This development was also viewed as an aid to assimilation and as a tool to combat vice and delinquency.

Organizations such as the Young Man's Hebrew Association, founded in 1854, championed healthful social activities. Other organizations followed such as educational alliances and settlement houses that supported productive activities for both girls and boys. This was particularly the case after the Young Women's Hebrew Association was founded in New York City in 1902 as an independent entity under the leadership of Mrs. Israel Unterberg.

YMHA's New York–based Atlas Athletic Club, founded in 1898, became specially important after it attracted more athletes from the Lower East Side. Basketball was introduced at the club in 1904, and its popularity spread with the formation of citywide leagues and competitions.

Basketball, invented in 1891 by James Naismith at a Springfield, Massachusetts, YMCA, became extremely popular during this period. With its emphasis on cooperation, teamwork, and discipline, the sport reinforced Progressive

Era values for moral and civic improvement. Basketball also met the sporting needs of urban youth and was soon the game of choice at settlement houses, gyms, and playgrounds.

The game was played behind wire fences to keep fans at bay, and court and ball dimensions were still vague. Basketball was an exciting, rough-and-tumble sport with few regulations—many of these did not come until after World War II.

In this period, the New York Public Schools Athletic League was started to promote competition, a notion that soon spread to other cities. The City College of New York also took up the sport, and many Jewish players of distinction developed their skills there, including Barney Sedran, Ira Streusand, and Harry Brill, all of whom in their later careers played professionally. However, during these years the differences between amateur and professional games were sometimes hard to distinguish. Basketball gave Jewish sportsmen a new independence and the ability to participate without fearing discrimination.

Basketball's popularity steadily increased throughout the 1920s at both the college and early professional levels. Prejudice was still encountered, particularly in the Ivy League where restrictive quotas operated against Jews. Yale eventually campaigned against the practice, perhaps more out of a desire for success that the Jewish players brought to the team. The game's impact also grew as more and more star players and coaches came to prominence, such as New York University star Nat Holman (1896–1995), who was a member of the Original Celtics (not the later Boston Celtics). Basketball became particularly popular on the East Coast, where the professional American Basketball League was created in 1925 and included teams such as the New York Celtics, Boston Whirlwinds, and the Cleveland Rosenblums.

Jewish athletes also achieved success in other sports during the 19th century, such as Barry Aaron in boxing. The Progressive Era, with its massive Jewish immigration, provided even more opportunities in sports such as boxing and baseball. Boxing heavyweight Joe Choynski achieved fame in the 1890s, and Harry Harris became bantamweight world champion in 1901. During the height of the era, Abe Attell was featherweight world champion from 1904 to 1912. In addition, between 1910 and 1919, there were four Jewish world champions in four different divisions.

ENTERTAINMENT

Besides sports, American Jews emerged from their immigrant roots and became instrumental in many other recreational and entertainment areas. The well-known Yiddish Art Theatre was founded in 1918 and produced actors and entertainers of note. Tin Pan Alley, with its popular sheet music industry, was also home to many Jewish songwriters such as Irving Berlin (1888–1989), who was one of America's most famous composers during the 20th century.

Berlin's initial fame came in 1911 with his *Alexander's Ragtime Band,* and was followed with successful musical revues including his World War I musical, *Yip Yip Yaphank,* in 1917. Fanny Brice (1891–1951) got her initial break in the 1915 Ziegfeld Follies, and Al Jolson (1886–1950) was famous by 1911 and by 1920 was America's highest-paid entertainer—long before his name became synonymous with the first talking film, 1927's *The Jazz Singer.*

Perhaps the most famous performer of the era was Harry Houdini (1874–1926), a Hungarian-born Jew whose real name was Eric Weisz. The son of a rabbi, Houdini became a major vaudeville performer, beginning as a magician and maturing into a stunt and escape artist whose escapes became legendary. Houdini always took his act to greater extremes, such as escaping from water-filled tanks, which eventually led to his Chinese Torture Cell escape while completely submerged.

The emergence of film and cinema, first in the form of the simple Vitascope of the 1890s, and after 1905 with the Nickelodeon, named after the nickel paid to view a short film, set precedents for the later silent film era. Film emerged during the Progressive Era as a major mass-entertainment source. During this period Louis B. Mayer got his start in the film business when he opened a nickelodeon in Massachusetts in 1907.

Harry Houdini, the "Handcuff King," posing in chains in 1905.

The business success of film led to rivalries, particularly after 1908, when the Edison Company attempted to establish a monopoly on film production. After 1912, this struggle led many Jewish New York and East Coast filmmakers to migrate westward to Hollywood. This move invigorated the Los Angeles silent film industry, and even combated anti-Semitism when more positive Jewish images appeared in movies. The 1915 film, *A Child of the Ghetto,* directed by D.W. Griffith, examined life on the Lower East Side of New York.

Also during this period, Jesse Lasky, Adolph Zukor, and Sam Goldwyn combined forces to produce the nation's first feature film, *The Straw Man,* in 1914, directed by Cecil B. DeMille. This collaboration later formed the basis of Paramount Studios. These developments in early American film set the stage for the transformation of the entire American film industry. By the 1920s, the six major movie studios that dominated American film production were all under eastern European immigrant Jewish ownership.

OTHER PROMINENT FIGURES

Bernard Baruch (1870–1965) was born in South Carolina. His father, a German-Jewish immigrant, was a well-known and successful Civil War surgeon on Robert E. Lee's staff. In 1881, the family moved to New York City, and Baruch attended the City College of New York, graduating in 1889. He took employment on Wall Street, quickly learned the business, and gained a seat on the New York Stock Exchange. He was a millionaire before age 30. By 1910, Baruch's stature as a Wall Street financier was well established, particularly after he took ownership of the international commodity firm H. Hentz Co. His Progressive credentials came during the Wilson administration, when he became a key adviser on defense production during World War I. He later assumed the important chairmanship of the War Industries Board, which gave him enormous power over the entire U.S. economy. His success during the Progressive Era made him a lifelong adviser to presidents.

Oscar S. Straus (1850–1926), German born, immigrated to America when he was four and was later educated at Columbia University, where he was a graduate of the law school. Straus first rose to prominence as the U.S. minister to the Ottoman Empire in the 1880s. He was a member of a highly influential New York City family with business interests in Macy's department store. Straus formally joined the Progressive Era when he became President Theodore Roosevelt's secretary of commerce and labor, a position he held from 1906 to 1909. He was the first American Jew to achieve cabinet rank. He continued his government service under the Taft administration, becoming U.S. ambassador to Turkey in 1909. In 1912, he ran unsuccessfully for governor of New York.

Henry Morgenthau Sr. (1856–1946) was another prominent German-born Jew in the early 20th century. He served as the U.S. ambassador to the Ottoman Empire beginning in 1913, and while there attempted to bring attention to the plight of the Armenians during the Armenian genocide. Morgenthau was also a lawyer and a successful businessman, and his descendants held important positions as well. His son Henry Morgenthau Jr. was secretary of the treasury from 1934 to 1945, and his grandson Robert Morgenthau was the District Attorney of New York from 1975 to 2009. His granddaughter Barbara Tuchman was also a noted historian and the winner of two Pulitzer Prizes.

Walter Weyl (1873–1919) was born to German Jewish parents in Philadelphia and was orphaned at an early age. He attended high school in Philadelphia and won a scholarship to the Wharton School at the University of Pennsylvania, from which he graduated at age 19. He then traveled to Europe and, upon his return in 1896, began graduate study at Wharton. He commenced the serious study of economics and quickly completed his doctorate, *The Passenger Traffic of Railways*.

Following graduate school, Weyl did statistical surveys for the Bureau of Labor. He also became interested in the labor movement and assisted John

Louis D. Brandeis

Louis D. Brandeis (1856–1941) was born into a family that immigrated to the United States from Prague, then part of the Austro-Hungarian Empire. The family settled in Louisville, Kentucky, and became successful grain merchants. Brandeis went to school locally and later studied in Germany. After returning to the United States, Brandeis entered Harvard Law School and graduated at the top of his class in 1877.

Brandeis joined the Boston, Massachusetts, law firm of Nutter, McClennen, and Fish. His law practice made him very successful and financially secure, and raised his public profile. Success enabled him to become involved in a number of other endeavors, including giving his support to a variety of personal privacy causes. His 1890 article "The Right to Privacy," published in the *Harvard Law Review,* remains one of its most famous submissions.

Fame as a litigator came in his 1908 *Muller v. Oregon* case, in which he defended an Oregon law regulating hours and wages for women. In addition to the customary legal precedents, Brandeis gathered sociological evidence in support of his arguments. This introduction of scientific and social material led this case to become known in legal circles as the Brandeis Brief and it broadened the concept of how evidence is legally perceived.

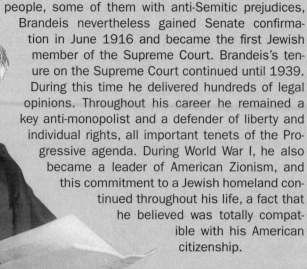

Brandeis's reputation as a committed Progressive drew the attention of President Woodrow Wilson, who first offered him a cabinet post that Brandeis refused. Wilson then nominated him to a seat on the Supreme Court in January 1916. Although his appointment was opposed by many people, some of them with anti-Semitic prejudices, Brandeis nevertheless gained Senate confirmation in June 1916 and became the first Jewish member of the Supreme Court. Brandeis's tenure on the Supreme Court continued until 1939. During this time he delivered hundreds of legal opinions. Throughout his career he remained a key anti-monopolist and a defender of liberty and individual rights, all important tenets of the Progressive agenda. During World War I, he also became a leader of American Zionism, and this commitment to a Jewish homeland continued throughout his life, a fact that he believed was totally compatible with his American citizenship.

Justice Louis D. Brandeis was the first Jewish justice on the U.S. Supreme Court.

Mitchell, leader of the United Mine Workers, in the writing of a pioneering history of the union movement. In addition, he did research for Wisconsin Progressive Robert LaFollette. From this time forward, he devoted his career to both journalism and economics. His book *The New Democracy,* published in 1912, became a Progressive manifesto, and brought him to the attention of *The New Republic* ownership. He joined the magazine as an editor in 1914, working with Herbert Croly and Walter Lippmann to make *The New Republic* a key vehicle for Progressive thought.

The outbreak of World War I led him to investigate the causes and consequences of the conflict, particularly the impact of nationalism in preventing a lasting peace. He was highly critical of the Treaty of Versailles, seeing it a recipe for future conflict. At the time of his death in 1919, Weyl was examining the rise of Japanese imperialism. Although he died at a relatively young age, the quality of Weyl's work made him a powerful Progressive intellectual. His ideas argued for the reformation of capitalism through planning and regulation, as opposed to its extinction on Marxist socialist terms.

Stephen S. Wise (1874–1949) was born in Budapest. He immigrated to the United States, initially settling in New York City, and attended the City College of New York; in 1901, he gained his Ph.D. from Columbia University. In addition, he was a Reform rabbi, and in 1900 moved to Portland, Oregon, to lead a congregation. His interest in social welfare made him identify with Progressive causes such as charitable efforts to improve the lives of the less fortunate. This work was recognized in 1903, when he was appointed Oregon's Commissioner of Child Labor.

In 1922, he helped found the Jewish Institute of Religion in New York City to train Reform rabbis. After his death, the Institute became part of Hebrew Union College. Wise also became an avid Zionist, which was at the time highly unusual for a Reform rabbi. His commitment made him a key player in the Federation of American Zionists. In 1920, he joined with other prominent American Jews such as Supreme Court justices Felix Frankfurter and Louis Brandeis to create the American Jewish Congress to promote Jewish interests and democratic ideals. He later became leader of the World Jewish Congress, which became a resistance group in the face of rising state anti-Semitism during the 1930s and 1940s.

SAMUEL GOMPERS

Samuel Gompers (1850–1924) was born to Jewish parents in London, England. His parents were recent arrivals from Holland. The family emigrated from England in 1863 and settled in New York City's Lower East Side where, along with his father, he joined the cigar-making trade. In 1872, he became a naturalized U.S. citizen and by 1875 was leader of his United Cigar Makers Union local. Gompers became a convinced union organizer, believing membership was the only way to raise and protect wages. Gompers and his union associates wanted to unify all the craft unions under a single banner to gain collective security. Following this credo, Gompers was instrumental in establishing the American Federation of Labor (AFL), becoming its president in 1886, a position he held until his death.

Gompers differed from the more radical industrial unionists and from socialists who saw the overthrow of capitalism as the only way to improve

Walter Lippmann

Walter Lippmann (1889–1974) was born in New York City to a second-generation German-Jewish family that was comfortably well off. At age 17 he went to Harvard, where he studied philosophy and languages. Bright and well connected, Lippmann took up the Progressive cause; in 1911, he became secretary to prominent muckraker Lincoln Steffens at *Everybody's Magazine*. In 1913, he published his first book, *A Preface to Politics*. The book's success brought him to the attention of Willard and Dorothy Straight, financial backers of *The New Republic*. He soon joined Herbert Croly and Walter Weyl as an editor there. Even with its limited circulation, *The New Republic* was extremely influential in Progressive circles.

Initially, the editorial board was committed to Theodore Roosevelt's Bull Moose variety of Progressivism, but by 1916 moved to support Woodrow Wilson's brand of New Freedom politics. In 1917, Lippmann became an assistant to Secretary of War Newton D. Baker, and, in 1918, gained his commission as a captain in military intelligence. From this post he advised President Wilson, contributed to the drafting of Wilson's famous 14 Points, and assisted with preparations for the Paris Peace Conference. At the end of the war Lippmann returned to *The New Republic*. In 1920, he joined the *New York World* as a writer, and later as editor. He remained an active political commentator throughout his life and often took opposing policies to subsequent presidential administrations. Toward the end of his life his opposition to the Vietnam war caused him to break with the Johnson presidency.

Walter Lippmann in an early-20th-century photograph.

labor's working conditions. Since the 1880s, Jewish immigrants had brought their socialist politics with them. This was reflected in organizations such as the *vereins*, and in unions, such as the United Jewish Trades created in 1888. However, Gompers thought that the American reality dictated different approaches that focused more on economic goals. By using tight local union organizing efforts, major improvements could be gained in wage earners' daily living conditions. If labor numbers were translated into votes, politicians would take notice and be favorably influenced. By maintaining an independent stance, the union would not be tied to any one political party and this increased its persuasive powers. Important objectives such as the drive for an eight-hour day could be better realized through nonpartisanship.

Economic ends remained the key to Gompers's philosophy. The growth of the union to over 3 million members by the time of his death gave the union important political clout. The height of Gompers's influence occurred during the Wilson administration, when he gained important collective bargaining concessions.

Gompers and the AFL also supported the war effort, which proved extremely helpful. The Wilson administration faced considerable socialist opposition to America's involvement, particularly after his 1916 campaign. This stance led to Gompers's appointment to the Council of National Defense during the war. From this position he mobilized labor in support of administration actions to defeat the Central powers. He also advised Wilson on labor matters during the 1919 peace negotiations.

Although an immigrant himself, Gompers, as a union advocate, argued for immigration restrictions. He deemed unrestricted immigration detrimental to union growth and higher wages. In this regard, he endorsed the Republican drive for quota controls after World War I. Samuel Gompers's career placed him in the national limelight throughout the Progressive Era and made him one of the period's most significant figures.

CONCLUSION

Jews established their place in American history, first as one of the most numerous immigrant groups of the period, and later as significant contributors to the American experience. The period's Progressive reform atmosphere also created the backdrop for Jewish involvement in American Democracy, although some within the community were attracted to more radical solutions that reflected certain European socialist political traditions. In addition, as these years unfolded, more and more of the Jewish population came from eastern Europe and Russia as situations there deteriorated before and during World War I. Jewish institutions and culture followed and thrived on America soil, strengthening the community in the face of many hardships. Individual Jews rose from both German-Jewish and eastern European roots to become significant personalities during the era.

Their success and influence far outpaced the overall Jewish representation in the general population. Beside adjusting to a new land and culture, Jews in the Progressive Era also encountered considerable prejudice and opposition; however, this did not prevent their assimilation and participation at all levels of American life and culture.

THEODORE W. EVERSOLE
NORTHERN KENTUCKY UNIVERSITY
AND UNIVERSITY OF CINCINNATI

Further Reading

Baker, Carol J. *Reforming Fictions: Native, African and Jewish Women's Literature and Journalism in the Progressive Era*. New York: Columbia University Press, 2001.

Buhle, Paul. *From the Lower East Side to Hollywood: Jews in American Popular Culture*. New York: Verso, 2004.

Burt, Elizabeth. *The Progressive Era: Primary Documents on Events from 1890 to 1914*. Westport, CT: Greenwood Press, 2004.

Chambers, John Whitecay. *The Tyranny of Change: America in the Progressive Era*. New York: St. Martin's Press, 2000.

Diner, Steven J. *A Very Different Age: Americans of the Progressive Era*. New York: Hill and Wang, 1998.

Dinnerstein, Leonard, Roger L. Nichols, and David M. Reimers. *Natives and Strangers: A Multicultural History of America*. New York: Oxford University Press, 2003.

Epstein, Lawrence J. *At the Edge of the Dream: The Story of Jewish Immigrants on New York's Lower East Side*. San Francisco, CA: Jossey-Bass, 2007.

Fink, Leon. *Major Problems in the Gilded Age and Progressive Era*. Lexington, MA: DC Heath, 1993.

Frankel, Noralee, and Nancy S. Dye, eds. *Gender, Class, Race and Reform in the Progressive Era*. Lexington, KY: University Press of Kentucky, 1994.

Goldstein, Eric L. *Price of Whiteness: Jews, Race and American Identity*. Princeton, NJ: Princeton University Press, 2006.

Gordon, Lynn D. *Gender and Higher Education in the Progressive Era*. New Haven, CT: Yale University Press, 1992.

Goren, Arthur A. *The Politics and Public Culture of American Jews*. Bloomington, IN: Indiana University Press, 1999.

Gould, Lewis L. *America in the Progressive Era, 1890–1914*. Harlow, UK: Pearson, 2001.

Higham, John. *Strangers in the Land: Patterns of American Nativism 1860–1925*. New Brunswick, NJ: Rutgers University Press, 2002.

Lee, Mordecai. *Bureaus of Efficiency: Local Government Reform in the Progressive Era*. Milwaukee, WI: Marquette University Press, 2008.

Levine, Peter. *The New Progressive Era*. Lanham, MD: Rowman and Littlefield, 2000.

McGerr, Michael. *A Fierce Discontent: The Rise and Fall of the Progressive Movement in America, 1870–1920*. New York: Free Press, 2003.

Mowry, George. *The Era of Theodore Roosevelt, 1900–1912*. New York: Harper and Row, 1958.

Painter, Nell Irvin. *Standing at Armageddon: A Grassroots History of the Progressive Era*. New York: W.W. Norton, 2008.

Rauchway, Eric. *The Refuge of Affections: Family and American Reform Politics*. New York: Columbia University Press, 2001.

Reiss, Steven. *Sports and the American Jew*. Syracuse, NY: Syracuse University Press, 1998.

Sadovnik, Alan R., and Susan F. Semel, eds. *Founding Mothers and Others: Women Educational Leaders during the Progressive Era*. New York: Palgrave Macmillan, 2002.

Slobin, Mark. *Tenement Songs: The Popular Music of the Jewish Immigrants.* Urbana, IL: University of Illinois Press, 1982.

Straughan, Dulcie M. *Women's Use of Public Relations for Progressive Era Reform: Rousing a Conscience.* Lewiston, NY: Edwin Mellen Press, 2007.

Thomas, William H. *Unsafe for Democracy: World War I and the US Justice Department's Covert Campaign to Suppress Dissent*. Madison, WI: University of Wisconsin Press, 2008.

CHAPTER 5

The Roaring Twenties and the Great Depression: 1920 to 1939

THE GREAT WAVE of Jewish immigration to America occurred between 1880 and 1924. From an American population of some 250,000 Jews in 1880, the Jewish-American population rose to an estimated 4.5 million in 1924, following the arrival, between 1900 and 1920, of some 2.5 million Jewish immigrants to America. During these years, Jewish national origins had shifted from central Europe to eastern Europe as conditions worsened in the crumbling Russian empire.

Many of these arrivals to New York City saw the Statue of Liberty on their way to Ellis Island for processing. In 1903, a plaque bearing American Jewish poet Emma Lazarus's poem "The New Colossus" was added. In many ways, one of its most famous lines, "Give us your tired, your poor, your huddled masses yearning to breathe free," captured the essence of the Jewish dream for America. The United States was a place where new beginnings could indeed happen. Once established on these shores, Jewish Americans representing only two to three percent of the overall national population made enormous strides and contributions to American life. Nevertheless not all Americans welcomed them.

In addition to World War I disrupting further immigration, the passage of the 1921 and 1924 Immigration Acts brought Jewish immigration to a near standstill, leading eventually to a reduction of new Jewish immigrant arrivals

Members of the American Jewish Congress during a Washington, D.C., meeting to discuss combating anti-Semitism on November 29, 1937. In the foreground, Jewish leader Rabbi Stephen Wise (left) of the Free Synagogue of New York confers with Christian Minister Harry A. Atkinson.

to only 10,000 per annum. Nativism had finally won the day. Jews no longer qualified under the new system as a favored national immigrant group. This occurred even in the face of tremendous postwar suffering brought on by the Russian Revolution and the subsequent civil wars that affected lives from Poland to Siberia. Eugenicist Dr. Lothrop Stoddard argued in his *Rising Tide of Color* (1920) that Jews were rightfully excluded, for they were part of the underclass that would only racially dilute America.

Surprisingly such prejudicial views found expression in important quarters during the 1920s. Henry Ford, the industrialist whose automobile helped shape American prosperity and development during the Roaring Twenties, also maintained through his newspaper, the *Dearborn Independent,* which ran from 1920 to 1927, a cultural campaign against the "International Jew." Ford even supported the publication of the "Protocols of the Elders of Zion," a vehement anti-Jewish tract and forgery. His views fueled anti-Semitic fires with claims that Jews were warmongers, anticapitalists, and a threat to the nation's morality. With the end of prosperity and economic hard times, these views expanded anti-Semitism nationally. Ford's notions were known to the Nazis and, in 1938, he was awarded the Grand Cross of the German Eagle for his pro-German sympathies.

Most Jews chose not to accept inferior status that would only further intolerance and lead to social rejection and systematic exclusion. Therefore in reference to immigration and integration, Jewish Americans tended to accept the idea of cultural pluralism as their best option. In the midst of many different ethnic groups it became harder to focus on one particular group as the source of all blame and hatred.

Such racial outbursts tended to come from ethnically homogenous lands, and America's racial complexity reduced the degree of anti-Semitism found in the country, but did not eliminate it entirely. Jewish intellectuals such as Horace Kallen, writing during this period, as well as the important jurist Louis D. Brandeis saw ethnic difference and cultural pluralism as an enrichment of American democracy and an enhancement of liberty that allowed for difference, but in an associative and cooperative society.

American Jews opposed the 1924 quota system as a discriminatory act to be opposed. Some scholars believed that as this statute took effect, it increased anti-Jewish sentiments and reduced the country's ethnic diversity through the use of its 1890 census yardstick. The law worked to preserve the nation's WASP (white Anglo-Saxon Protestant) orientation, which in the eyes of many American Jews made assimilation more problematic.

In addition to existing anti-Jewish sentiments, the eastern European Jewish immigrant influx seemed more different and exotic than other immigrants, and this brought about increased anti-Semitic attitudes. With these attitudes flowed a series of negative stereotypes that viewed Jews as products of the ghetto: greedy, vulgar, physically weak, dirty, and clannish. To combat these prejudices, Jewish associations were formed to help the newly arrived secure jobs, homes, healthcare, and other services that might make the transition to America less difficult.

Resentment against Jews increased during the Progressive Era, and some social restrictions became more common. By the 1920s and 1930s, discrimination increasingly affected Jewish opportunities in certain professions and corporate business. Many Jews also faced higher education quotas that prevented Jewish enrollment in many universities, including the Ivy League. Harvard and Yale reduced Jewish-student numbers during the 1920s and 1930s substantially, and other private colleges followed. Many American writers such as F. Scott Fitzgerald, Ernest Hemingway, T.S. Eliot, and Ezra Pound perpetuated negative Jewish characterizations in their novels and poetry.

AMERICA AS A THREAT TO JEWISH IDENTITY

From 1924 on, easy access to America was essentially closed. Faced with degrees of bigotry and intolerance, many Jews also encountered additional non-racist threats to their identity, primarily stemming from a general freedom of movement and an ability to assimilate not found elsewhere. This situation could well pose problems in defining what it meant to be Jewish. In

This synagogue in North Philadelphia housed two different congregations in succession in the late 19th century and into the 1920s, but later became a Baptist church.

this environment, many Jews simply lost religious fervor. As figures for the 1920s indicate, there was but one synagogue for every 1,300 Jews, whereas for Christians during this era, there was a church for every 220 people. Furthermore, in many American cities, there were a large number of Jews who simply choose a secular life.

Given their diverse European backgrounds, Jewish Americans also lacked a central Jewish leadership, and rabbis from different areas were not necessarily accepted by other congregations. Rabbinical training became an important solution to this divide, which was reflected in the founding of the American Reform movement in 1875 and the founding of what became Hebrew Union College. However, Judaism was not unified by this development and divisions persisted, leading to separate Conservative and Orthodox movements. American Conservative Jews organized the Jewish Theological Seminary in 1886; for Orthodox Jews, Yeshiva University was not started until 1927.

By the 1920s, Conservative Judaism represented the core direction of American Judaism, which essentially represented a mingling of Reform and Orthodox teachings. In time, further compromises modernized services, including the use of English and abbreviated praying. Synagogues became more Americanized as they attempted to improve attendance and strengthen observance. This would reduce the use of Yiddish as the main means of communication, particularly with the young members of the congregation.

Lacking a core religious unity, some Jewish Americans chose to define their cultural identity through the Yiddish language and shared social traditions as well as common approaches to encounters with prejudice and intolerance. The search for a cultural identity became a key element in adjusting to the American experience, which was a primary goal of individuals such as Mordechai Kaplan. In 1922, Kaplan founded the Society for the Advancement of Judaism as a social vehicle for building communities by creating shared social and recreational outlets. Such organizations had an easier time reaching their audiences due to the fact that many Jews chose to live in areas where a sense of protection and unity was felt.

During the 1920s and 1930s, as a new generation of Jewish Americans emerged, its members found social accommodation easier. Native-born Jews who were more acculturated to and knowledgeable about American culture looked for a better sense of belonging and greater levels of inclusion and acceptance. This was most clearly observed in residential patterns that saw Jews in New York City move

Eve *was a magazine that sought to address Jewish-American women's interests in the 1930s.*

Prohibition and Jewish Gangsters

The passage of the Eighteenth Amendment in 1919, which led to a prohibition of the sale, transport, and consumption of alcoholic beverages, defined the 1920s and 1930s. Enforced through the Volstead Act, Prohibition proved a great folly that increased alcohol consumption and criminalized those that consumed illegal drink. Crime rates increased in all areas and American prisons were crowded with Volstead violators.

Prohibition also provided a virtual gold mine of easy profits for the bootleggers who supplied alcohol, and whose gangs brought new levels of criminality to America. When President Roosevelt secured the repeal of the Eighteenth Amendment in 1933, the return of alcohol sales proved to be one of the Democratic Party's most popular programs, particularly in hard economic times.

Although there were Jewish criminals operating before the Roaring Twenties, Prohibition opened the door of opportunity to Jewish gangsters who now saw a method to earn huge profits. These gangsters emerged from the ethnic neighborhoods of New York's Lower East Side and Brooklyn, and from Los Angeles, Chicago, Philadelphia, Detroit, and other major American cities where there had been considerable Jewish settlement.

Famous Jewish gangsters Meyer Lansky and Bugsy Siegel established themselves as prominent bootleggers during these years. Abraham Bernstein made the Purple Gang in Detroit a major criminal enterprise with national connections. Others such as Dutch Schultz, Moe Dalitz, Abner Zwillman, Louis Buchalter, and Harry Greenberg expanded their enterprises and forged links with Italian-run gangs such as the Lucky Luciano organization. These links were further cemented during the 1930s. The ultimate goal was a cooperative national criminal syndicate that maximized profits from the many illegal activities that they engaged in such as gambling, prostitution, and murder for hire.

The rise in anti-Semitic feeling during the 1930s, stimulated by desperate economic circumstances and the rise of Nazism, created causes for concern for American Jews. Attitudes were poisoned by the likes of Father Coughlin in radio broadcasts, and by the growth of America's own Nazi offshoots, the German-American Bund and William Pelley's Silver Shirts.

Some have even credited Jewish gangsters such as Meyer Lansky with combating these anti-Jewish forces with their own brand of force and intimidation. The coming of World War II and America's entry into the conflict ultimately silenced these fascist organizations. However, many Jewish gangsters promoted American participation, frequently being denounced as agents of international Communism in the process. After World War II and the establishment of the state of Israel, contributions were made by characters like Lansky toward the success of a Jewish homeland.

away from the cramped and impoverished Lower East Side to new, although still predominantly Jewish, neighborhoods such as in Brooklyn and the Upper West Side. Many of these neighborhoods had a more suburban middle-class feel that reflected the growing success and upward mobility some of America's Jews were achieving.

Some scholars have defined this accommodation process as part of a commercialization of Judaism. One such example was found in the transformation of the bar mitzvah from a simple process on the road to adulthood to an elaborate social affair. In addition, educational opportunities were promoted both within the community and through the public school systems as a means to reach the bourgeois threshold. During this era children also took on a greater focus within the family, which brought about greater spending on their welfare and upbringing.

After the collapse of Wall Street in 1929 and the coming of the Great Depression that dominated economic life during the 1930s, the Jewish drive for social and economic acceptance faced new hurdles. Hard times increased anti-Semitic incidents as social tensions rose. Many upwardly ambitious Jews who had achieved middle-class success and white collar jobs now faced the brutal facts of unemployment.

These Jewish women patronized a temporary store that gave them access to kosher meat and other foods in the "cooperative colony" of former city-dwellers in Jersey Homesteads, Hightstown, New Jersey, in November 1936.

The job crisis also severely affected Jewish garment workers, an occupation that employed as many as a third of New York's Jews. The failure of the Bank of the United States in 1930, a primarily Jewish bank that held the savings of 20 percent of New York's Jewish population and 10 percent of the savings of American Jews nationally, left large sections of the Jewish-American community wiped out. Thousands of Jewish businesses went bankrupt, and many Jewish Americans who had tasted prosperity during the 1920s now felt the reality of joblessness and a complete reversal of fortunes.

For the remaining jobs, hiring quotas meant that finding a job was difficult, and many Jews were driven to accept public assistance—a demeaning affair. Employment discrimination affected even the most qualified, including Jewish doctors and lawyers who faced poor prospects. Many within New York and other areas did seek assistance from Jewish Mutual Aid Societies and the assorted federations that had developed during the Progressive Era. There were also *landsmanschaften* (local or hometown societies) that tried to offer assistance and aid to those in need. Often, though, the severity of the crisis meant that demand exceeded the existing resources and soon funds were depleted. Many community facilities were also hurt as there were no funds for expansion and building, and further, many existing social programs had to be reduced or curtailed.

In the 1920s and 1930s, the many Jewish communities found within the United States attempted to preserve certain traditions and practices as part of their Jewish identity. For religiously minded Jews, the most significant tradition was the *mitzvot*, which represented over 600 obligations as outlined in the Torah and Talmud. These commandments involved testimonies and the judgments and rules that shaped behavior and expression of faith. Fulfilling such a range of obligations was difficult, and the degree of obligation varied among people and circumstances.

VOTING PATTERNS

During the Depression, Jewish Americans made use of their increased voting powers, particularly in large cities, to give their political weight to the Democratic Party. Evidence of this party identification was seen as early as the 1928 election, when Jewish Americans supported the Al Smith campaign. Although an Irish Catholic, Smith spoke some Yiddish, and he had an open door policy toward the appointment of Jews to state and other offices, and and was pro-immigrant and pro-religous minority.

In 1932, the Jewish vote clearly shifted to Franklin D. Roosevelt, who received 82 percent of Jewish votes cast. This vote increased to 86 percent in 1936. Such support was recognized—during his administration, Roosevelt appointed more Jews to high office than any president before him. With the rise of Nazism and the mistreatment of European Jews in Germany, and then in Europe after 1940, Roosevelt tried to loosen the Quota Act restrictions, but he was hampered by Congress, which opposed any major changes to immigration policy. This situation was particularly seen in the 1939 case of the SS *St. Louis* when its cargo of Jewish refugees were denied entry into the United States and subsequently were forced to return to Europe, where they became a propaganda victory for Hitler. The events of World War II and the discovery of the Holocaust made the existence of this restrictive policy a source of much later criticism. Events of the 1930s also convinced many American Jews to support the Zionist idea of a Jewish homeland in Palestine. From the mid-1930s, American Jewish support for Zionist groups and charities grew, and even the Reform movement reversed its Zionist opposition in 1937.

POPULAR CULTURE

The important role played by Jewish Americans in shaping American popular culture materialized early, and was evident during the Progressive Era. In composing and, in particular, in musical theater, by the 1920s and 1930s the names Jerome Kern, Irving Berlin, Lew Fields, Richard Rodgers, Lorenz Hart, and George and Ira Gershwin were well known.

As a group, there has rarely been such a creative force in American music as potent and pleasing to the public at large. Jerome Kern composed for both the stage and the screen and wrote, among his many compositions, hits such as *Show Boat* (1927) and *Swing Time* (1936, starring Fred Astaire and Ginger Rogers). Irving Berlin composed over 3,000 songs including classics such as "God Bless America" and "White Christmas." Lew Fields, a vaudeville performer who initially teamed with Joe Weber, was a film and Broadway comedian and musical producer whose talents

Irving Berlin, the composer of over 3,000 songs, including "God Bless America," at the piano in 1948.

Composers Richard Rodgers (left) and Lorenz Hart collaborating on a project in 1936. They wrote large numbers of musical comedies for Broadway, averaging four original shows per year 1920–30.

were well recognized, particularly the Field and Weber stereotypical takes on the immigrant experience.

Richard Rodgers composed hundreds of songs and wrote over 40 musicals, often in collaboration with Lorenz Hart as his lyricist and Oscar Hammerstein as producer and director. Some of Hart's hits included "Blue Moon" (1934), "The Lady is a Tramp" (1937), and "My Funny Valentine" (1937). Brothers George and Ira Gershwin teamed up to shape American music during the 1920s and 1930s. George Gershwin also composed classical standards such as *Rhapsody in Blue* (1924) and *Porgy and Bess* (1935), in addition to Broadway musicals such as *Show Girl* (1929) and *Of Thee I Sing* (1930) and a cornucopia of popular songs including "Fascinating Rhythm" (1924) and a parade of compositions for Ella Fitzgerald. Until George's early death ended the partnership, Ira Gershwin wrote the lyrics for many of his brother's tunes. His songs included "I Got Rhythm" (1930) and "Embraceable You" (1928), which became classics. Many of his songs were recorded by artists such as Ella Fitzgerald, Billie Holiday, and Frank Sinatra.

An actor, comedian, and singer, Al Jolson was one of the nation's biggest stars during this period; by 1920, he was the highest-paid entertainer in

America. His starring role in *The Jazz Singer* (1927)—the first "talkie"—made him famous. Eddie Cantor also gained fame as an actor and singer-songwriter, becoming a leading performer during the 1920s in the *Ziegfeld Follies*. His move to Hollywood made him a featured artist following hits such as *Whoopee* (1930). Fanny Brice also received the accolades of the era from her many singing performances as part of the *Ziegfeld Follies*. She had a wide audience from her radio skits and songs, which included her popular hit, *Second Hand Rose* (1921). In film, she starred with Judy Garland in the popular *Everybody Sing* (1938). Sophie Tucker was another star of similar magnitude with hits such as "My Yiddishe Momme" (1925) and film appearances in *Honky Tonk* (1929) and *Broadway Melody* (1938).

From the 1880s, the Yiddish Theater helped train talent and provided early stage experiences for actors who later joined the mainstream theater in the 1920s and 1930s. Stereotypical comedy roles gave way to more complex performances in English. Aaron Hoffman's play W*elcome Stranger* (1920) introduced more serious themes such as anti-Jewish sentiment. Hoffman was joined by other playwrights such as Montague Glass, author of *Potash and Perlmutter, Detectives* (1926), and Elmer Rice, creator of *Street Scene* (1928). These works indicated a move away from a purely Jewish milieu in order to appeal to a broader audience.

Another important playwright during this era was S.N. Behrman, who was noted for his high comedies and film scripts for Greta Garbo. Behrman also wrote about more penetrating issues involving the Jewish-American experience. In addition, George S. Kaufman made his mark primarily in collaboration with others. For example he wrote the highly successful play *Stage Door* (1936) with Edna Ferber. He also wrote the extremely popular Marx Brothers' film, *A Night at the Opera* (1935).

Many critics feel the 1930s unleashed a more serious political turn in Jewish writing, such as was reflected in Clifford Odets's *Awake and Sing* (1935). Odets's plays confronted poverty, survival, and family manipulation

This poster for a federal WPA Yiddish Theater Unit production in Chicago dates from the late 1930s.

Actress and singer Fanny Brice behind the camera in an undated photograph.

in a manner that encouraged the idea that through art, higher intellectual levels could be reached that actually questioned or transformed society. Such sentiments allowed plays to become vehicles for social commentary and protest, which seemed appropriate for the Depression era.

Another prominent art form that emerged during the 1930s was modern dance. Many American Jewish women saw dance as an effective vehicle for both political and artistic expression. Influential women such as Sophie Maslow, Anna Sokolow, Lilian Shapero, Lily Mehlman, and Nadia Chilkovsky promoted the modern dance movement. Skills were perfected at New York's Henry Street Settlement, Kinderland, and during the 1920s, at the Neighborhood Theater, where Martha Graham offered classes. Modern dance was redefined as a political art essential to the culture of the masses, and became part of the Communist Party's efforts to bring class consciousness to the people. The New York Workers International Relief even provided a Workers' School of Music and Dance—with lessons priced at 10 cents—to spread the political message. Dance had become a tool of the revolution and many American Jewish women became keen performers and advocates of dance as liberationist exercise.

In addition to the theater, American Jewish writers began to have an impact within the world of American fiction. At the end of the Progressive Era, Abraham Cahan, although principally a Yiddish writer, wrote *The Rise of David Levinsky* (1917) in English. This well-received work captured the dilemmas associated with the loss of heritage as one rose and became successful in America. As the 1920s unfolded, the best-known Jewish writer, playwright, and screenwriter was Ben Hecht. His novel *A Jew in Love* (1920) established his humorous approach to serious issues. Yet it was Hecht's screenwriting that made his reputation. He received the first Oscar awarded for Best Screenplay for writing the 1927 film *Underworld*. He furthered his credits with numerous other important efforts including coauthoring the script for

The Front Page, which became a successful film in 1931. In 1932, Hecht wrote the screenplay for the highly influential gangster film *Scarface*, which created an entire film genre. In a lengthy career that lasted into the 1960s, six of Hecht's films were nominated for Academy Awards.

As the 1930s progressed, more socially aware writing emerged. Nelson Algren's *So Help Me* (1933) and *Somebody in Boots* (1935) both, from the perspective of the outsider, captured the lower depths of American life. Albert Halper gave an appropriate proletarian realism to his settings and characters in books such as *Union Square* (1933). However, the most important writer of the period was Nathanael West, who combined humor with surrealism in his writing. He gained critical success with works such as *Miss Lonely Hearts* (1933) and *A Cool Million* (1934), but is remembered best for *The Day of the Locust* (1939), which explored the illusion of Hollywood.

AMERICAN JEWS AND HOLLYWOOD

Jewish Americans made important early contributions to the development of the American film industry, which evolved into a huge business by the 1920s—investments in the mid-1920s totaled over $2 billion. Carl Laemmle's creation of Universal Studios in 1914 in many ways set the stage for others to follow. Cinema attendance made such investment possible: 40 million in weekly ticket sales in the early 1920s rose to over 100 million in 1929. There were over 800 film releases a year during this decade.

Silent black-and-white films remained the major product, but films were becoming more elaborate with longer and costlier production capacities. All film genres were represented, appealing to the variety of American tastes by ranging from romances to westerns and comedies. The basis for this expansion can be attributed to the growth of the large studios.

Film became big business with the arrival of the "big five" studios that controlled over 90 percent of film production and releases. The key studios also built up a steady creative workforce through the introduction of studio contracts that tied stars to long-term commitments. Ownership of these major studios often rested with Jewish Americans, who made Hollywood the center of the film industry. These studios included Warner Brothers founded in 1923 by Jack, Harry, Albert, and Sam Warner. Warner Brothers produced *The Jazz Singer* (1927), the first talking film.

Paramount Studios, formed in 1927, was controlled by film pioneers Adolph Zukor and Jesse Lasky. Metro Goldwyn Mayer Pictures came into existence in 1924, and 20th Century Fox emerged in 1935 when Darryl Zanuck joined Twentieth Century Films with the older Fox Studios. In this period the fifth major studio was RKO Pictures (Radio-Keith-Orpheum), formed in 1928 by the RCA Corporation, then led by David Sarnoff. In the late 1940s, RKO's ownership passed to industrialist and aviator Howard Hughes. In addition to the big five, another important Jewish-owned, small studio was Columbia

This 1916 photograph brought together a number of early Hollywood moguls, including (from left to right): Jesse L. Lasky, Adolph Zukor, Samuel Goldwyn, Cecil B. DeMille, and Al Kaufman.

Pictures, started in 1919 by Jack and Harry Cohn. Columbia's influence grew in the late 1920s and 1930s, largely due to the films of Frank Capra.

Although many studios were Jewish controlled, the owners shared an American immigrant or first-generation history that shaped their worldview. They often used film to demonstrate their Americanism and felt that their common touch gave them special insights into American culture. This understanding included an appreciation of American values, ideals, and—particularly important for film sales—the public's likes and dislikes. Their creative approach was middle-brow and was structured to achieve the biggest audience share. As the 1930s unfolded, film also offered escape for millions from the drudgery and desperation of everyday Depression life.

SPORTS AND THE AMERICAN JEWISH EXPERIENCE

As with other areas of American popular culture, sports were another avenue in the American Jewish process of acculturation. Participation in sports as an athlete or fan provided a key way to counter blatant anti-Semitism that perpetuated negative Jewish stereotypes. In addition, sports recognized indi-

Jewish Boxing Legends

Benny Leonard (1896–1947) was a product of New York City's Lower East Side who fought under the nickname "Ghetto Wizard." Leonard learned to fight in the streets and developed his skills in neighborhood boxing gyms. After turning professional, he became one of the most highly regarded lightweight fighters ever. Leonard took the championship at age 21 in 1917, and held it until 1925, with an unofficial career record of 157 wins with 69 knockouts and only 11 losses. He had great hand speed, was lightfooted, and had the psychological skills in the ring that made him a hard fighter to beat. Although a Lightweight, he challenged Jack Britton for the Welterweight Championship in 1922, but lost on a disqualification for hitting his opponent while he was down. He later became involved with the National Hockey League and also became a boxing referee. Leonard died in the ring in 1947 from a heart attack while refereeing a fight.

Barney Ross (1909–67) (real name Dov Rasofsky) was born in New York City but was raised in Chicago. The son of a rabbi who was murdered in a robbery attempt, Ross took to boxing as a way to make money. He became a professional at age 19 and fought under the name Ross to protect his mother's and his family's sensibilities. Ross gained his first title in 1933 when he defeated Tony Canzoneri for both the Lightweight and Jr. Welterweight titles. He eventually became the first fighter to achieve three championships in different weight classifications. Ross finally ended his boxing career in 1938 after a 15-round decision to Henry Armstrong. In 81 fights, he was never knocked out, and his career posted an impressive record of 72 wins and four losses. In the atmosphere of the 1930s, with the rise of Nazism, Ross made a point to show that Jews could fight back. During World War II, he demonstrated his courage by joining the Marines. In brutal combat on Guadalcanal, he single-handedly killed 22 Japanese to save his comrades. This bravery earned him the Silver Star and true hero status. His wounds led to a dependence on morphine and, later, heroin, which he beat in the postwar period.

Lew Tendler (1898–1970), who came from South Philadelphia, is regarded by many aficionados as the best left-handed fighter in boxing history. He is also considered the best fighter not to win a championship, largely due to the fact that he fought in the same class and era as Benny Leonard. Tendler had his first professional fight at age 15 and went on to fight in the Bantamweight, Lightweight, and Welterweight divisions. Known as a quick and hard puncher, Tendler fought until 1928 and established his reputation with two classic contests against Leonard, which he lost on late-round decisions, the last in 1923 in front of 60,000 fans at Yankee Stadium. In 1924, he fought Michael Walker for the Welterweight crown and lost in the 10th round. Tendler ended boxing with a record of 59 wins and 11 losses. In retirement, he became a successful restaurateur in Philadelphia.

Gertrude Ederle, swimming Gold medalist in the 1924 Olympics, in the early 1920s.

vidual achievement and promoted an individual's home community. Jewish athletes embraced all sports including the important American sports of baseball, basketball, and boxing. In America's national game of baseball, the most famous Jewish-American athlete was Hank Greenberg, who joined the Detroit Tigers in 1933 and challenged Babe Ruth's single-season home run record in 1938. Greenberg's career was shortened by army service in World War II, but his achievements led to his election to the Baseball Hall of Fame in 1954.

Sports grew in the 1920s and 1930s to include intercollegiate athletics, particularly basketball and football. Even in more exotic sports, American Jewish athletes excelled. For example, New York's Sidney Frumkin trained in Mexico and became the first successful American bullfighter. There was also the occasional negative portrait of Jewish-American involvement in sports as seen in the character of New York's Arnold Rothstein. He gained fame as the gambler, speakeasy owner, and businessman who introduced business principles to the gangsters' domain. His notoriety in sports came at the beginning of this era and involved the accusation that he fixed the 1919 World Series played between the Chicago White Sox and the Cincinnati Reds. He was also accused of manipulating horse races in the 1920s, particularly events featuring his own horse Sporting Blood.

In the world of collegiate sports, Jewish-American athletes, especially those seeking admission to private universities, faced steep levels of discrimination and rejection. This rested on the introduction of quota systems that denied entry to many American Jewish athletes. The issue affected Harvard and Yale especially. Harvard argued that the increase in the number of Jewish students enrolled from 7 percent in 1900 to 21 percent in 1922 created imbalances and made the quota system necessary.

However, the presence of successful student athletes at other public institutions was duly reported in the press and there were many notable success stories from this period. Benny Friedman became an All-American quarterback at the University of Michigan in the mid-1920s. At the University of Wisconsin, Louis Behr received the Kenneth Sterling Award in 1928, recognizing his achievements in basketball. In football, which became a popular sport in the 1930s, similar fame was achieved by Marshall Goldberg at Pittsburgh and Sid Luckman at Columbia.

Women athletes also made their presence known during these decades. Jewish-American women became more visible as opportunities developed for them to show their sporting abilities. The settlement houses, Jewish Educational Alliances, Young Women's Hebrew Associations, and many other community-based facilities opened the world of sports and competition to women. In swimming, Charlotte Epstein, who in 1917 organized the New York Women's Swimming Association, became a keen promoter and administrator of the sport and a major influence in the Olympic movement.

Many Jewish-American women stars emerged such as Aileen Riggin, who at age 14 won a Gold medal in diving at the 1920 Antwerp Olympics; at the 1924 Paris Olympics, she added to her medal collection in both swimming and diving. Gertrude Ederle also established herself at the 1924 Olympics, winning Gold in the 400-meter relay freestyle, and in 1926 became the first woman to swim the English Channel. In track and field, Lillian Copeland won amateur titles starting in 1925 and later won Olympic medals: Silver in the discus at the 1928 Amsterdam Olympics, and Gold at the 1932 Los Angeles Olympics.

CONCLUSION

The 1920s and 1930s represented a coming of age for American Jews as they became more fully integrated into American life. This second generation lost—through the Americanization process—those distinctive features that set the immigrant apart. This would, over time, have a negative impact on the Yiddish press, which had established deep roots in urban areas such as New York City and other East Coast cities where most American Jews had settled. American Jews increasingly absorbed the language, style, manners, and values of the dominant American culture. This was evident in the attitudes and beliefs of the Jewish moguls who owned the Hollywood movie studios. Their experiences prepared them to be crucial purveyors of Americanism. The studio heads' rise from the garment and retail trades gave them the tools to be in tune with public tastes, perhaps more so than other Americans, including the intellectuals and other cultural critics.

In addition, by the 1920s, hard work and application delivered new levels of prosperity for America's Jews. This can be seen in the drive toward higher education. Between 1890 and 1925, Jewish college enrollment grew at a fantastic rate—five times that of the general population. This delivered new levels of professionalization to American Jewish communities. American Jews became major contributors to all levels of American popular culture, including education, and they became stars in many different sports.

The coming of the Depression delivered hardship and a temporary reversal in Jewish-American fortunes as financial collapse and unemployment affected many households. The period galvanized the political identities of the American Jewish communities, and many became attached to Franklin D. Roosevelt's Democratic machine, while others became involved in the more radical politics of the era. In many different arenas, American Jews became prominent proponents of progressive social change.

The introduction of the 1920s' immigration quota system stemmed the tide of Jewish immigration, which would have terrible consequences, in light of Nazi persecution and World War II's subsequent devastation of European Jewry. During these years only about 100,000 Jews were admitted to the United States, which sentenced many others to the coming Holocaust. Discrimination continued to exist in American life and anti-Semitism remained an issue, but greater assimilation saw its harsher aspects slowly reduced. Judaism, without a central religious rabbinical tradition, also evolved to accommodate American experiences, often falling more in line with the other major American religions. Although only two to three percent of the national population, Jewish Americans had a disproportionate impact upon American life and institutions that would grow even more impressive in the decades ahead.

THEODORE W. EVERSOLE
NORTHERN KENTUCKY UNIVERSITY
AND UNIVERSITY OF CINCINNATI

Further Reading

Brodkin, Karen. *How Jews Became White Folks and What that Says for Race in America*. New Brunswick, NJ: Rutgers University Press, 1999.

Cohen, Joseph. "Yiddish Film and the American Immigrant Experience," *Film and History*, v.28, 1–2 (1998).

Cohen, Sarah B., *From Hester Street to Hollywood: The Jewish Americans of Stage and Screen*. Bloomington: Indiana University Press, 1988.

Dalin, David, and Alfred J. Kolatch. *The Presidents of the United States and the Jews*. New York: Jonathan David Publishers, 2000.

Dimont, Max I. *The Jews in America*. New York: Simon and Schuster, 1978.

Diner, Hasia. *In the Almost Promised Land: American Jews and Blacks, 1915–1935*. Baltimore, MD: Johns Hopkins University Press, 1995.

Dinnerstein, Leonard. *Anti-Semitism in America*. New York: Oxford University Press, 1995.

Feldstein, Stanley. *The Land That I Show You: Three Centuries of Jewish Life in America*. New York: Doubleday, 1978.

Finkelstein, Norman H. *Forged in Freedom: Shaping the Jewish American Experience.* Philadelphia, PA: Jewish Publication Society, 2002.

Gabler, Neal. *An Empire of their Own: How the Jews Invented Hollywood.* New York: Crown, 1988.

Gay, Ruth. *Unfinished People: Eastern European Jews Encounter America.* New York: W.W. Norton, 2001.

Gonzales, Juan L. *Racial and Ethnic Groups in America.* Dubuque, IA: Kendall/Hunt, 1996.

Goren, Arthur A. *The Politics and Public Culture of American Jews.* Bloomington, IN: Indiana University Press, 1999.

Gurock, Jeffrey S. *Judaism's Encounter with American Sports.* Bloomington, IN: University of Indiana Press, 2005.

Handlin, Oscar. *The Uprooted: The Epic Story of the Great Migrations that Made the American People.* Philadelphia, PA: University of Pennsylvania Press, 2002.

Hertzberg, Arthur. *The Jews in America.* New York: Columbia University Press, 1998.

Howe, Irving and Morris Dickstein. *World of Our Fathers: The Journey of East European Jews to America and the Life They Found and Made.* New York: New York University Press, 2005.

Levine, Peter. *Ellis Island to Ebbetts Field: Sport and the American Jewish Experience.* New York: Oxford University Press, 1993.

Lipset, Seymour. *American Pluralism and the Jewish Community.* New Brunswick, NJ: Transaction, 1990.

Meltzer, Milton. *The Jewish Americans: A History in Their Own Words.* New York: Thomas Crowell, 1982.

Parrish, Michael E. *Anxious Decades: America in Prosperity and Depression, 1920–1941.* New York: W.W. Norton, 1994.

Rogin, Michael. *Blackface, White Noise: Jewish Immigrants in the Hollywood Melting Pot.* Berkeley, CA: University of California Press, 1998.

Sachar, Howard. *A History of the Jews in America.* New York: Knopf, 1992.

Whitfield, Stephen J. *American Space, Jewish Time.* Hamden, CT: Archon, 1998.

CHAPTER 6

World War II and the Forties: 1939 to 1949

NAZI GERMANY INVADED Poland in 1939, setting off a chain reaction that became World War II, and American Jews entered the most tumultuous and transformative decade in their history. While their fellow Jews in Europe and North Africa were displaced at best or destroyed at worst, American Jewry would move from the margins to the mainstream of society.

When Japan attacked the U.S. naval base at Pearl Harbor, Hawaii, on December 7, 1941, U.S. Congress declared war on Japan and its allies Germany and Italy. Over half a million American Jews joined the American armed forces and millions more participated in the war effort at home. When America's Jewish soldiers returned home from the war, they—like so many World War II veterans—earned college degrees, entered professions, purchased homes in the suburbs, and contributed their share of children to the postwar baby boom.

After 1924, the gates to America had virtually closed to Jewish refugees from Europe, and by 1939, a majority of American Jews had been born in the United States. Increasingly, the children of Yiddish-speaking American Jews used English as their first (and often only) language. Similarly, the children of Orthodox immigrant Jewish parents became less-observant members of Conservative or Reform congregations, or simply non-observant, secular Jews.

These experiences—the end of immigration, participation in the military, and the breakdown of ethnic Jewish neighborhoods—helped integrate much of American Jewry into the broader national culture. In another dimension, however, the war reinforced Jewish particularism, or more specifically, a sense of Jewish peoplehood. Confirmation of the Holocaust, the massive slaughter of European Jewry by Nazi Germany and its allies and collaborators, ended the decades-old debate about whether American Jewry should support Zionism. American Jewish leaders who formerly opposed the creation of a Jewish homeland in Palestine now accepted the argument that, without a homeland, Jewry in other parts of the world could never be secure, even if American Jewry could protect itself. In November 1947, the United Nations voted to partition the British-administered territory of Palestine into Jewish and Palestinian Arab homelands. On May 14, 1948, Israel declared its statehood (a step beyond "homeland" that made it an independent nation). The Truman administration immediately recognized the Jewish state. The vast majority of American Jews were euphoric.

When the surrounding Arab nations declared war on the new nation of Israel, American Jewry united in support for it by volunteering to fight in the Israel Defense Force, by purchasing and shipping surplus World War II armaments to help the Jewish state fight back, and by supporting Hadassah Hospital in Jerusalem, where the wounded were taken for care. Against steep military odds, Israel survived. Many American Jews believed that they should have acted more vigorously to save their fellow Jews from the Holocaust. Now they took pride in having helped in the fight for the survival of Israel. For the next several decades, concern for the survival of Israel would provide American Jews with a shared focal point for their identity.

From the darkness of the Great Depression, World War II, and the Holocaust, American Jews emerged by 1949 as the world's largest, wealthiest, most secure, and most unified Jewish community and the lifeline supporting the survival of Israel. This remarkable result came at the tragic expense of 6 million of Europe's Jews, many of whom were family members of those lucky enough to live in America. As a result, American Jewry adopted a new motto, "Never Again," pledging that the destruction of a Jewish community anywhere in the world would never recur.

LINGERING EFFECTS OF THE DEPRESSION, 1939

Since the arrival of Jews in New Amsterdam in 1654, American Jews have viewed themselves as having a moral obligation to care for their needy at home and abroad. By 1939, most American cities with more than a few thousand Jewish residents had established a local Jewish welfare federation charged with coordinating fundraising and distribution of support to Jewish-oriented social service agencies. In the early 1930s, many Jewish charities became overwhelmed by the demands they faced, and despite significant donations by wealthy Jewish leaders and the efforts of the federations to help them raise funds, they could not keep up with the ever-increasing demands for aid to Jews in need.

By 1939, a number of American Jewish organizations had taken on the additional burden of caring for Jews overseas. The American Jewish Joint Distribution Committee ("the Joint") tried to meet the increasing call for food and medical supplies for European Jews being crushed by Nazi oppression in German-occupied lands and by local anti-Semites in other European nations. They were also urged to support the needs of the *Yishuv*, the Hebrew term for Jews living in British-administered Palestine.

At the same time, New Deal relief and employment programs, some of which were channeled through community agencies, helped Jewish agencies meet their domestic obligations. Jewish agencies and federations joined other religious-based charities to form community chests or United Way organizations. However, full employment would not completely return to the Jewish community—or the nation—until 1941.

CONCERN FOR EUROPEAN JEWS

By 1939, reports from Europe were deeply troubling to many in the American Jewish community. In 1933, Adolf Hitler was appointed chancellor of Germany and began implementing the Nazi anti-Semitic measures he had promised. German Jews were slowly but systematically deprived of their legal rights, property, physical safety, and, for some, their lives. News of this persecution reached America in the mid-1930s and, while somewhat neglected by the secular press, received intense coverage in the American Jewish press.

Despite the dire news, many in the Jewish-American community refrained from pressuring the U.S. government to act on behalf of German Jews. Reluctant to stir charges that American Jews were "dual loyalists" who cared more about their co-religionists abroad than about America's domestic problems, and knowing that the great majority of Americans opposed increasing immigration while the nation was still suffering from high unemployment, the majority of American Jewish communal defense groups chose not to advocate for lowering the barriers to Jewish immigration into the United States. The American Jewish Committee leadership in particular preferred quiet, closed-door diplomacy at the White House and with cabinet members, seeking to influence President Franklin D. Roosevelt to send aid to Jews in need.

By 1939, however, the political landscape of the America Jewish community began to change. Led by Rabbi Stephen S. Wise, the American Jewish Congress preferred to mobilize public opinion through rallies, calling for a lifting of the Jewish immigration quotas from Germany and Poland in order to save lives. In 1938, a group of Orthodox rabbis marched on Washington,

Political and religious leaders leaving the White House after discussing efforts to help German and Austrian refugees with President Roosevelt on April 13, 1938. Pictured left to right are Joseph P. Chamberlain, George S. Messersmith, Rabbi Stephen S. Wise, Henry Morgenthau Sr., Rev. Samuel Cavert, Rev. Michael J. Ready, Frances Perkins, and Louis Kenedy.

D.C., hoping to see Roosevelt and to ask him to lower immigration barriers by executive decree, but the president declined to meet with them. Jewish organizations also began reaching out to the Protestant churches for support in lobbying for rescue.

In the end, nothing would convince Congress and FDR to make Jewish rescue a national priority. Congress had made it clear that it would not lower the barriers to immigration. Isolationists made it clear that they opposed any American involvement in the war. The State Department dragged its feet in issuing visas to European Jews, even when the annual quota went unfilled. No matter which path the Jewish organizations took in advocating for rescue of European Jews in 1939 and 1940, their arguments could not move Washington.

American Jews' Response to the Beginnings of the Holocaust

When World War II broke out in Europe in 1939, the United States was in the midst of the Great Depression and widespread isolationist political sentiments meant that most Americans did not want to become involved in the military conflict. European information on the Nazi campaign to expel Germany's Jewish population began to spread in America shortly after the 1938 night known as Kristallnacht (night of the broken glass), in which Jewish businesses and property were destroyed. Stories of an ultimate plan to exterminate Jews, known as the Final Solution, also began to circulate. American Jewish communities, however, had limited power and central organization due to widespread anti-Semitism in American society at the time. The information received little attention in the American press and many dismissed it as simply rumors and exaggerations. The U.S. State Department, which had helped block early information on the Holocaust, would not confirm that information until 1942, when approximately half a million Jews had already been killed.

Those Jewish Americans who were gravely concerned and sought to bring their European relatives to the United States encountered almost insurmountable bureaucratic barriers against all Jewish refugees, termed the "paper wall," established by the U.S. State Department. Many Americans supported the policy of blocking Jewish refugees, fearing that the admittance of such large numbers would increase the intense job competition and unemployment problems created by the lingering Great Depression. Jewish Americans had long endured propaganda blaming them for the country's economic and other difficulties and widespread discrimination in employment, business, and housing. Economic conditions, isolationism, and long-standing anti-Semitism in the U.S. government and general public all contributed to the sometimes muted response of Jewish Americans to news of the Holocaust's beginnings.

Some Jewish-American leaders did protest German treatment of the Jews, but widespread indifference hurt their attempts to publicize early Holocaust information and spur the U.S. government and public into action. Fears of increasing anti-Semitism through attention-drawing protests and the realization that the United States was not likely to pursue military intervention in any case caused many Jewish-American leaders to place less emphasis on the issue than they might have otherwise. This belief was supported by the fact that those few early demonstrations that did occur received little publicity or general support. Thus, many Jewish organizations focused on gaining postwar aid for those who survived. The U.S. government's official policy of bureaucratic obstruction would not officially be lifted until 1944, when rising Jewish protests as more information reached the U.S. and the work of the Treasury Department headed by Henry Morgenthau resulted in the creation of the federal War Refugee Board.

WAR COMES TO AMERICA

The Japanese attack on Pearl Harbor and U.S. entry into the war ended American Jews' enforced period on the sidelines. The United States declared war on Germany and Italy, Japan's two main allies, and the Jewish community mobilized at every level to participate in the fight against Nazism, fascism, and the destruction of European Jewry.

At a minimum, 550,000 self-identified Jews either volunteered or were drafted into the U.S. military, forming a percentage of the nation's armed forces that exceeded the proportion of Jews in the American population. The U.S. military had a policy that each member of the armed forces should be able to observe his or her religion while in uniform and to receive the burial rites of his or her religion should they die in combat. Accordingly, on each individual's identification tag, affectionately dubbed their "dog tag," the military engraved a "P" for Protestant, a "C" for Catholic, or an "H" for Hebrew, anachronistically using the polite 19th-century term for "Jewish." The men and women who registered their religion as Judaism received dog tags with an "H." Some Jews, anticipating the treatment they might receive if captured by the Nazis, indicated that no religious identification should be engraved on their tag. For this reason, it will never be known for certain how many Jews volunteered or were drafted during the war.

The National Jewish Welfare Board conducted surveys to document the exact number of Jews who fought in the war and published stories about American Jewish soldiers and sailors who were killed, wounded, or awarded medals. The board's efforts were a response to decades of scurrilous charges that Jews were either war profiteers who never fought but prospered when others did, or unassimilated immigrants and radicals who cared more about European Jews and socialist revolution than American patriotism, or simply cowards.

One of the stories the Jewish Welfare Board and other Jewish organizations were proud to tell was that of the German Jews who had arrived before 1924 or under the quota and had volunteered for the U.S. military. Many of the men in this group, including future secretary of state Henry Kissinger, proved invaluable as translators during the invasion of Germany.

THE MILITARY AND THE JUDEO-CHRISTIAN TRADITION

Until World War II, the U.S. military had a reputation as being unfriendly to members of the Jewish faith. The army did not recognize Judaism as an equal religion until the Civil War, when Congress finally voted to allow Jewish chaplains to serve. Relatively few Jews attended the military academies at West Point or Annapolis. Christian officers paid little heed to the religious needs of Jewish enlisted men, and many Jews who served in the military believed that their religion had blocked their path up the ranks.

However, the need for millions of men and women to serve in World War II forced a change in attitude. While the term *Judeo-Christian tradi-*

tion had been coined in 1899, its use did not become more commonplace until the 1920s and 1930s, particularly as a means to promote interfaith harmony during the Depression. In brief, the term *Judeo-Christian tradition* implies that the two religions share a common belief in ethical monotheism, the value of the individual, and respect for a shared set of moral values grounded in the Ten Commandments. The military adopted the phrase and implemented policies based on the concept to promote unity and morale during World War II.

To encourage interfaith cooperation, the military trained all its chaplains in a single program at Harvard University's Divinity School. It required that the priests, ministers, and rabbis who volunteered consider themselves soldiers, sailors, or marines first and clergymen second. Each was required to serve all the men and women they en-

This 1948 illustration commemorated an interfaith group of U.S. Army chaplains who perished together while helping save soldiers on a torpedoed troopship in 1943.

countered, not only members of their own faith. In classrooms, dining halls, and dorm rooms, the rabbis, priests, and ministers taught each other the rituals they needed to know—for example, a chaplain who was a priest might have to preside over the funeral of a Jewish soldier in the absence of a Jewish chaplain, or a Jewish chaplain might have to give last rites to a dying Catholic soldier. When the army built chapels on its expanding network of bases, it specified that no permanent religious symbols be affixed to the altars or the buildings so that soldiers of all faiths could feel comfortable praying within them. More than one chapel had a flag on the podium inscribed with the words, "Have we all not one God?"

Under the influence of President Roosevelt and of his successor, Harry Truman, the military became a true American religious and ethnic melting pot, at least for whites. High casualty rates created opportunities for Jews to rise in the ranks. The military had to choose the best qualified, or the most willing,

American Jewish Chaplains at War

American Jewish chaplains are among the unsung heroes of World War II. Each rabbi who served was a volunteer. Jews formed approximately four percent of the armed forces population, and so the military authorized the Jewish Welfare Board to recruit and certify 311 rabbis to fill four percent of the chaplaincy. These rabbis were spread over five continents and among more than half a million Jewish personnel. Often flying or traveling in an open jeep to three or four services in a single day, they exhausted themselves to provide Sabbath and holiday services, deliver kosher food, conduct burials and other life-cycle ceremonies, and write condolence letters to the families of Jewish men killed in combat. After the Normandy invasion of France in 1944, the Jewish chaplains were, more than any other individuals, faced with the added burden of trying to provide food, clothing, and prayer books to the Jews who emerged from hiding in the wake of Allied successes in the field.

After the Allied invasion of Germany in early 1945, a handful of Jewish chaplains were among the first to enter liberated Nazi death camps. They would never forget what they saw. Chaplain David Max Eichhorn reported from Dachau in early May 1945:

We saw the 39 boxcars loaded with the Jewish dead in the Dachau railway yard, 39 carloads of little, shriveled mummies that had literally been starved to death; we saw the gas chambers and crematoria, still filled with charred bones and ashes. We cried not merely tears of sorrow. We cried tears of hate. Combat hardened soldiers, Gentile and Jew, black and white, cried tears of hate.

After the Nazi surrender, the United States occupied most of the southern portion of Germany, which included Munich and Nuremberg. Approximately 12 million homeless persons—refugees, prisoners of war, German civilians, and Jews who had survived the death camps—lived in Displaced Persons (DP) camps in the Allied-occupied zones of Germany and Austria. Within months, all were repatriated to their homes, but the 200,000 or so Jewish DPs had no surviving families to help them, and they were unwelcome in the communities from which they had been driven. American military policy dictated that all DPs were to be treated the same. The chaplains provided evidence to supporters at home that the Jewish survivors needed their own camps and better rations if they were to recover physically and spiritually from the years of starvation and terror to which they had been subjected.

Jewish leaders and humanitarian groups persuaded President Truman to appoint a commission of inquiry, led by Earl Harrison, into the issue. The members of the Harrison Commission visited the DP camps in the American Zone, escorted by Jewish chaplain Samuel Klausner. In its final report, the commission recommended the separate Jewish camps and improved conditions in them that the chaplains had advocated.

U.S. military chaplain Samuel Blinder reads a Torah scroll from among hundreds of stolen Jewish and Hebrew books discovered by American forces in Germany in July 1945 after the Nazi surrender.

to serve without consideration as to religious or ethnic background. When the army selected pilots for its air force (today, a separate branch of the service), educated Jews came to represent a disproportionate number of airmen. Jews who were too old for combat served in supply and distribution centers or in clerical roles. Many of those with experience in retail and business became supply officers. Hollywood screenwriters, many of them Jews, were assigned to write propaganda releases or to make patriotic films to boost morale among the troops.

While African Americans continued to serve in segregated units, and did so until 1948, Jews from cities like New York, Philadelphia, and Chicago who had lived in predominantly Jewish neighborhoods found themselves sharing barracks with Americans they had never encountered before: farm boys from Kansas or sons of West Virginia coal miners. While there were instances of overt anti-Semitic behavior on the part of Christian officers and soldiers, most Jewish servicemen reported that they experienced less hostility than expected. Occasionally, a Jewish GI would report that a backcountry infantryman would ask (usually with honest intent) to see his horns. These became teachable moments for the Jewish men to show that, other than a difference in

Among the many Jews who flew for the U.S. Army in World War II was First Lieutenant Leo S. Bach (front row center), who served as a bombardier on a B-17 with the 381st Bomb Group. After being shot down by the German Luftwaffe, Bach survived being held as a prisoner of war in Germany and later wrote a memoir about his experiences.

religious beliefs or customs and where they came from, they were no different from their fellow soldiers. In combat, Jews showed the same level of courage and endurance as their Christian comrades, and few combat units had serious conflicts between Jews and Christians when in battle.

With guidance from organizations such as the Jewish Welfare Board, the military did its best to respect the religious requirements of Jewish GIs. At training camps in the United States it was relatively easy to provide kosher meals to those men and women whose observance required it. Providing kosher meals under combat conditions, especially in remote locales overseas, was more difficult. Wherever possible, the military shipped kosher foods provided by the Jewish Welfare Board to Jewish chaplains in the field, who then distributed it to Jewish servicemen within reach.

JEWISH AMERICANS ON THE HOME FRONT
Jewish Americans participated in rationing and material sacrifices at home, worked in the factories, manufactured the munitions, and served in the merchant marine—measures that, by 1943, gave the United States and its allies a distinctive edge in battle and finally pulled the nation out of the Depression. Not many large industrial enterprises such as automobile or aircraft manufacturing belonged to Jewish owners, but Jews were leading

figures in small and medium-sized companies in textiles, clothing, food distribution, and material recycling (better known as the junk business). These industries provided the military with essential goods it needed to keep the troops supplied.

Jews were among those groups that found an opportunity in wartime both to perform public service and to gain employment by working in federal agencies. Tens of thousands of Americans worked in Washington, D.C., helping coordinate the war's economic, military, social, and political dimensions. Jews played a prominent role in Roosevelt's New Deal administration, urging him to continue social reform even in wartime. By the 1940s, Jews had developed a reputation for supporting liberal causes, and Roosevelt had an easy time keeping their support.

RELATIONS WITH PRESIDENT ROOSEVELT

At the same time, only one Jew served in FDR's cabinet. Roosevelt appointed his long-time friend and neighbor Henry Morgenthau, Jr., to serve as secretary of the treasury. Morgenthau would later press Roosevelt to issue an executive order to allow refugee Jews in Europe to enter the United States outside the quota system. In 1944, Roosevelt asked Morgenthau to serve on his newly created War Refugee Board, which had some success in persuading neutral nations to accept European Jews fleeing extermination.

While Jews other than Morgenthau did not sit in FDR's official cabinet, they were close to him in other ways. At the suggestion of Special Counsel Samuel Rosenman, Roosevelt appointed an informal group of advisers, known as his "brains trust" (later shortened to "brain trust") that, besides Rosenman, included Jews Benjamin V. Cohen, Felix Frankfurter, and James Warburg. FDR also counted on advice from Sidney Hillman, head of the Amalgamated Clothing Workers, when he wanted the view of organized labor on economic or political issues.

Roosevelt's close relationship with Jews, their near-universal support for his policies, and his conduct of a war against Germany provoked isolationists and anti-Semites to accuse Roosevelt of selling out America's interests in favor of "international Jewry." Some even accused him of having Jewish ancestry—asserting that the name Roosevelt had originally been Rosenfeld. Throughout his presidency, Franklin Roosevelt was the target of hate from those who also hated Jews.

In part, this undercurrent of antiwar sentiment on the right helps explain Roosevelt's unwillingness to define saving European Jews as an American war goal. He was quite aware that Jews were an especially vulnerable target. When confirmation of the Holocaust could no longer be ignored, Roosevelt promised that, at the war's inevitable conclusion, those responsible for these atrocities would be severely punished. But he still refused to lift the quota restrictions by executive decree, or to divert American warplanes to bomb the tracks to the death camps, or to define liberating the camps as a specific war aim. Finally, at the urging of Morgenthau and the War Refugee Board, FDR agreed to open Fort Oswego, an unused military training camp in upstate New York, for the temporary housing of 1,000 Jews trapped in American-occupied Italy, but with the promise that, at war's end, they would return to Europe.

Some historians have argued that FDR showed indifference to the plight of European Jews; others point to the limits set on his ability to act, given congressional and State Department opposition and his understandable fear that public support for the war would erode if he defined it as one to save the Jews. American Jewish opinion itself was divided on these issues, again as reflected in the different approaches of the American Jewish Committee on the one hand, and the more vocal American Jewish Congress in pressuring, or not pressuring, Roosevelt to allow refugees in or to bomb the tracks to the camps.

By 1943, however, there was an even stronger call to action coming from a radical Jewish cadre known as the Bergson Group, led by Peter Bergson, son of the chief rabbi of Palestine. The Bergsonites demanded the formation of a Jewish army to fight under its own Jewish flag and whose primary mission would be to rescue the remnant of Jewry still alive in Europe. Bergson recruited American supporters such as playwright Ben Hecht and illustrator Arthur Szyk to call for direct Jewish action independent of the military policies of the Allied nations. Eventually, the British did allow a Jewish Brigade, composed

Reporters, including an American, writing beside a pile of human bones outside a crematoria at Buchenwald after the concentration camp was liberated in April 1945. Confirmation of the Holocaust forced Roosevelt to promise retribution and strengthened American Zionism after the war.

The U.S. Army's 80th Division found these starving survivors at Buchenwald when they liberated the camp. Among those pictured is author Elie Wiesel (seventh from left in the second row).

primarily of Jews from the *Yishuv* in Palestine, to form a special unit in the British army and to operate under British command.

PEACE AND THE POSTWAR YEARS AT HOME

The war in Europe ended in April 1945 with Germany's unconditional surrender. In August, the United States dropped two atomic bombs on Japan and, a few days later, the war in the Pacific ended. Jewish soldiers, sailors, and Marines had acquitted themselves well, undermining the stereotype of Jews as slackers, profiteers, and loyal only to their co-religionists. They had volunteered in large numbers and shown bravery under fire. Some rose to the rank of general or to command squadrons of ships. On the home front, they shared the sacrifices and worked the overtime hours to assure American victory abroad. Having overcome anti-Semitism and racial hatred abroad, the returning Jewish soldiers (and especially their chaplains) determined to end the social discrimination against Jews that had characterized the 1920s and 1930s.

Again with the prodding of their chaplains, many Jews began to see the ethical connections between fighting against racial hatred in Germany and condemning racial segregation at home. African-American soldiers had already resolved to redress America's racial inequalities upon their return to the United States, and the modern Civil Rights Movement can be traced to their newfound confidence. It was the experience of fighting alongside black soldiers and especially their role in liberating the death camps that influenced many Jewish-American veterans to join the Civil Rights Movement of the 1950s and 1960s.

GETTING AHEAD

Idealism aside, most soldiers of every background wanted to get back to normal life. The sudden return of 13 million servicemen and women to the civilian economy raised fears that they would form a pool of unemployed reminiscent of the Depression years. These fears proved false. The economy benefited from pent-up demand for consumer goods that had been delayed by war for four years during which food was rationed, private automobiles were not manufactured, and homebuilding came to a standstill. The increased productive capacity built up in the United States to meet war requirements could now be turned to meeting consumer demand at home. Most of the European economy had been ravaged by war, and the fact that the United States had sustained virtually no damage to its industrial infrastructure established the nation as the world's leading exporter of food and manufactured goods. Returning servicemen who were willing and able to work immediately found jobs waiting for them.

Another form of stimulus to the economy came in 1944, when Congress passed the Servicemen's Readjustment Act, more commonly known as the GI Bill. This legislation provided funds to support college or vocational education for returning veterans, and one year of unemployment compensation for those who needed it. The bill also provided low-interest loans for returning veterans to buy homes and start businesses.

Tens of thousands of American Jewish GIs, and millions all told, took advantage of these programs to fulfill their dreams of receiving a higher education and entering a profession or business. In light of the discovery of Nazi atrocities against Jews, many institutions of higher education that before the war had imposed limits on Jewish enrollment quietly dropped them. Jews could enter schools of law, medicine, dentistry, and accounting on the same basis as other applicants. Few hospitals denied Jewish doctors admitting privileges any longer, and medical schools began to accept Jews on their faculties in significant numbers. Before the war, American Jews had been associated with retail businesses, garment manufacture, and organized labor. By the end of the 1940s, a generation of American-born Jewish men and women had laid the groundwork for a new image of the Jew as a white collar professional.

The provisions of the GI Bill that granted low-interest home loans to veterans had a profound effect on the United States in general. More than 2 million returning veterans purchased new homes during the 1940s and 1950s, many of them in emerging neighborhoods away from the older Jewish neighborhoods in city centers where the Jewish GIs had grown up. For example, the Grand Concourse neighborhood in the Bronx offered luxury rental apartments to young couples who had grown up in tenements on the Lower East Side or in Brownsville, Brooklyn.

The newly laid-out tracts of thousands of small, inexpensive single-family houses in Levittown on suburban Long Island, New York, became a destination for returning Jewish GIs who dreamed of owning their own home. More adventuresome yet were the men and women who, having seen the Sunbelt states during their military service, decided to relocate to San Diego, Miami, or Phoenix.

The returning Jewish GIs contributed their share of births to the baby boom of 1945–50. Marriage and birth rates for almost every American ethnic group rose in this period, as did incomes. But the changes that came with suburbanization and affluence provided challenges to traditional Jewish family and community cohesion. No longer crowded into predominantly Jewish neighborhoods such as Maxwell Street in Chicago or Blue Hill Avenue in Boston, the younger generation of Jewish Americans found themselves living increasingly among non-Jewish neighbors, much as they had done in the military.

While that wartime experience helped make the transition to more cosmopolitan living situations easier, it also meant that grandparents no longer lived as conveniently near their children and grandchildren. Family social support networks grew looser, and the burdens of caring for family members became more isolated and challenging as members lived farther away from each other.

POSTWAR AMERICAN JUDAISM

Following the adage that "there are no atheists in foxholes," many returning Jewish GIs resolved to pay more attention to religious observance than they did before their years of service. As they moved into newly developed, ethnically mixed communities—thanks to the GI Bill—they maintained their connections to Judaism through the suburban synagogue. For many before the war, the urban synagogue had been a place used strictly for prayer on the Sabbath and holidays. Few women attended, and those traditional women who did sat separately from the men.

Having left old patterns behind, postwar American Jews reconfigured the synagogue into a community center, a place not only for prayer, but also for family involvement. Suburban synagogues offered Hebrew schools on Sunday or after public school; youth social groups for teenagers; adult education courses; a social hall for bar and bat mitzvah parties, anniversaries, holiday parties, and bingo games; and in some cases recreational facilities.

Exodus and *Exodus*

The Jewish Holocaust survivors remaining in the Displaced Persons (DP) camps in the U.S. Zone of Occupied Germany had nowhere to go. At first, thousands tried to return to their homes in Poland, Romania, and elsewhere, only to find that they were unwelcome targets of violence and even murder. Nor could they immigrate to the United States, where Congress chose to keep in place the national origins quotas that excluded all but a handful of Jews each year. Most of the survivors wanted to go to the promised Jewish homeland in Palestine, which was administered by the British under a mandate from the United Nations. Responsive to Arab objections to allowing any part of Palestine to become a Jewish homeland, the British barred all but a few thousand Jews from immigrating to Palestine.

For thousands of younger Jews who foresaw no future in a Europe "drenched in Jewish blood," and no prospect of coming to the United States, Palestine would not be denied to them. With the assistance of clandestine Zionist groups organized in Palestine, the Jewish Brigade of the British Army and American Jewish chaplains throughout the American Zone of Occupation, the *Brichah* or "flight" from the DP camps to Palestine began.

Despite the official U.S. policy denying assistance to those who defied British law by trying to reach Palestine, American Jewish chaplains such as Herbert Friedman, Samuel Klausner, Eli Bohnen, Joseph Shubow, and others assigned to Occupied Germany helped prepare and transport Jewish men, women, and children to Italy for the risky trip by sea to Palestine.

The best known of these voyages was that of the *Exodus 1947*. After risking the perils of a truck trip from Germany to Italy, boarding the barely seaworthy *Exodus*, and steaming under British surveillance to the port of Haifa in Palestine, the British invaded the ship and forced its passengers to disembark and board British ships for a return voyage to France. When the French government refused to accept the refugees, Britain returned them against their will to DP camps in the British sector of Occupied Germany.

Led by expressions of outrage by Jewish leaders, members of every American religious faith began to turn against Britain. British public opinion began to change as well. By 1947, under pressure from the United States and the United Nations, the British government concluded that it was fruitless to try to reconcile Arab resistance to Jewish longings for a homeland in Palestine and told the United Nations that, as soon as possible, it wanted to terminate its mandate obligations there. The United Nations then voted to partition Palestine into two homelands, one for Palestinian Arabs, and one for Jews.

The story of the *Exodus* was made famous in a book by the same name by American Jewish author Leon Uris, and later made into a movie starring Paul Newman. The book and movie would later be called "the single most effective piece of Israeli public relations in the United States."

Two women leave a synagogue on West 23rd Street in New York City after special D-Day services on June 6, 1944. American Judaism in the 1940s now included Orthodox, Reform, Conservative, and Reconstructionist branches.

The typical Reform and Conservative synagogue became a community center as well as a house of worship, or what historian David Kaufman has called "a shul with a pool."

The Jewish Welfare Board developed a network composed of Young Men's Hebrew and Women's Hebrew Associations (JYs) and helped these local facilities to expand their recreational, social, and religious offerings in response to the changes in Jewish demographics. They particularly supplied guidance to the newly constructed JYs in the suburbs, often called not YMHAs, but Jewish Community Centers, or JCCs. In later years, many JCCs would evolve into luxury recreation centers open to non-Jews and Jews alike.

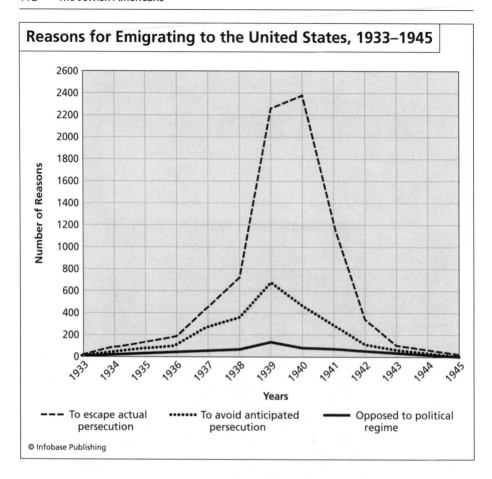

Reasons for Emigrating to the United States, 1933–1945

Number of Reasons

Years

- - - To escape actual persecution   •••••• To avoid anticipated persecution   —— Opposed to political regime

© Infobase Publishing

By the 1940s, Judaism as a religion in America had added a fourth movement, Reconstructionism, to its three main branches: Orthodox, Reform, and Conservative. Orthodoxy was the first and, in those times, only form of Judaism in America, brought by the Sephardic settlers in New York, Newport, Philadelphia, Charleston, and elsewhere on the Atlantic seaboard. With the influx of German Jews came classic 19th-century Reform, with its more abbreviated services and a willingness to speak the language of the worshipers (first German, and later English) as well as the Hebrew used in prayer. Conservative Judaism began to flourish in the United States around 1900. It struck a balance between traditional observance and an acceptance of modern culture. Reconstructionist Judaism, based on the ideas of Rabbi Mordecai Kaplan (1881–1983), views Judaism as a progressively evolving civilization, rather than a fixed set of theological ideas and observances. Kaplan defined the movement during the 1930s and 1940s, and it grew to the point of establishing a seminary in 1968. Today, Reconstruction remains the smallest of the main branches of American Judaism.

THE BIRTH OF ISRAEL AND AMERICAN JEWISH RESPONSE

Until confirmation of the Holocaust, the American Jewish community was divided between Zionists and anti-Zionists, although the number of anti-Zionists decreased throughout the 1930s. The American Council for Judaism, the leading American Jewish anti-Zionist group, was closely associated with Reform Judaism. Members of the council feared that an embrace of Zionism would imply dual loyalties or disloyalties on the part of American Jews. While they could accept that Europe's displaced Jews and those living in Palestine longed for a homeland, they would not advocate for American diplomatic action to secure it.

Other organizations such as the American Zionist Organization, Hadassah (the Women's Zionist Organization), the American Jewish Congress led by Rabbi Stephen S. Wise and then Rabbi Abba Hillel Silver, the Jewish War Veterans, and the Jewish Labor Committee all believed that establishment of a Jewish homeland—a place that Jews could defend by military and political means, as could other nations—was the only way to prevent another Holocaust. They asked the Jewish public to join them in speaking up for establishment of a Jewish homeland in its traditional site, Palestine, with Jerusalem

Jewish-American veterans of World War II volunteered for service in the future Israel Defense Forces after the end of the war, joining up with groups like these Jewish Brigade recruits shown around 1945.

as its capital, as the British had promised in the Balfour Declaration of 1917. In a white paper in 1939, the British government revoked this promise, severely limiting Jewish immigration to Palestine in order to appease the Arab opposition. Jewish groups pressured the U.S. government to convince the British to allow immigration to Palestine of the Jews still left in DP camps in occupied Germany.

The British saw access to Middle Eastern oil and passage through the Suez Canal as central to survival of their empire. At the same time, Britain was America's primary ally in confronting the Soviet Union, which quickly replaced Nazi Germany as the military and ideological enemy of democratic ideals. By 1947, it was clear that the Soviet Union and the United States would compete for world leadership, if not domination, and America would need British support in the struggle. Neither FDR nor Truman was inclined to force the British to open the gates to further Jewish settlement. Jewish hopes for a homeland in Palestine, which appeared to be the only solution to Europe's perennial "Jewish Problem," even to former anti-Zionists, were at an impasse.

When the United Nations voted to accept Britain's request to take back the mandate in Palestine, relieving the British of responsibility to keep peace between Jews and Arabs, the international body announced its intention to divide the territory into homelands for each group, after which it would withdraw. American Jews foresaw that the new Jewish political entity would face serious threats to its very survival. Surrounded by hostile Arab states and Palestinian Arabs who believed, as did the Jews, that the land was historically theirs, a Jewish state or other political entity would be met with the same hostility that Jewish settlements had met in previous decades. Some American Jews who had served in the U.S. military volunteered for service in what would become the Israel Defense Forces between 1945 and 1948. Others raised funds, purchased weapons and supplies, hired ships, and brought the contraband to the Jewish settlers in Palestine, running the British blockade.

Critical to the success of an independent Jewish state was its diplomatic recognition by the United States and, secondarily, by the Soviet Union. If those two great powers recognized the right of a Jewish homeland to become a Jewish state, joining in the United Nations and exercising the same rights as other nations, the centuries-long dream of restoration of a Jewish nation in the Holy Land would have a far better chance of coming true. Without American recognition, all those who did not want to see the creation of a specifically Jewish state in Palestine would have fuel for their argument that the state was illegitimate.

Accordingly, all Jewish groups who supported the creation of a Jewish state tried to find a way to persuade President Harry Truman, Roosevelt's successor in 1945, to recognize the new state immediately upon its declaration of independence, which was scheduled for May 14, 1948. While he appeared to waver before Israel's declaration of independence, Truman announced the United States' diplomatic recognition of the Jewish state within hours of its formation.

As predicted, neighboring Arab states attacked Israel the next day. The Israeli army was outnumbered by a factor that might have been as high as 100 to one. Led by David "Mickey" Marcus, an American who had graduated from West Point, the Israeli army was able to repel the far superior Arab forces. The Israeli navy, led by another American volunteer and Annapolis graduate, Paul Shulman, managed to sink the Egyptian flag vessel *Emir Farouk*, assuring that the newly formed state could receive supplies from friends abroad.

The stunning triumph of Israel's armed forces became a source of pride for Jews all over the world. Organizations such as Hadassah, the largest Jewish women's organization in the United States, were now free to send medical supplies to its hospital in an independent Jewish nation. Sales of Israel bonds to support the new nation's economy soared. The ancient prayer intoned by Jews around the world at the Passover Seder, "Next Year in Jerusalem," was for the first time in more than 2,000 years a reality. American Jews rejoiced at the fact that, as a people, they had—like Irish, Italian, Czech, Polish, or other ethnic Americans—a permanent home in America and a homeland to claim as an emotional base, even though few, if any, American Jews actually went to live there.

CONCLUSION

The euphoria spawned by Israel's creation in 1948 would lead to a new unity within the American Jewish community. The arguments between gradualists and militants, Zionists and anti-Zionists, ended. Justice Louis Brandeis's dictum that there was no contradiction between Zionism and Americanism appeared now to be a prophecy. The survival and success of Israel became the glue holding together all segments of the American Jewish community. That unity would not survive.

MICHAEL FELDBERG
THE HISTORY CONSULTANCY

Further Reading

Bendersky, Joseph W. *The Jewish Threat: Anti-Semitic Politics of the U.S. Army*. New York: Basic Books, 2001.
Diner, Hasia R. *The Jews of the United States: 1654–2000*. Berkeley, CA: University of California Press, 2004.
Dinnerstein, Leonard. *Anti-Semitism in America*. New York: Oxford University Press, 1995.
Goren, Arthur A. *The Politics and Public Culture of American Jews*. Bloomington, IN: Indiana University Press, 1999.

Hertzberg, Arthur. *The Jews in America*. New York: Columbia University Press, 1998.

Moore, Deborah Dash. *G.I. Jews: How World War II Changed a Generation*. Cambridge, MA: Harvard University Press, 2006.

———. "Worshipping Together in Uniform: Christians and Jews in World War II." The 2001 Swig Lecture. San Francisco, CA: Swig Judaic Studies Program at the University of San Francisco, 2001.

Sarna, Jonathan D. *American Judaism: A History*. New Haven, CT: Yale University Press, 2005.

Shapiro, Edward S. *A Time for Healing: American Jewry since World War II*. Baltimore, MD: Johns Hopkins University Press, 1992.

Sachar, Howard. *A History of the Jews in America*. New York: Knopf, 1992.

Urofsky, Melvin I. *American Zionism from Herzl to the Holocaust*. Lincoln, NE: University of Nebraska Press, 1995.

CHAPTER 7

The Fifties: 1950 to 1959

BY THE END of World War II, Jews exerted a definite presence in American social life, politics, and popular culture. Milton Berle was on television, Herman Wouk was an established author, and Jews had served in Congress, the Senate, the Supreme Court, and several presidential cabinets. Jewish-American soldiers served valiantly in the armed forces alongside their fellow citizens and returned from World War II seeking normalcy, stability, and full integration into modern American life. A Jewish state had survived turbulence and war against all odds, and seemed poised to become a major American ally in the Middle East. American Jews at the beginning of the 1950s had much to look forward to.

As Edward Shapiro has argued, two major themes characterize the 1950s for American Jews. First, rapidly growing social and economic mobility allowed large numbers of American Jews to move into the middle class. Second, American Jews came up with a variety of strategies and approaches to adapt to these new and unprecedented conditions.

THE RISE OF THE JEWISH MIDDLE CLASS

The Jewish working class began to disappear as Jews achieved unprecedented economic mobility and ascended rapidly into the American middle class. By 1955, 96 percent of Jews answered in surveys that they worked in non-manual occupations, compared to 38 percent of other Americans. Unlike their parents and grandparents, most American Jews in the 1950s were native born and members of the middle class. They spoke fluent English and sought acceptance in every aspect of American life and culture.

American Jewish soldiers, like their comrades throughout the country, were given new educational opportunities upon their return with the passage of the postwar GI Bill. In the early postwar period, 24 percent of Jewish men and 13 percent of Jewish women were college graduates. By 1957, this figure had risen significantly to 29 percent of Jewish men and 16 percent of Jewish women. Jewish Americans enrolled in colleges and universities at rates much higher than those of the general population. Jews who enrolled in institutions of higher education also encountered non-Jews much more frequently than they would have in their urban environments. Many Americans met Jews for the first time at their colleges or universities.

World War II, the effects of the GI bill, and the Jewish transition into the middle class helped to eliminate many of the lingering anti-Jewish prejudices from the 1930s and 1940s. According to one poll, by 1950, less than one-tenth of the American population objected to friendships with Jews. Americans were also more comfortable with the idea of Jews ascending politically. A 1959 poll demonstrated that more Americans were comfortable with voting for a Jew for president than voting for a Roman Catholic or a Protestant woman. Anti-Semitism continued to decline during the 1950s, as American Jews became increasingly entrenched in mainstream American society and culture. Whereas one-fifth of Americans polled in 1948 had said that they did not want Jews as neighbors, only two percent of Americans held the same opinion in 1959. These developments paved the way for American Jews to fully integrate into American society and to become part of the growing middle class in the new suburban neighborhoods.

JEWISH SUBURBANIZATION

Across America, rapid relocation to the new suburbs began immediately after the war. Abraham Levitt, a Jewish American, together with his sons William and Alfred Levitt began planning what was at the time the largest private housing project in American history: Levittown, on Long Island in New York. Levitt and his sons went on to build tens of thousands of affordable homes for families seeking to take advantage of postwar prosperity and leave the crowded cities. The housing boom in suburbia, the increased prosperity of the postwar period, and the rise of the automobile led to the mass migration of Americans from the cities to the suburbs.

The GI Bill and federal loans made suburban housing affordable for many Jewish Americans. Jews relocated to the suburbs at a much higher rate than other Americans. It is estimated that between 1945 and 1965, one out of every three Jews left the cities for the suburbs. By 1960, a majority of the Jewish-

Austrian immigrant Victor Gruen's 1956 Southdale Shopping Center in Edina, Minnesota, which was still in use when this photograph was taken in June 2009, influenced the direction of American suburban development for decades. Gruen has been called the "inventor of the mall."

American population lived in the suburbs. During the 1950s, a full two-thirds of American Jews lived in the suburbs of America's 10 largest cities. In contrast, it was not until 1970 that the majority of Americans lived in suburbs instead of cities. Not only did Jews migrate to the suburbs, but they also became highly mobile and increasingly geographically dispersed across the country. For example, both the urban and suburban Jewish populations of California and Florida experienced tremendous growth during the 1950s.

Jewish infrastructure relocated to the suburbs together with the vast majority of American Jews. Suburbanites built new synagogues and community centers and established B'nai B'rith lodges, Hadassah chapters, religious schools, and scout troops in their new communities. In 1956, Victor Gruen, an Austrian Jew who had escaped Nazi Europe in 1938, designed Southdale, America's first fully-enclosed shopping mall, in suburban Minneapolis. The institution of the enclosed shopping mall would soon come to define the suburban American lifestyle.

Since Jews were less concentrated in suburban towns than in major cities, Jews and non-Jews mixed more readily in the suburban environment. These encounters had a dramatic effect on Jewish-American lifestyles and patterns of observance. Albert Gordon's study, *Jews in Suburbia* (1959), famously defined the suburbanization movement as a transition from Judaism to Jewishness. In other words, Gordon argued, American Jews in the 1950s began to shift away from defining their Jewish identity around religious observance, and instead began to define themselves as culturally Jewish.

CHANGING PATTERNS OF OBSERVANCE

Religion became a defining element of Americanism during the 1950s. In 1954, Congress added the words *under God* to the Pledge of Allegiance. Two years later, Congress reintroduced the phrase *in God We Trust* to U.S. currency, which had not appeared since the Civil War. As Americans throughout the United States became increasingly religious, American Jews expressed their religious leanings by building a vast number of synagogues and by affiliating with them in greater numbers than ever before. Between 1947 and 1959, Jews built 99 new synagogues in the New York suburbs alone. In fact, Jews spent over $50 million on new synagogues nationally between 1945 and 1952. Though only about 18 percent of American Jews attended weekly services (according to a 1958 survey), American Jews joined synagogues in large numbers and participated in an increasing number of social activities organized by synagogue committees. In the 1950s, about 51 percent of American Jews were members of a synagogue—the highest rate of affiliation at any point in American Jewish history.

The major function of synagogues in the new suburban environment became the celebration of life-cycle events, social gatherings, and Jewish education. The synagogue replaced the Jewish street of the city as the new center of Jewish-American life and culture. Jewish parents turned to the new suburban synagogues to educate their children and to provide them with a sense of Jewish identity. The number of children enrolled in synagogue schools more than doubled during the 1950s. Approximately 40 percent of suburban Jewish children were enrolled in supplementary Hebrew schools during the 1950s, compared to only 23 percent of urban Jewish children.

Synagogue architecture took on a distinctly suburban look during the 1950s, reflecting the new functions of the suburban synagogue. Large parking lots were installed to provide for members who drove their cars to services and to synagogue functions, lawns were added to allow for outdoor activities, social halls were expanded to facilitate large social gatherings and events, classrooms and educational wings were added for growing Hebrew schools and adult education programs, and a movable wall was added between the sanctuary and the social hall to accommodate fluctuating patterns in attendance.

The 1950s were a period of significant institutional and organizational growth for the American Jewish community. Each denomination expanded dramatically, though some developed more than others. The Conservative movement in particular grew tremendously during the 1950s as newly suburban Jews flocked to synagogues that promised the best of both worlds: semi-traditional observance with a full acceptance of the modern American lifestyle. During the 1950s and 1960s, the number of Conservative synagogues in the United States grew by 450, more than the growth of Reform and Orthodox communities combined. The expansion of the Conservative movement during this period reflects the new patterns of Jewish observance that the movement institutionalized during the 1950s. In 1950, the Conservative Committee on Jewish Law and Standards ruled that Jews could drive on the Sabbath, provided they were driving to synagogue. The decision permitting Sabbath driving reflected the fact that the Conservative movement was becoming a largely suburban phenomenon and marked a major break with the Orthodox movement. Soon after, the committee permitted limited use of electricity on the Sabbath, as well as mixed-gender seating in the synagogue. In 1954, the same committee decided to allow women to be called upon to the Torah to recite the preliminary blessings.

By mid-century, membership in Conservative synagogues accounted for over half of the American Jewish population. In addition, the Conservative movement created new organizations and venues to increase synagogue affiliation. In 1948, Conservative leaders founded the Ramah summer camps for

The Conservative congregation of Beth Sholom in Elkins Park, a suburb of Pennsylvania, was one of the earliest in the area to move to a suburban location in the 1950s. They soon commissioned Frank Lloyd Wright to build this landmark synagogue, which was completed in 1959.

children and teenagers. A few years later, the movement started a network of Solomon Schechter Jewish day schools. In 1957, a world council of Conservative synagogues was created, uniting the Conservative movement under a single umbrella organization.

OTHER MOVEMENTS

The Reform movement also grew during the 1950s. With new leaders like Rabbi Maurice N. Eisendrath (1902–73), president of the Union of American Hebrew Congregations (UAHC), and Nelson Glueck (1900–71), president of the Hebrew Union College–Jewish Institute of Religion (HUC-JIR), the Reform movement carried out a major institutional expansion driven by large gains in membership. By 1955, the union had 520 congregations and 255,000 affiliated families. Under Glueck, the HUC-JIR opened new branches in Los Angeles and in Jerusalem to complement already existing branches in Cincinnati and New York. The Reform Central Conference of American Rabbis (CCAR) hired its first executive director, Rabbi Sidney Regner, in 1954. Following the lead of the Conservative movement with the Ramah camps, Reform also dramatically expanded their youth activities during the 1950s. They opened the first dozen National Federation of Temple Youth (NFTY) summer camps, and NFTY membership grew rapidly as a result.

Orthodox Jews also moved to the new suburbs, though in smaller numbers than their Conservative and Reform counterparts. There they began to battle the Conservative congregations for the affiliation of the next generation of American Jews, insisting on stricter standards of Orthodoxy. However, most of the growth of Orthodox affiliation during this period was due to the influx of refugees and Holocaust survivors into American cities and suburbs.

The 1950s also saw the beginning of the new Reconstructionist movement. The Jewish Reconstructionist Federation (JRF) was established in 1955, and individual congregations across the nation began to affiliate with the new denomination.

Women gained many new opportunities and roles in every denomination during the 1950s. In particular, women were given increased access to Jewish knowledge and education. In 1954, Stern College opened as a women's college within Orthodox Yeshiva University. In the Conservative and Reform movements, the Bat Mitzvah became an increasingly common educational experience for young Jewish girls. In addition, women in the Conservative movement became increasingly integrated into Jewish ritual practice after the 1954 ruling that allowed them to be called up to the Torah.

The Jewish Federation movement also experienced tremendous growth during the 1950s. Each city founded its own communal organization to distribute funding to the local community and to unite all of the synagogues and communal organizations without regard to denomination or level of observance. In Baltimore, it was The Associated; in Pittsburgh, the United Jewish

Federation; in Boston, Combined Jewish Philanthropies; in Philadelphia, the Jewish Federation. Each of these local organizations was loosely connected to the national body, United Jewish Communities.

JEWISH LITERATURE IN THE 1950s

Jewish Americans published many books during the 1950s that were popular and influential across the nation. Herman Wouk, an Orthodox American Jew born in New York to immigrant parents, became a best-selling novelist in the 1950s with his *The Caine Mutiny* (1951), *Marjorie Morningstar* (1955), and *This is My God* (1959). Wouk won the 1952 Pulitzer Prize for Fiction with *The Caine Mutiny*, and the novel was later made into a popular movie starring Humphrey Bogart, Van Johnson, and Fred MacMurray.

Each year brought influential new books from young Jewish writers. In 1951, Sydney Taylor published *All-of-a-Kind-Family*, the first juvenile book on a Jewish theme to be mass marketed to non-Jewish Americans. In 1952, Bernard Malamud published his first novel, *The Natural*, the story of an extraordinarily gifted baseball player. Malamud would go on to publish many influential novels in the 1950s, most famously *The Assistant* in 1957.

In 1953, playwright Arthur Miller made national headlines with *The Crucible*, a thinly veiled attack on the activities of Senator Joseph McCarthy and the House Un-American Activities Committee. The play was, on the surface, a retelling of the Salem Witch Hunts of 1692. However, Miller made his true intent clear. He wrote of his play: "The more I read into the Salem panic, the more it touched off corresponding ages of common experience in the fifties." In *The Crucible*, Miller sought to parallel the use of specious evidence and the demonization of Communists in America with the persecution of so-called witches in the 17th century.

In 1955, sociologist and American Jewish writer Will Herberg published his *Protestant-Catholic-Jew*, a book that created a framework for the sociological study of religion in America. In his book, Herberg argued that Catholicism, Protestantism, and Judaism were America's three great faiths and ought to be treated as equally valid religious expressions. The book was highly influential and came to define the way that Judaism was viewed in the postwar environment—as one of many important American religions.

Pulitzer Prize–winning playwright Arthur Miller in a photo from late in his career.

In 1954, novelist Saul Bellow won his first National Book Award with *The Adventures of Augie March*, published in 1953. Leon Uris came out with *Exodus* in 1958—the biggest bestseller in American history since Margaret Mitchell published *Gone with the Wind*. In 1959, Philip Roth's debut novel *Goodbye, Columbus and Five Short Stories* was published. *Goodbye, Columbus* chronicled the relationship between lower-class Neil Klugman and affluent, assimilated Brenda Patimkin. The book was a commercial and critical success, winning Roth the National Book Award in 1960.

In addition to achieving literary fame, American Jews also became influential in the academy. Brandeis University, founded in 1948, rose to prominence in the 1950s and became known across the nation for its commitment to academic excellence. The 1950s also saw the first stirrings of Jewish Studies as a new academic discipline. Malcolm Stern researched the genealogy of early American Jewry in the early 1950s and published his findings in *Americans of Jewish Descent*. In 1956, Edmund Wilson published "The Need for Judaic Studies" in his collection of essays *A Piece of My Mind*. The essay recommended that Jewish Studies become a part of the university curriculum. The development of Jewish Studies programs in the academy indicated the degree to which Jews had become comfortable with their American identity. Jews no longer needed to abandon their Jewishness to become fully American; rather, they could simultaneously identify both as Jews and as middle-class Americans.

While American Jews writing in English achieved literary and academic fame, Jews who wrote in Yiddish were seeing their audiences and their profits dwindle. American Jewish writers such as Jacob Glatstein and Kadya Molodovsky wrote stunning works of postwar poetry and prose in Yiddish; however, these works were largely ignored in the United States because they were not in English.

POPULAR CULTURE IN THE 1950s

Across the United States, anti-Semitism began to weaken as Jews entered mainstream American culture. Many Americans encountered Jews for the first time on radio and television, in major league sports, in politics, in medicine, and in popular music and film.

Prominent American Jewish cultural figures in the 1950s included Milton Berle, in the midst of his transition from radio celebrity to television star; and Mickey Katz, star of the 1951 Broadway review *Borscht Capades*. At the height of Berle's popularity, 5 million people watched "Uncle Miltie" every week. Katz, on the other hand, was famous throughout the American Jewish world for his "Yinglish" parodies of classic American songs, including "Haim afn Range" and "Duvid Crockett, King of Delancy Strit."

Another major television phenomenon during the 1950s was *The Goldbergs*, a television sitcom that was broadcast for six years (1949–55) to tre-

Milton Berle

Milton Berle (1908–2002) became an icon of early American television. As the host of NBC's *Texaco Star Theater* (1948–55), Berle was well-known to millions of Americans across the country as "Uncle Miltie" and "Mr. Television." He was born Mendl Belinger in 1908 to Moses Belinger, a paint and varnish salesman, and Sarah Glantz Belinger in Manhattan. Young Mendl appeared in several silent films before changing his name to Milton at age 16.

In the 1920s and 1930s, Berle gained fame on the vaudeville stage, appeared in several popular Hollywood films, and became a well-known nightclub and radio comedian. In 1948, Berle accepted an offer from NBC to host its new show, *Texaco Star Theater.*

Milton Berle and his wife Ruth Cosgrove at a movie premiere in 1979.

Within two months, Berle had become television's first superstar. The show reached the number one slot on the Nielson ratings and reportedly had about 80 percent of the viewing audience watching the show every Tuesday night. After the first season, both Berle and the show's producers won Emmy Awards. Berle went on to appear in many other television shows, specials, and movies, including *It's a Mad, Mad, Mad, Mad World* in 1963. In 1984, Berle became one of the first seven people to be inducted into the Television Hall of Fame. Berle died in 2002 at the age of 93 at his home in Los Angeles.

mendous popular acclaim. The show was the first television series to feature a Jewish family as main characters. *The Goldbergs* was originally created by Gertrude Berg (1899–1966), who starred in the series as Molly Goldberg, the matriarch of the Goldberg family. For a generation of Jewish Americans who were embarking on their ascent into the middle class, the Goldbergs symbolized the quintessential American Jewish family. Episodes of the show demonstrate the family's move from the largely Jewish Bronx to the suburbs of Connecticut, their adoption of the new social customs of their neighbors, and their gradual assimilation into mainstream American society. By providing American Jews with a positive model of acculturation, *The Goldbergs* helped American Jews to be more comfortable about their transition into middle-class America. Gertrude Berg attributed the success of her show to its reassuring way of dealing with complicated issues such as politics, religion, and communal identification. "You see, darling," she replied to an interviewer in 1956, "I don't bring up anything that will bother people. That's very important. Unions, politics, fund-raising, Zionism, socialism, inter-group relations, I don't stress them . . . After all, aren't such things secondary to daily family living? The Goldbergs are not defensive about their Jewishness, or especially aware of it."

At Berg's request, the writers of *The Goldbergs* were careful to avoid potentially problematic topics concerning Judaism. The Goldberg family does not observe Shabbat, keep a kosher kitchen, or speak Yiddish in their home. Most episodes did not address the subject of Judaism at all. For example, when Molly's son Sammy gets married, the ceremony is not shown. Instead of hearing the rabbi bless the marriage, the television audience hears a 10-minute discussion about the caterer. Though there were episodes that dealt with ostensibly Jewish subject matter, the writers of the show cast the topics in a mainstream American light. For example, a Passover episode focused exclusively on how many portions of gefilte fish Molly would need for a growing number of guests instead of demonstrating holiday rituals or discussing the importance of the holiday. *The Goldbergs* thus reflected the growing feeling among American Jews that cultural Judaism ought to replace traditional Jewish observances and lifestyle patterns.

Despite the Hollywood blacklist of the early 1950s, American Jews continued to produce and star in many popular films. Though filmmakers shied away from Jewish subjects in the early 1950s, they began to once

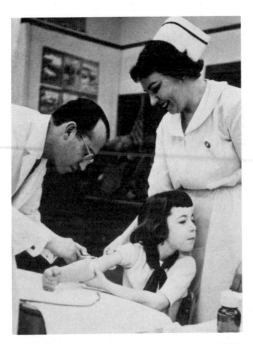

Dr. Jonas Salk vaccinating a young girl around 1955, when he became known worldwide for developing a polio vaccine.

again touch upon Jewish subjects in the latter part of the decade in films such as *Marjorie Morningstar* (1958), *The Diary of Anne Frank* (1959), and *Exodus* (1960).

American Jews were also prominent in major league sports, science, and music during the 1950s. Henry (Hank) Greenberg, famous for his refusal to play on Rosh Hashanah, was admitted to the Baseball Hall of Fame in 1956. In 1955, Dr. Jonas Salk, another Jewish American, made headlines when he announced his discovery of the first effective polio vaccine. The vaccine revolutionized pediatric medicine. In 1957, Jewish composer Leonard Bernstein completed his *West Side Story*, which opened to widespread critical acclaim on Broadway. The following year, Bernstein was named the conductor of the New York Philharmonic Orchestra.

In addition to achieving prominence in popular culture and sports, Jews were also key leaders during the early years of the Civil Rights Movement. Joel and Arthur Spingarn, two Jewish-American brothers, led the National Association for the Advancement of Colored People (NAACP) from 1930 to 1966. In 1954, when the U.S. Supreme Court issued its revolutionary ruling in *Brown v. Board of Education*, Jewish organizations such as the Anti-Defamation League issued statements supporting integration. The Reform Union and the Convention of Conservative Rabbis both declared their unanimous support for the Court's decision.

As Jews became increasingly incorporated into American cultural life, they continued to be largely insecure about their newly acquired social status. American Jews were skeptical of the decline of anti-Semitism during the 1950s and exaggerated the extent of anti-Jewish sentiment that remained. The trial of Julius and Ethel Rosenberg, which took place between 1950 and 1953, exacerbated these fears and made many Jews eager to assimilate further into American society in order to escape being branded a Communist.

McCARTHYISM AND "THE CRIME OF THE CENTURY"

Wisconsin senator Joseph R. McCarthy began his career with a speech in Wheeling, West Virginia, in which he accused the State Department of harboring known Communists. McCarthy's speech was just the beginning of years of persecution for Communists, Communist sympathizers, socialists, and radical activists of all political stripes, who were accused (usually falsely) of aiding the Soviet Union in the Cold War. Between 1953 and 1954, McCarthy led the U.S. Senate Permanent Subcommittee on Investigations and publicly accused Communists and former Communists of being a danger to America.

Jewish Americans, who had been disproportionately involved in the American Communist Party in the 1930s, feared that McCarthy would soon turn on them and spur an American neofascist movement. Though McCarthy never attacked Jews specifically for their Jewish affiliation, his speeches and political activities made many Jewish Americans fearful for their newly acquired middle-class security.

In 1953, Julius and Ethel Rosenberg were executed for treason. The Rosenbergs remain to this day the only civilians executed for espionage in the history of the United States. The case began in the summer of 1950 when Julius and Ethel Rosenberg were first arrested and charged with passing classified information about the atomic bomb to the Soviet Union. Both Rosenbergs had long-standing ties to the Communist Party; Julius, in particular, had been active in the Young Communist League while he was an undergraduate at City College during the Great Depression. David Greenglass, Ethel's younger brother, was also arrested by federal agents. Greenglass pleaded guilty and told detectives that his sister and her husband had recruited him as a spy for the Soviet Union.

In January 1951, Julius and Ethel were indicted, along with Morton Sobell. The Rosenberg trial opened on March 6, 1951, in federal court in New

Julius and Ethel Rosenberg in a March 1951 photograph taken soon after the jury's guilty verdict at the U.S. Court House in New York City.

Excerpts from the Rosenberg Trial Transcript

SUMMATION OF EMANUEL BLOCH FOR THE DEFENSE: Now I want to conclude very simply. I told you at the beginning and I tell you now that we don't come to you in this kind of charge looking for sympathy. Believe me, ladies and gentlemen, there is plenty of room here for a lawyer to try to harp on your emotions, especially so far as Ethel Rosenberg is concerned; a mother, she has two children, her husband is under arrest. No, because if these people are guilty of that crime they deserve no sympathy. No, we want you to decide this case with your minds, not with your hearts, with your minds. . . . I say that if you do that, you can come to no other conclusion than that these defendants are innocent and you are going to show to the world that in America a man can get a fair trial.

SUMMATION OF IRVING SAYPOL FOR THE PROSECUTION: Ladies and gentlemen, you have heard statements of defense counsel here concerning the injection of Communism in this case. I repeat again, these defendants are not on trial for being Communists. I don't want you to convict them merely because of their Communist activity. Communism, as the testimony has demonstrated, has a very definite place in this case because it is the Communist ideology which teaches worship and devotion to the Soviet Union over our own government. It has provided the motive and inspiration for these people to do the terrible things which have been proven against them. It is this adherence and devotion which makes clear their intent and motivation in carrying out this conspiracy to commit espionage. We ask you to sustain the charge of the grand jury in a verdict of guilty against each of these three defendants, on one basis and one basis alone; the evidence produced in this courtroom as to their guilt of the crime of conspiracy to commit espionage; that proof as to each defendant has been overwhelming. The guilt of each one has been established beyond any peradventure of doubt.

I am a firm believer in the American jury system. I have confidence in the perception of the jury of twelve intelligent American citizens. I am confident that you will render the only verdict possible on the evidence presented before you in this courtroom—that of guilty as charged by the grand jury as to each of these three defendants.

York City. The prosecutor was Irving Saypol, assisted by Roy Cohn, who would later become an aide to Senator Joseph McCarthy. The lawyers for the Rosenbergs' defense were Emanuel and Alexander Bloch, a father-and-son team. All of the principal actors in the trial, including the defendants, key witnesses for and against them, the judge, and all of the prosecution and defense lawyers, were Jewish. However, the jury was composed entirely of non-Jews. This imbalance would later lead to accusations of anti-Semitism after the guilty verdict was made public. American Jews also feared that the case would fuel American anti-Semitism and cause Americans to associate Jews with Communism and treason.

The jury delivered its guilty verdict on March 28, and on April 5, 1951, Judge Irving Kaufmann sentenced Julius and Ethel Rosenberg to death. American Jews were, by and large, shocked by the death sentences and fought hard to have them repealed. A few even accused the court and the jury of being anti-Semitic. In addition, the Communist Party organized a worldwide campaign to overturn the death sentence for the Rosenbergs. Some American Jewish organizations, such as the American Jewish Committee, feared reprisal and openly supported the court's verdict. Ultimately, however, the Supreme Court refused to hear the case and President Dwight Eisenhower denied a petition for clemency. On June 19, 1953, Julius and Ethel Rosenberg were executed in New York's Sing Sing Prison.

THE LEGACY OF DESTRUCTION AND REDEMPTION

Between 1945 and the early 1950s, approximately 150,000 Jewish Holocaust survivors immigrated to the United States from the Displaced Persons camps of Europe. Despite the vast numbers of survivors who immigrated, remembering the Holocaust had yet to become a part of mainstream American Jewish consciousness during the 1950s. Many American Jews felt guilty because they had not suffered during the Holocaust like their European brethren.

At the same time, American popular culture during the 1950s tended to present the Holocaust in a way that ignored the issue of Jews and Jewish victimhood altogether. For example, the award-winning film *Stalag 17* (1953) showed the condition of POWs in Germany without mentioning anti-Semitism or European Jewry even once. Americans were also reluctant to embarrass West Germany, an ally in the Cold War, by drawing too much attention to its recent past. In addition, many Americans did not support the unrestricted immigration of Holocaust survivors to America. In one 1948 poll, 60 percent of the respondents believed that a "special limit" should restrict the number of Jewish displaced persons allowed to immigrate to the United States. These attitudes toward Holocaust memory and DPs among mainstream American society led many American Jews to downplay the importance of discussing the Holocaust publicly.

The Jewish-American relationship to Israel was also problematic during the 1950s. Zionist leaders in the early 1950s were baffled by the failure of American Jews to move to the new State of Israel en masse. They failed to see that American Jews had become increasingly comfortable with their new economic and social position in the United States and were not interested in emigration. Instead, American Jews expressed their support for Israel through institutional means. By the end of the 1950s, there were 18 major American

The Rosenberg Trial Verdict

CLERK: Mr. Foreman, have you agreed upon a verdict?

FOREMAN: Yes, your Honor, we have.

CLERK: How say you?

FOREMAN: We, the jury, find Julius Rosenberg guilty as charged. We, the jury, find Ethel Rosenberg guilty as charged. We, the jury, find Morton Sobell guilty as charged.

CLERK: Members of the jury, listen to your verdict as it stands recorded. You say you find the defendant Julius Rosenberg guilty, Ethel Rosenberg guilty, and Morton Sobell guilty and so say you all?

JURORS: Yes.

COURT: My opinion is that your verdict is a correct verdict, and what I was particularly pleased about was the time which you took to deliberate in this case. I must say that as an individual I cannot be happy because it is a sad day for America. The thought that citizens of our country would lend themselves to the destruction of their own country by the most destructive weapon known to man is so shocking that I can't find words to describe this loathsome offense.

PROSECUTOR: The conviction of the defendants in a criminal case is no occasion for exultation. It has been said that the Government never loses a case—because if there is a conviction the guilty are punished, and if there is an acquittal, the presumption of innocence must permanently prevail. The conviction of these defendants, however, is an occasion for sober reflection. That you the jury so considered it is evidence from the fact that you deliberated for six and a half hours last night, and the nature of your requests as to the evidence and the identity of the witnesses amongst other things demonstrates that you complied throughout with the instructions of the learned Court; and that your conclusion is a mature, a reflected one. . . . The jury's verdict is a ringing answer of our democratic society to those who would destroy it. First, because a full, fair, open and complete trial—in sound American tradition—was given to a group of people who represented perhaps the sharpest secret eyes of our enemies. They were given every opportunity to present every defense and I would fight at all times for their right to defend themselves freely and vigorously. Secondly, your verdict is a warning that our democratic society, while maintaining its freedom, can nevertheless fight back against treasonable activities. . . .

Jewish organizations dedicated primarily to the political and economic support of Israel. Fundraising for Israel and Israeli causes became a major part of the work of nearly every American Jewish organization. These efforts were largely successful. Between 1946 and 1962, the United Jewish Appeal (UJA) raised over $1 billion dollars to support Israel.

In July 1956, the Suez Canal crisis brought Israel to the forefront of U.S. politics and created a new relationship between the United States and Israel. After the United States and the United Kingdom withdrew their support for the construction of the Aswan Dam in Egypt, Egyptian forces, led by Colonel Gamal Abdel Nasser and allied with the Soviet government, seized and nationalized the Suez Canal. Britain and France secretly enlisted Israeli support for an attack on Egypt in the Sinai Desert. Israel agreed and invaded Egyptian-held Sinai and Gaza on October 29, 1956, surprising the rest of the world. The Eisenhower administration quickly forced a ceasefire through the United Nations and issued a warning to Israel to immediately withdraw. Across the United States, American Jews sent telegrams to President Eisenhower and staged rallies urging the United States to support Israel. The Suez Canal crisis thus marked the first time that the American Jewish community united politically in support of Israel. The affair also raised American consciousness about Israel's position in the Middle East and its security needs.

CONCLUSION

Approximately 5 million Jews lived in the United States in 1950. During the next decade, these Jews would undergo many changes in their lifestyles, communal affiliations, and culture. They would move to the suburbs, change their religious affiliations, and become a part of the growing American middle class. They would send their children to afternoon Hebrew schools, build new synagogues, and become part of mainstream American culture. They would watch Milton Berle and Gertrude Berg on television, advocate for the State of Israel, and fear for the fate of the Rosenbergs. The postwar period in Jewish-American history was a dynamic era in which American Jews sought to fundamentally redefine the very notion of what it meant to be a Jew in America. In the new synagogues, organizations, and culture created during the 1950s, American Jews became a part of the cultural life of mainstream American society while still maintaining their distinct identity as a community.

DEBRA CAPLAN
HARVARD UNIVERSITY

Further Reading

Bial, Henry. *Acting Jewish: Negotiating Ethnicity on the American Stage and Screen*. Ann Arbor, MI: University of Michigan Press, 2005.

Diner, Hasia R. *The Jews of the United States: 1654–2000*. Berkeley, CA: University of California Press, 2004.

———. *A New Promised Land: A History of Jews in America*. New York: Oxford University Press, 2000.

Excerpts from the Transcript of the Trial of Julius and Ethel Rosenberg. New York, Printing House Press. Available online courtesy of the UMKC School of Law, URL: http://www.law.umkc.edu/faculty/projects/FTRIALS/Rosenb/ROS_TRIA.HTM. Accessed December 2009.

Finkelstein, Norman H. *American Jewish History: JPS Guide*. Philadelphia, PA: Jewish Publication Society, 2007.

Gordis, David M. and Dorit P. Gray, eds. *American Jewry: Portrait and Prognosis*. West Orange, NJ: Behrman House, 1997.

Norwood, Steven H. and Eunice G. Pollack, eds. *Encyclopedia of American Jewish History*. Denver: ABC-CLIO, 2008.

Raphael, Marc Lee, ed. *The Columbia History of Jews and Judaism in America*. New York: Columbia University Press, 2008.

Shandler, Jeffrey. *While America Watches: Televising the Holocaust*. New York: Oxford University Press, 1999.

Shapiro, Edward S. *A Time for Healing: American Jewry since World War II*. Baltimore, MD: Johns Hopkins University Press, 1992.

Weber, Donald. *Haunted in the New World: Jewish American Culture from Cahan to The Goldbergs*. Bloomington, IN: Indiana University Press, 2005.

CHAPTER 8

The Sixties: 1960 to 1969

SOME JEWISH AMERICANS who came of age during the 1960s recall from their youth a short, quaint phrase: *"Sha!* Still!" Usually snapped at children, it forcefully commanded them to "Be quiet!" Yet, its composition is more interesting. These two syllables—the first a Yiddish expression, the second an English word—mean the same thing, with similarly strong effect. Recited in succession, however, they represent the change from an immigrant Jewish culture to a homegrown American one. They also resound a 1950s admonition: Jews could be fully vested Americans as long as they quietly blended with the majority.

At mid-century, the majority of Jewish-American adults were native born. U.S. emergency immigration laws expired in 1951, though the intent was revived under the Refugee Relief Act of 1953. Jewish immigration to the United States dwindled to several thousand annually, a trend that would last into the 1960s. Between 1964 and 1968, an estimated total of only 39,000 sought permanent residency status in the United States. Jewish-American culture was torn between the desire to capitalize on an economy big enough to embrace anyone who subscribed to mutually shared (perhaps homogenized) values and the need to sustain cherished—and rapidly vanishing—traditions inculcated by several immigrant generations.

Holocaust survivors continued to enter the United States (sometimes after a stay in Israel) and were quickly absorbed by their families and the Jewish philanthropic network. As the 1960s began, however, Jewish Americans had not yet come to meaningful terms with the *Shoah* (the Holocaust). Painful narratives needed to filter through several emotional spheres: internal, between survivors, among families, and to the public. The film *Diary of Anne Frank* (1959) and author Elie Wiesel's *Night* (1960) opened conversations about the Shoah, but the Jewish Publication Society, a leading publisher, printed only one book on the topic from 1950 to 1965.

Increasingly detached from the immigrant narrative, Jewish Americans embraced a present laden with new opportunities—and optimism. Massive wartime industries finally put an end to the Great Depression, and victory propelled massive economic growth. "GI Jews" (as Deborah Dash Moore calls Jewish World War II veterans) had left their often packed, segregated urban communities and emerged from their military service with a broader perspective, shared with their peers from across the ethnic spectrum. They took advantage of low-cost housing loans and educational benefits to physically and materially vacate the old neighborhoods.

JEWISH GEOGRAPHY AND DEMOGRAPHY

Jewish Americans chosen venue was most often the suburbs, and communities like Long Island's iconic Levittown. Constructed by a family of Jewish developers, it set the physical parameters: acres of small, modern homes—limited to a few basic floor plans—and frequently replacing forests and farms. Yet, the term *suburbanization* simplifies Jewish population movement.

Some families, for example, sought leafier and more-affluent urban neighborhoods, such as Pittsburgh's Squirrel Hill. Just outside Boston, they moved into Newton and Brookline (President John F. Kennedy's birthplace), both dating to the 1600s. More recently, Detroit's Oak Park originally was settled during the 1840s. No Jew lived there for 100 years afterward, but as housing developments emerged, it and nearby Huntington Woods attracted a substantial minority.

The American Jewish population also spread beyond its center in the northeastern corridor. The biggest demographic shift was westward. GIs, who might have never ventured there independently, discovered the Golden State during their Pacific tours. The charms of Southern California beckoned—beaches, mountains, perpetual sunshine, and an already-established Jewish community—and many vowed to return. While New York held primacy, Metropolitan Los Angeles counted an estimated 250,000 Jewish residents in 1950, and 400,000 a decade later. It thus became the second-largest Jewish city in the United States, surpassing Philadelphia (331,000), Chicago (282,000), Boston (150,000), Detroit (89,000), Cleveland (88,000), Greater Washington, D.C. (80,900), and Miami (80,000). The downturn in Rust Belt manufacturing hastened this westward movement in the 1970s and beyond, and places like Phoenix and Las Vegas benefited.

Critical Dates 1960–69

1960　Elie Wiesel publishes an English-language edition of his memoir, *Night*, the first of his many books written to keep the memory of the Holocaust alive.

1960　Release of the film *Exodus*, based on Leon Uris's novel, fosters identification with the state of Israel among Jews and Christians alike.

1962　Reform movement opens the Religious Action Center in Washington, D.C., dedicated to the pursuit of social justice and religious liberty.

1962　Zalman Schachter founds B'nai Or, forerunner of the Jewish Renewal Movement, in an effort to revitalize Jewish prayer.

1964　The American Jewish Conference on Soviet Jewry and the Student Struggle for Soviet Jewry are established, initiating a successful campaign to release Jews from Soviet bondage. Over 1.5 million Soviet Jews eventually emigrate to Israel, the United States, and western Europe.

1965　Abraham Joshua Heschel walks arm-in-arm with Martin Luther King and other black leaders in the Civil Rights march from Selma to Montgomery, Alabama.

1965　*Nostra Aetate*, an official Catholic statement on the Jews issued as part of Vatican II, marks a turning point in Catholic-Jewish relations as the Church decries hatred, persecution, and displays of anti-Semitism.

1967　Six-Day War between Israel and its Arab neighbors brings the Jewish state to the forefront of American Jewish consciousness. Amid fears of another Holocaust, American Jews raise $430 million for Israel. After the war, tourism and emigration to Israel rise dramatically.

1968　Students in Massachusetts form Havurat Shalom, devoted to fellowship, peace, community, and a "new model of serious Jewish study." It serves as a forerunner of the Jewish counterculture and the *havurah* movement (Jews that assembled to facilitate Shabbat and holiday prayer services).

1968　Reconstructionist Rabbinical College in Philadelphia opens. It is the first rabbinical seminary to admit women students.

1969　Association for Jewish Studies founded, marking the growth of Jewish studies on college campuses across the country.

Opting for "idealistic careers and early marriages," as contemporary writer John Updike observed of this generation, young Jewish couples likewise nurtured the baby boom. Yet, if boomers (and, particularly, their older siblings) are credited with rebellion, their parents actually may have started them on that path. Anthropologist Karen Brodkin writes: "Part of the attraction suburbia had for my mother was its emphasis on young families that were starting out—no elders, no in-laws, no parents. Like being your own boss, or in the context of her friends, being accepted as an adult, a competent woman-person. This version of Jewish womanhood was a social position, a political identity, invented by my parents and their circle. . . . Mothers weren't supposed to be working, certainly not as career women, but my mother and her friends, as well as most other teachers, were doing just that."

Through a lifestyle change that diverged significantly from that of their parents, these young couples inadvertently gave their children permission to break away, too. Nor did the happy suburbanite mode fit that entire generation. A group of creative Jewish Americans who entered the 1960s as working adults—beat poet Allen Ginsberg, essayist Susan Sontag, comedians Mort Sahl and Lenny Bruce—could neither claim a "typical" Jewish background, nor did they necessarily wish to pursue one. Yet, their work spoke to the historic Jewish role of "outsider" that, in fact, made the 1960s a far more open, inclusive decade.

A NEW INFRASTRUCTURE

Young adults may have left the Jewish urban core, but as their parents might have warned them metaphorically, not without their "galoshes." The first study of intermarriage across religious lines occurred during the late 1950s and blared a new warning for rapidly assimilating Jewish Americans. Maybe out of habit, or for warm cultural associations bound with families, or because the community had provided protective gear against years of anti-Semitism, this generation felt the need to create a Jewish infrastructure—but one that would match changing times and new environs. Children were the intended beneficiaries. As sprawling churches rose in the suburbs and trendier neighborhoods, equally impressive synagogues became the vehicle for maintaining Jewish identity. These palaces of worship gilded the long-held notion of America as a religious country.

Not everyone found these new surroundings compelling, however. Fleeing the city, but distrusting suburbs that lacked traditional Jewish definitions, the *Skvirer* Chasidim (originally from the Ukraine) carved their own village out of Ramapo, New York. The resulting town officially became known as New Square. Similarly, after several unsuccessful attempts during the 1960s, the insular Hungarian Satmars built Kiryas Joel in 1976. Situated in Monroe, New York, it took its name from their rabbi, Joel Teitelbaum. Its first language remains Yiddish.

The Washington, D.C., Jewish Community Center building as it looked soon after it opened in 1925. After restoration in the 1990s, it again became a very active center for urban Jewish life.

Generally, the Jewish infrastructure—kosher food purveyors and restaurants, as well as old Federation and Jewish Community Center (JCC) buildings—remained in the cities. The urban unrest of the mid- and late-1960s ultimately put an end to this relationship. Although some of these Jewish businesses and organizations eventually moved outward, others were never duplicated to the same extent, or with the same geographic centrality. One happy ending occurred in Washington, D.C., during the 1990s, when the JCC bought back and lovingly restored the dignified 1925 stone building it had vacated nearly 30 years earlier. Attracting both residents and the daytime population of commuters in this mostly African-American city, the JCC counts several hundred thousand visitors annually.

The new Jewish infrastructure of the 1960s focused on families and youth. With synagogues as conduit, Conservative Judaism became the largest movement, boasting 800 affiliates in 1965—twice the number it had counted at mid-century. Reform Judaism also grew, but not as rapidly, from 442 temples in 1951, to 664 in 1966. The appeal of Conservative Judaism lay in its position as a bridge between valued tradition and an evolving American lifestyle.

Yeshivot (institutions for the study of classical Judaism) provided religious training to Orthodox youth for centuries, but the Conservative movement now created its own brand. As an offshoot of its United Synagogue Commission on Jewish Education, one of the first Solomon Schechter Day Schools was chartered in Far Rockaway, New York, in 1951. Twenty-eight such institutions existed by the late 1960s, enrolling 5,000 students; by the early 1980s, there were 65, with a combined student enrollment of 12,000.

Another constituency, not entirely overlapping, was United Synagogue Youth. Fed by the synagogues at large and their Hebrew schools, it paralleled the National Council of Synagogue Youth (Orthodox) and National Federation of Temple Youth (Reform). All flourished during the era, further enhancing their missions by channeling members into associated summer camps. Independent Jewish groups also engaged Jewish children. Perhaps the largest was the B'nai B'rith Youth Organization, but Young Judea, Habonim, and others (aligned to Israeli/Zionist political parties) counted followers, too.

Ironically, at the same time that Conservative Judaism strengthened both formal and informal options for Jewish education, it liberalized liturgy. Select services, often on Friday night, were conducted in English and sometimes accompanied by a choir. These observances attracted their own constituencies and, during later decades, put the "big tent" philosophy to test.

Religious movements also developed regional structures that, in some instances, sent emissaries into the hinterlands to organize new Jewish communities. By the end of the sixties, these outposts included both exurbanites and younger folks who wanted to get "back to the land". Not too long afterward, the outreach-oriented Chabad sought to reclaim cities and establish a presence on college campuses, where religious observance may have reached a low.

Post–World War II parents left a Jewish legacy, largely through the denominational synagogue movements and their related youth/educational branches. Yet, few "lay people" contributed in uniquely creative or ideological ways. Dependence on a growing network of rabbis, educators, and other communal professionals yielded the sought-after Jewish infrastructure for much of the 1960s.

CHILDREN OF THE 1960s
Jewish social and political activism during the 1960s is evident, yet the extent of student leadership may be understated. If Tom Hayden authored the Port Huron Statement (1962), Robert Haber and Todd Gitlin also were ranking leaders in Students for a Democratic Society (SDS). Berkeley activist Jack Weinberg had been arrested before Mario Savio returned to the legendary intersection of Bancroft and Telegraph Avenues at Berkeley; together, their resistance inspired the Free Speech movement. And by the time Jerry Rubin and Abbie Hoffman applied guerrilla theater to social protest under the Yippie banner, Jewish Americans were synonymous with the New Left.

Part of the reason, of course, was exposure. Some were "pink diaper babies" imbued with and sympathetic to their parents' union or socialist backgrounds. Jewish youth populated the campuses as never before. No longer exclusively the children of immigrants, some were second-generation college educated; the vast majority, however, benefited from the combination of traditional learning values and a public education system, then quite possibly in its prime. A 1965 study by the Bureau of Census asked school-aged children about their future aspirations. Approximately 86 percent of the 330,000 Jewish youngsters expressed the desire to attend college, compared with 53 percent of the general student population.

Jewish-American activist Abbie Hoffman (center) on the campus of the University of Oklahoma during an antiwar protest in 1969.

Many Jewish students of the early and mid-1960s took their inspiration from the Civil Rights Movement, which then welcomed biracial participation. Idealistic youth could relate to the familiar theme of oppression—and to the hope offered through organizing. After all, quite a few of their immigrant grandparents had been union members and leaders. Political transference to a plight different than their own also imposed a separation from Jewish identities that they judged outdated or too isolationist. According to one estimate, more than half of the white Freedom Riders who traveled Mississippi on buses during the summer of 1964 to register black voters were Jewish. The tragic capstone of this experience was the murder of three young Civil Rights workers—James Chaney, Andrew Goodman, and Michael Schwerner, the first African American, and the latter two Jewish.

Within a short time, the Civil Rights Movement appeared less welcoming to outsiders. One recalls the common saying, "Two Jews, three opinions." African Americans only recently had been given the chance to be public—and political. Young black leaders started to challenge Martin Luther King Jr.'s inclusiveness and theologically based notions of passive resistance. The Civil Rights Movement found itself diversifying politically, yet turning inward.

Armed with an increasing repertoire of organizing strategies, Jewish youth embarked on other crusades. The Free Speech movement and Students for a Democratic Society initially forged connections with the Civil Rights Movement, but later articulated broader issues. Joined by Americans from various strata, Jewish (and other) youth also began protesting U.S. policy in southeast Asia.

Women entered all issues and interest groups, but often in spite of education, they toiled as second-class citizens within their respective movements. Margery Tabankin, the first female president of the National Student Association and later director of the federal VISTA program, recalls an eagerly awaited visit by Tom Hayden: "The first thing he handed me was his dirty laundry and asked me if I would do it for him." Increasingly, women realized that it was time for a room of their own.

Jewish women assumed various public roles in the Women's Liberation movement. Despite the popular campus phrase, "never trust anyone over 30," it triumphed because of its intergenerational nature. Those who grew up during different eras or who were experiencing different cycles of life could impart personally meaningful aspects of feminism: its sexual, political, and economic contexts.

Contacting fellow Smith College alumnae for a reunion, the movement's early theoretician, Betty Friedan, ended up writing a path-breaking book. *The Feminine Mystique* (1963) poignantly conveyed women's ennui in the supposedly happy, family-centered suburban lifestyle.

During the same year, journalist Gloria Steinem went undercover as a Playboy bunny to report on that glorified brand of sexploitation. Her professional desire to dig beneath gender roles was a maternal family legacy, inherited from a suffragette grandmother and a clinically depressed mother.

Attorney Bella Abzug realized her calling behind a *mechitza* (women's partition in a traditional synagogue) when

Politician Bella Abzug in one of her iconic hats at a press conference in 1971.

she was 13—and was denied the right to say the *kaddish* prayer for her recently departed father. Crowned with her trademark hats, the flamboyant Abzug represented the 19th (later, 20th) congressional district of New York 1971–77, before it was usual for women to do so.

These feminist leaders constantly combined and connected, forging with others a powerful national community. Abzug began first, as one of two organizers of the precocious antiwar group, Women Strike for Peace (1961). She, Friedan, and Steinem appeared among National Women's Political Caucus (1971) founders, while the early leadership rosters of both the National Organization for Women (1966) and the National Abortion Rights Action League (1968) included Friedan. *Ms.* magazine (1972) retained the passions of founders Gloria Steinem and Letty Cottin Pogrebin.

Betty Friedan in 1964, the year after the publication of The Feminine Mystique.

RUMBLINGS AMONG THE "ESTABLISHMENT"

Many of the tidal waves associated with the 1960s first washed ashore during the late 1950s. *Brown v. Board of Education*, Rosa Parks, and the Montgomery bus boycott publicly introduced the term *civil rights*. Given a long history of discrimination, the organized Jewish community responded earlier, and perhaps more positively, than most others. The American Jewish Committee adopted a supportive position and, in 1959, the Reform movement approved the presence in Washington, D.C., of a social action center to further civil rights and other progressive causes.

Yet, the response was not uniform; distance from political pressure points may have encouraged freer thinking. For reasons of regional history and civic culture—perhaps mixed with a tinge of fear—southern Jews were less likely to endorse the Civil Rights Movement. And in moving to the suburbs, young Jews also left older and less-affluent coreligionists in the urban neighborhoods, where they felt increasingly powerless against inner-city ills. Some small Jewish-owned businesses remained, selling the same products to a changing clientele. The Civil Rights Movement both bolstered and embittered people of

Gloria Steinem

In the April 7, 1969, issue of *New York* magazine, Gloria Steinem traced the development of her feminism, linking her story to the discovery of her Jewish grandmother's activism. A portion of that article, "After Black Power, Women's Liberation," is excerpted below.

What's a nice girl like me doing in a movement like this? I guess the real question is why it took me so long. I was about 34 or 35 before the light began to dawn. I had identified with every other social justice movement in the world first. I think that often happens to women—we identify with other underdogs, even if we don't know why—but there was no women's movement out there really, and nothing told me to take females as a group seriously. That's especially ironic because I had a Jewish suffragist grandmother, Pauline Perlmutter Steinem, who died when I was about five. She had addressed Congress, but nobody told me about that. They told me that she was a wonderful woman who kept a kosher table, had four sons, and was a pioneer of vocational education—different measurements of success—but not that she was also the first woman to be elected to a Board of Education in the state of Ohio, as a suffragist on the same ticket with the socialists and the anarchists. I didn't know this until a feminist historian in Toledo wrote a monograph about her. In a way, feminism rediscovered my grandmother for me. I think a lot of us have women in our families who aren't talked about. They were the feminists.

It was really the women who had come out of the Civil Rights Movement, who realized that sex was a caste system just as race was, who introduced me to feminism. Betty Friedan had already written The Feminine Mystique *in 1963. It was very important for homemakers in the suburbs who were well educated and wanted to get into the paid labor force, but I thought, "I've always been in the labor force, and I'm still getting screwed." I didn't see how that message applied to my life. Then younger feminists came along with an analysis that included all females—a revolution and not a reform—and it made sense of my own life.*

color, and the friction between black and white urban dwellers exploded. The urban unrest of the middle and late 1960s effectively ended Jewish connections to the inner-city, at least for several decades. In Detroit and other places, they began leaving the relatively new, "close-in" suburbs for communities farther from the urban core.

Rabbi Abraham Joshua Heschel was a pivotal figure in transitioning Jewish Americans from civil rights to the broader field of human relations. Born in Poland of a Chasidic dynasty, Heschel fled Europe just weeks before World War II began, but lost his sisters to Hitler's death camps. He spoke in the United States from his "pulpit" as a Jewish Theological Seminary faculty member. Most Americans know Heschel from a famous photo: a white-bearded rabbi walking arm-in-arm with the Reverend Dr. Martin Luther King Jr. in the 1965 march from Selma to Montgomery. Their acquaintance began in 1963, and both were soon counted among early Soviet Jewry advocates. At around the same time, Heschel consulted with Rome on what became Vatican II's "Declaration on the Relationship of the Church to Non-Christian Religions"— a monumental reversal of supercessionism and anti-Semitic teachings.

Heschel's passions evolved from theology, but his stance was distinctly activist—and peaceful. United by a "professional brand" that each had developed separately, Heschel and King built a deeply meaningful friendship. What transpired between them occurred at the grass roots, to varying degrees, all over the nation: clergy-led networks—bound by personal amity—and calmly devoted to social change. They went under different names: ecumenical councils, interfaith coalitions, ministerial associations. These networks may have started with all-Christian groups (as the term *ecumenical* implies), but they later opted for inclusiveness. Their adherents were mostly middle-aged suburbanites, not inclined by temperament or social culture toward rabid protest. Gazing back at their parents' religious practices and having underwritten Jewish institutions specifically for their children, they now desired their own spiritual expressiveness—and found it in universalist social action. People of diverse backgrounds came together for "dialogues" to ease their differences. By the 1970s, these networks also bore nonprofit service and advocacy programs, including food pantries and fair housing councils.

FINDING JUDAISM THROUGH ETHNICITY

As African Americans and, in the West, Chicanos (Latinos) converted difficult histories into cultural identities, Jewish Americans reconsidered the assimilationist mode. Foreign affairs presented an intermediary step: an emotional and physical distance that nevertheless offered the opportunity to advocate, nationally, on behalf of uniquely Jewish causes. Furthermore, the evolving issues allowed them a "politically correct" position. With the twin causes of supporting Israel and freeing Soviet Jewry, Jewish Americans could pride themselves on being democratic, communally oriented, and progressive yet anti-Soviet (an important factor as the Cold War continued and McCarthyism lingered in recent memory).

The 1960s opened with the film *Exodus*, portraying an appealing Jewish communal lifestyle (the collectives or *kibbutzim*)—before the back-to-the-land movement. The *realpolitik* was also vividly depicted. With hostile neighbors surrounding the Jewish state, native Israelis did not have time for American social graces. They cultivated the image of *sabras*, prickly pear cacti: thorny on the outside, sweet on the inside. The overwhelming majority of Jewish Americans supported Israel politically, emotionally, and financially, in

part as an actualization of the slogan "Never Again!" (referring to the Holocaust foremost and, indirectly, anti-Semitic victimization).

The Six Day War of June 1967 began with Egypt, Jordan, and Syria preparing for a major attack. Egypt alone amassed 100,000 troops and 1,000 tanks
in the Sinai. Realizing that this action would be devastating, the Jewish state
struck first. The fact that Israel shattered its enemies in less than a week—and
recaptured Jerusalem (and other strategic territories) after a 2,000-year forced
exodus—seemed miraculous; Jews around the world exhibited a strong eth-
nic-cultural pride. The American community raised $430 million (including
bond purchases) for Israel, twice as much as during the previous year's campaign. The 1957 total was $181 million, showing only incremental growth un-
til the Six Day War.

The event also brought visible exchanges between Jewish Americans and
Israelis. American students in their teens and early 20s soon worked on *kibbutzim* over their breaks, and Orthodox high school graduates attended specially oriented *yeshiva* programs there. Instead of journeys of self-discovery to
San Francisco, young adults might "find themselves" in Israel.

Yet, the Middle East again offered realpolitik. The vast majority of Israelis
who fought in the Six Day War had been born around the time of independence (1948) or earlier. With a major conflict anticipated at least once each
decade, some grew battle weary. The first noticeable wave of Israeli immigrants occurred in the late 1960s and early 1970s. Many found jobs waiting
in the growing network of Jewish-American religious schools and summer
camps. Together, new educators and growing ethnic pride impacted curricula. Besides an infusion of Israeli culture (including dance, food, and song),
modern Sephardic/Israeli Hebrew pronunciation replaced the classic Ashke-
nazic/Yiddish.

SOVIET JEWRY

By contrast to these occasional lightning bolts from Israel, the effort to free
Soviet Jewry was a snowball building into an avalanche. It took the Jewish-
American public the better part of two decades to become fully aware of the
situation in the Soviet Union, and, during an era of increasing empowerment
here, realize their organizing potential. The results, however, elevated Jewish
Americans to new political heights.

Information leaks seldom flow from totalitarian regimes. With the Soviet
Union as a World War II ally and a small, but committed core of Jewish-
American socialists and communists active in the United States, word of
Joseph Stalin's purges remained concealed. His successor, Nikita Khrush-
chev, publicly revealed these horrors in 1956. Hinting at political liberal-
ization, the new Soviet leader also made economic promises. Among the
most popular was his vow to replace the austere Soviet diet through better
agricultural production.

These efforts failed, but Jews bore some of the consequences: they were disproportionately scapegoated for economic crimes and conspiracies. A controversy that attracted far broader attention surfaced during 1957 when, under the guise of wheat scarcity, Soviet Jews were prohibited from baking their Passover *matzot*, or unleavened bread. The situation was known to only a few Jewish-American leaders who quietly, but unsuccessfully, tried to resolve it; then, before Passover 1964, Rabbi Yehuda L. Levin, chief rabbi of Moscow, publicly appealed to the West for ritual rations. Few *matzot* reached their intended destinations, and Soviet policy vacillated, depending on the unpredictable combination of internal activities and external pressures. Still, the issue was moving—and evocative. At around the same time, the Ukrainian Academy of Science published an offensive anti-Semitic tract, *Judaism without Embellishment* (1963). The Western press and even Communist newspapers railed against the book until it was withdrawn.

These two episodes, in such close juxtaposition, raised global consciousness. Many feared that Jewish life in the Soviet Union would not survive. What had been a network of 3,000 synagogues prior to the Russian Revolution dwindled from 450 at Stalin's death to fewer than 100 by 1963—and 60 a decade later. Major Jewish organizations in the United States soon seized the cause of Soviet Jewry, but wavered on both political turf and methodology.

The movement to free Soviet Jews utilized a wide range of organizing tools and media, such as poster art and even billboards, like this one created by Jewish-American activists in Los Angeles.

Combined with a mid-1960s distrust of the "establishment," the movement thrived, instead, at the grass roots. The Cleveland Committee on Soviet Anti-Semitism, for example, later morphed into the impassioned (and, what some described as "militant") Union of Councils for Soviet Jews. Meanwhile, college fervor was tapped by a middle-aged British Jew, Jacob Birnbaum, whose apartment near Yeshiva University served as headquarters for the fledgling Student Struggle for Soviet Jewry.

Other organizations—and their local chapters—formed, with the cause embracing an exceptionally wide range of constituents. More American Jews had come from Russia than any other country, so the historic connection was obvious. Others believed that the act of rescuing Soviet Jewry was an opportunity to compensate for their collective impotence during the Holocaust. With the revelations of Stalin's atrocities, some "red diaper babies" wished to formally sever their past ties to the Soviet Union. The very visible Soviet Jewry movement of the late 1960s also offered a final call to activism for young people: religious youth and Jewishly identified high school students who yearned for involvement, but were not old enough to join other movements or who held values that conflicted with dominant protest modes.

Powered by widespread sentiment, the "Leningrad trials" of 1970 unleashed a rush of Jewish-American energy. The incident revolved around nine Soviet Jews and two Christians sentenced to long prison terms for allegedly plotting to hijack a Soviet plane to Israel. Whereas the economic scapegoating of the late 1950s affected more people and was probably just as egregious, political momentum catapulted this particular episode into a major rally.

Historian William Orbach and others have noted that the Soviet Jewry movement added new organizing tactics to the Jewish-American standards of fundraising and "quiet diplomacy." Activists carefully monitored the status of Prisoners of Conscience, Jewish "refuseniks" who wanted to leave the Soviet Union; held local teach-ins and demonstrations; picketed Russian diplomats and events (such as Bolshoi Ballet performances). Youth gathered over dinners that simulated Russian prison diets. Such widespread, demonstrable support won political allies. The Jackson-Vanik Amendment to the Trade Act of 1974 tied favored trade status to human rights; it was specifically aimed at the Soviet Union—and Prisoners of Conscience seeking emigration. But even more significant, it gave Jewish Americans far greater confidence in their ability to effect political change.

JEWISH AMERICANS IN FILM

During the 1960s, Hollywood films reflected the degree to which Jews *as Jews* had entered into the mainstream of American culture. As noted earlier, the Jewish entrepreneurs who founded the fabled Hollywood studios in the 1920s and headed them through the 1950s produced few films that had specifically Jewish content. The 1960s saw the emergence of Jews as leading characters with a full range of identifiably Jewish behaviors. The change began as Americans developed a widespread consciousness of the Holocaust. The 1961 trial of Adolph Eichmann in Jerusalem focused the world on the horrors of Nazism. Hollywood had already made a movie of *The Diary of Anne Frank* in 1959. *Judgment at Nuremberg* appeared in 1961 and *The Pawnbroker* in 1965, each of which portrayed their Jewish characters sympathetically. The Cold War alliance between the United States and Israel assured the success of the Hollywood blockbuster *Exodus* (1960), which glorified post–Holocaust Jewish emigration to Israel. *Cast a Giant Shadow* (1966), a romanticized account of American David "Mickey" Marcus, commander of the Israeli army during Israel's War of Independence, starred the handsome (and Jewish) Kirk Douglas.

A noticeable break from the past was that most Jewish celebrities of the 1960s kept their given names. They generally had been spared Ellis Island "interpreters" who mangled foreign sounds or decided that Anglicization was the quickest leap into the melting pot. But the decline in institutionalized anti-Semitism helped most of all. During a December 2008 interview with *Los Angeles Times* reporter Rachel Abramowitz, Dustin Hoffman described his acting breakthrough: director Mike Nichols cast him in *The Graduate* (1967), even though the script called for a blond, blue-eyed, white Anglo-Saxon Protestant. "I always thought there was a kind of cloaked racism in what we call leading men," said Hoffman, speaking about the casting practices of a studio system that was crumbling as he was coming of age as an actor. Hoffman played a variety of characters in his career, most of them not specifically Jewish. Yet, his roles imbued a certain cultural sensibility—up-front but not stereotypic—to which Jewish Americans could relate.

Barbra Streisand entered through a different route. Her Oscar-winning performance in *Funny Girl* (1968) cast her, quite naturally, in the biographical/musical role of burlesque star Fanny Brice (born Fania Borach, 1891–1951). *Fiddler on the Roof* had opened on Broadway a few years earlier. Both productions spoke to a nostalgia for eastern European or immigrant Jewish culture—increasingly left to memory.

Perhaps no film illustrates better the self-confidence American Jewry had attained by the end of the 1960s than Mel Brooks' *The Producers* (1968). This farce about two stereotypical Jewish types—the greedy Hollywood producer and the nerdy Jewish accountant—managed to make fun of Hitler and Nazism and turn its stereotypical Jewish characters into heroes. *The Producers* allowed American Jews to laugh at themselves and feel good about it, knowing that the rest of America was laughing with them, not at them.

JEWISH AMERICANS IN POPULAR MUSIC

The cultural genre most associated with the 1960s is rock and roll music. Beginning in the late 1940s, some pioneering Jewish Americans nurtured its two musical parents: folk, and rhythm and blues (R&B). Moe Asch, son of the

Barbra Streisand

Widely recognized for her vocals, actress and singer Barbra Streisand has played a number of Jewish characters in popular films, including in her breakout role in *Funny Girl* (1968), where she played Fanny Brice. *The Way We Were* (1973) cast her as Katie Murovsky, a passionate, hard-working, left-wing activist attending college during the 1930s who falls in love with and later marries her temperamental and cultural opposite, Hubbell Gardner (Robert Redford). *Yentl* (1983) hearkened to early-20th-century eastern Europe. The leading role is a young girl who attends a yeshiva—disguising herself as a boy—because it is the only way to attain the rigorous education she fervently desires.

Barbra Streisand strikes a pose for the camera in 1962.

Perhaps one of Streisand's greatest legacies, besides her long, extremely successful career in music and film, was defying seemingly intractable images. In a 1997 interview, designer Isaac Mizrahi called her "One of my icons. She was kind of a misfit, and yet she convinced everyone she was beautiful, including me. She *is* beautiful, but she's not the prototypical ideal of female beauty." In paying tribute to Streisand during the Kennedy Center's Lifetime Achievement Award in 2008, Queen Latifah echoed those sentiments.

Yiddish writer Shalom Asch, started Folkways Records (later affiliated with the Smithsonian Institution) to elevate the words and music of such legends as Pete Seeger and Woody Guthrie. From the R&B side, the Chess Brothers brought to public attention bluesy African-American artists, who influenced the next generation's rockers.

Jews also acted as behind-the-scenes navigators during the early years of rock. The Beatles owed their American debut and at least part of their ensuing global fame to their manager, Brian Epstein, whom Paul McCartney later named the "fifth Beatle." By the time Epstein died at the age of 32 in 1967, the group was a phenomenon that had made a lasting contribution to the music world. Though later imprisoned on murder charges, Jewish-American Phil Spector contributed significantly to music production. Known for his "Wall of Sound," Spector also promoted a number of Motown groups.

As the 1960s evolved, young Jewish Americans became among the most influential singer-songwriters. Most fell into the folk or soft rock category, but beyond that point, it is not easy to collectively describe the lyrics or sounds of Leonard Cohen, Peter Yarrow (Peter, Paul and Mary), Carole King, Neil Diamond, Paul Simon and Art Garfunkel, and Bob Dylan. Born Robert Zimmerman, Dylan never denied his background, but refused to represent Judaism (or anything else, for that matter). His attitude was individualistic. He glided from folk to amped-up folk-rock—recording, along the way, the country-sounding *Nashville Skyline* with Johnny Cash—while refuting genre connections. For example, his 2009 CD, *Together through Life*, leans toward the blues.

However classified, Dylan's influence is beyond dispute. In a March 1966 interview, music critic Nat Hentoff quantified it: "More and more performers, from Joan Baez to the Byrds, considered it mandatory to have an ample supply of Dylan songs in their repertoires; in one frantically appreciative month—last August—48 different recordings of Dylan ballads were pressed by singers other than the composer himself." Everyone wanted to claim him. A little-known fact of the 1960s is that the iconic music festival, Woodstock, actually occurred in Bethel, New York. Dylan lived in the namesake community, and the event was supposed to have been homage.

Regardless of their outsized talents as singer-songwriters, however, Jewish Americans were absent from the era's major rock 'n' roll groups. (Among the very few exceptions were Cass Elliott of The Mamas and the Papas and The Band's Robbie Robertson, born Jaime Robert Klegerman to a Jewish father and Native-American mother.) One observation: much of 1960s music was associated with place. From the British invasion forward, audiences identified distinctive Motown (Detroit), California, and southern sounds. Jewish-American culture at that time swayed toward universalism and mobility, away from parochialism. Whatever the reason, regional music disappeared in the 1970s and 1980s. And even the hard rock, heavy metal groups such as Kiss, Van Halen, and Guns N'Roses claimed Jewish band members.

CONCLUSION

The 1960s were a decade of enormous upheaval in America and the world. So it was for the American Jewish community. The Jewish religion as practiced in America underwent redefinition in the 1960s, as Jewish women brought feminist analysis to bear on what they perceived as the patriarchal nature of Judaism. To the surprise of most prognosticators who predicted increasing assimilation, some younger Jews from suburban middle and upper class families began returning to traditional practices and Orthodox synagogues. Others supported the idea that it takes 10 adults (male and female alike) for a prayer service, but not necessarily the presence of a rabbi—the Havurah movement. *The First Jewish Catalog*, homemade Passover *haggadot* (books containing the order of service of the traditional Passover meal) and other manifestations of the Jewish Counterculture reflected the growing divide between Jewish generations.

These same students insisted that Jewish education be strengthened, Hebrew school curricula be made more interesting, and all-day Jewish schools receive communal funding. These students were the first to benefit from the creation of Jewish Studies programs at major, secular universities, which themselves were responding to pressure to create ethnic studies programs for African Americans, Latinos, and other groups. Jewish students and faculty were at the forefront of developing women's studies, black studies, and other courses focused on those they felt had been left out of the American history curriculum.

The decade of the 1960s were best-known for the Civil Rights Movement and the political divisions created by the Vietnam War. Jews of every age tended to be pro-civil rights and against Vietnam. The 1930s had converted most Jews into Democrats and their liberal tendencies continued unabated. Jewish youth were doubtless far more radical than their parents, and provided disproportionate numbers of protesters to the civil rights and anti-War movements. It was Jewish college students who insisted that the American Jewish community oppose the oppression of their fellow Jews in the Soviet Union.

Historian Michael E. Staub notes, "No other American decade during the 20th century has been so strongly defined by Jewish-led and Jewish-sponsored social activism or so deeply informed by Jewish culture." Whether it was Abby Hoffman and Students for a Democratic Society disrupting universities, Lenny Bruce disturbing nightclub audiences with his profanity-laced attacks on their middle-class complacency, Betty Friedan telling American women to break out of their cocoons, or Senator Abraham Ribicoff at the 1968 Democratic National Convention accusing Chicago Mayor Richard Daley and the Chicago police department of using "Gestapo tactics," American Jews were at the forefront of every major political, cultural and intellectual upheaval of the 1960s.

LYNN C. KRONZEK
INDEPENDENT SCHOLAR

Further Reading

American Jewish Committee. *American Jewish Yearbook.* Published annually since 1899. Available online, URL: http://www.ajcarchives.org. Accessed November 2009.

Brodkin, Karen. *How Jews Became White Folks and What that Says About Race in America.* New Brunswick, NJ: Rutgers University Press, 1998.

Cott, Jonathan, ed. *Dylan on Dylan: The Essential Interviews.* London: Hodder & Stoughton, 2006.

DeGroot, Gerard J. *The Sixties Unplugged: A Kaleidoscopic History of a Disorderly Decade.* Cambridge, MA: Harvard University Press, 2008.

Diamond, Etan. *And I Will Dwell in their Midst: Orthodox Jews in Suburbia.* Chapel Hill: University of North Carolina Press, 2000.

Goldstein, Sidney. "American Jewry, 1970: A Demographic Profile." In *American Jewish Yearbook* (1971). New York: American Jewish Committee, 1971.

Jewish Women's Archives, "Jewish Women and the Feminist Revolution," Available online, URL: http://www.jwa.org. Accessed November 2009.

Orbach, William M. *The American Movement to Aid Soviet Jews.* Amherst, MA: University of Massachusetts Press, 1979.

Raphael, Marc Lee. *Profiles in American Judaism: The Reform, Conservative, Orthodox, and Reconstructionist Traditions in Historical Perspective.* San Francisco, CA: Harper & Row, 1984.

Sarna, Jonathan D. *American Judaism: A History.* New Haven, CT: Yale University Press, 2004.

Shapiro, Edward S. *We Are Many: Reflections on American Jewish History and Identity.* Syracuse, NY: Syracuse University Press, 2005.

Slezkine, Yuri. *The Jewish Century.* Princeton, NJ: Princeton University Press, 2004.

CHAPTER 9

The Seventies: 1970 to 1979

A MAJOR THEME for American Jewish communities in the 1970s was reflection: they reconsidered what was important about being Jewish and how they wanted to live that Jewishness. Women and men wrestled with "big picture" issues like their relationship to Israel, the role of women in Judaism and society at large, and the meaning of rituals in their lives. On a more mundane level, they also considered whom to marry, where to live, and how to educate their children. For some, Jewishness played a foundational role in their decisions, while others thought of it as simply an accident of birth. Thus, different individuals and families came to vastly different conclusions, and the result was a diversification of American Jewish life.

In the 1970s, American Jews inhabited a wider spectrum with respect to Judaism than ever before: lifestyles ranged from secular with almost no ties to the Jewish community, to a growing movement to embrace traditional modes of Orthodoxy and even Hasidism (or "ultra-Orthodoxy"). In 1970, Jewish Americans who affiliated themselves with an organized movement mostly identified with non-Orthodox groups: 33 percent were Reform, 42 percent were Conservative, and 11 percent were Orthodox. As the decade wore on, the Conservative movement declined and the Reform movement gained membership. Observers have suggested that this gradual shift was one of a "disappearing middle": some American Jews became less religiously observant and socially involved, while others increased their religiosity and involvement. But the popularity of an intermediate lifestyle that primarily privileged being American, while unreflectively retaining some Jewish customs, began to wane. Many of these "middle" Jews became less religiously observant, although they often self-consciously chose to be involved in Jewish communal life in other ways. Others chose to become more religiously observant and involved, but fewer and fewer floated along in a complacent and unexamined American Jewish existence.

JEWISH DEMOGRAPHICS

By the 1970s, assimilation into American ways of life had become a prominent possibility. Demographics suggested that American Jews were an economically and socially successful group. Most were middle class, and, like other white Americans, many had moved from cities out to the suburbs in the 1950s and 1960s. By the end of the 1970s, only a tiny percentage of American Jews could be considered working class. Statistics suggest that the average Jewish-American parents were slightly older than their non-Jewish peers, and Jewish communities experienced lower birth rates than the national average. As a group, Jewish Americans were highly educated: in the 1970s, about 80 percent of Jews attended college, compared to 34 percent of non-Jewish Americans. About 20 percent of university faculty were Jewish, a remarkable number when compared with the percentage of Jews in the overall population (three percent). Although many of these statistics were cause for optimism, they also meant that it had become easier for Jewish Americans to jettison their Jewish identification altogether.

Other demographics incited explicit concern for the future of Jews and Judaism. As Jews became more and more integrated into non-Jewish American life, intermarriage grew as a concern. Ironically, seemingly positive phenomena like Jewish Americans' economic and social success and decreasing anti-Semitism in the United States contributed to the problem of Jewish survival in the face of intermarriage. When Jews married non-Jews—and they did so at higher and higher rates during the decades after World War II—they often left behind Judaism or chose to raise their children outside the Jewish tradition. During the 1970s, the rate of intermarriage had increased to about 30 percent. The low birth rate among Jewish families (around 2.3 children per couple, which barely reached the rate of replacement) added to the concern. This was especially discomfiting because the family—and especially the women in the family—had become the main locus of the continuation of Judaism. As Jewish communities were no longer self-contained and even no longer geographically together, the home became the last and best location for older generations to pass Judaism to younger generations. When Jews married non-Jews, they most often did not keep Jewish homes. Some people even expressed their concern for Judaism's slowly dwindling numbers in catastrophic language: they bandied about dramatic phrases like "finishing what Hitler started," which signaled how important the issue was to them. Even observers who were more circumspect, like those in the Jewish magazines *Midstream* and *Commentary*, recognized intermarriage as a significant problem facing the Jewish community as a whole. Some called it the "community's dirty laundry," while others called for ameliorative measures to prevent the total alienation of mixed couples and families. By the end of the 1970s, Jews across the religious continuum disagreed about how to react, but they concurred that the survival of the Jewish people was at issue.

CULTURAL JUDAISM

Jewish ethnicity and religion, for many years and in many historical and cultural contexts, were inseparable; conceptually and in lived experience, they were one and the same. But during the 1970s, many American Jews faced a personal choice in participation in Jewish ethnic life and Jewish religious life. They could choose to practice and believe in Jewish religion, which might mean going to synagogue each week or even each day. Or they could choose to be part of Jewish culture, which could mean reading books by Jewish authors, seeing Woody Allen films, or eating kugel or latkes at home. Some could even disavow Judaism and Jewish heritage altogether.

From this view, the 1960s, especially before the Six Day War in Israel (1967), marked a time of a middle-way American Judaism. One woman explained her perception of that experience: "There was a time, not too long ago, when all that was expected of a nice Jewish girl growing up in America was that she marry a nice Jewish boy and have nice Jewish children; if she was an especially good Jewish girl, she would also keep kosher, or at least have two sets of dishes. That is the world into which I was born. My parents had already moved out of the ghetto in Chicago into a middle-class neighborhood

For Jews in the 1970s, foods and rituals such as having latkes and a menorah at Hanukkah became more of a self-conscious choice.

Annie Hall

In *Annie Hall* (1977) filmmaker Woody Allen created a humorous contrast between a Jewish and non-Jewish family. Alvy, played by Allen, has Easter dinner with his girlfriend Annie in the scene excerpted below.

Annie's mom: It's a nice ham this year, Mom.

Annie: (Smiling) Oh, yeah. Grammy always does such a good job.

Annie's dad: A great sauce.

Alvy: It is. (Smacking his lips) It's dynamite ham.

Grammy stares down the table at Alvy: a look of utter dislike. Alvy tries not to notice.

Annie's mom: We went over to the swap meet. Annie, Gram and I. Got some nice picture frames. . . .

Grammy continues to stare at Alvy; he is now dressed in the long black coat and hat of an Orthodox Jew, complete with mustache and beard. . . . The conversation continues . . . Then Alvy, leaning his elbow on the table, looks out toward the camera.

Alvy: (To the audience) I can't believe this family. Annie's mother. She really is beautiful. And they're talking swap meets and boat basins, and the old lady at the end of the table (pointing to Grammy) is a classic Jew-hater. And, uh, they, they really look American, you know, very healthy and . . . like they never get sick or anything. Nothing like my family. You know, the two are like oil and water.

The screen splits in half. On the right is Alvy's family, busily eating at the crowded kitchen table. They eat quickly and interrupt one another loudly. On the left the Halls in their dining room. . . .The two families start talking back and forth.

Annie's mom: How do you plan to spend the holidays, Mrs. Singer?

Annie's dad: Fast?

Alvy's father: Yeah, no food. You know, we have to atone for our sins.

Annie's mom: What sins? I don't understand.

Alvy's dad: Tell you the truth, neither do we.

where Jews could acculturate along with second-generation Greek, Irish, and Italian families." From her perspective in the 1970s, however, this set of ideas had begun to change. Not only had women's roles changed, but there were fewer and fewer obstacles to complete assimilation. Jewish observance would have to be an active choice, not simply a default position.

Jews in America began to drift out of the middle and toward the extremes. Some began to let ritual observance slide away. They organized their lives around being American, and only secondarily concerned themselves with being Jewish. But they did not necessarily give up their Jewish identities completely; in fact, most chose to live their lives

Filmmaker Woody Allen was among a number of Jews in the arts in the 1970s who explored issues of Jewish identity.

as "culturally Jewish." Since American Jews did not necessarily live in Jewish neighborhoods, work in certain occupations, or send their children solely to Jewish schools; including cultural Jewish forms in their lives became a choice rather than a default position. Cultural Judaism included art, literature, film, food, language, support for Israel, and a plethora of everyday ways of connecting with other Jews. While there had been Jewish arts, food, and language as long as there had been Judaism, some American Jews began to see participation in these areas as a way of being Jewish. They might not attend synagogue or believe in God, but many American Jews wanted to continue being Jewish through other cultural forms that were meaningful to them.

For instance, Jewish studies in universities grew rapidly during the 1970s. Although the trend had started in the 1960s, by the mid-1970s, Jewish Studies had established itself as a widespread and legitimate academic discipline. More than 300 universities offered courses, and 40 had Jewish Studies majors. These courses taught not only sacred texts, but also Jewish literature, history, and languages. While these classes helped students acquire Jewish knowledge, they did not significantly increase religious observance or combat assimilation.

Jewish art and literature, too, grew in popularity. The critically acclaimed authors Cynthia Ozick and Philip Roth, for instance, both portrayed American Jewish characters who actively wrestled with their identities. In 1978, the

Nobel Prize–winning novelist and short story writer Isaac Bashevis Singer in 1988. Singer wrote in Yiddish, and some of his works drew from his childhood in Poland.

Yiddish writer Isaac Bashevis Singer, an American Jewish immigrant from Poland, received the Nobel Prize for Literature for his work, which often featured Jewish characters and treated themes of Jewishness. Jewish comedians and filmmakers like Woody Allen (born Allan Konigsberg) explicitly and humorously dealt with issues of Jewish identity and family, and the Jewish public responded. American Jews' growing public identification with these art forms demonstrated both a new comfort in a public Jewish identity and a desire to explore Jewishness through art.

Not all cultural Jews were necessarily secular Jews, however. Secular Judaism, which also grew during this period, is the interest in Jewish culture and history, but the explicit denial of a theistic religion. Some American Jews who were decreasing their religious observance did not hold the tenets of religious Judaism (secular Jews), but others continued to believe in God and simply found cultural ways of connecting with their Jewishness to be more fulfilling. Both groups saw an upswing of interest in Jewish history, languages, and art during the 1970s.

INCREASED RELIGIOSITY

On the other end of the spectrum were the Jews who chose to increase their Jewish commitment in religious and social ways. As the American Jewish

A Return to Traditional Judaism

In 1977, journalist Ellen Willis wrote about her brother Michael's turn from a secular, experimental lifestyle like that of many of his American peers in the 1970s to traditional Judaism. Michael was visiting Jerusalem after seven months of traveling, and unfulfilling jobs at home before that, when he had this awakening.

He wrote in a letter: "I haven't written because I'm having trouble describing what's happening . . . I've never given much thought to the existence of God—my [drug] experiences had left me with the idea that there was 'something' there, but I never thought it was knowable or explainable (and if it was explainable certainly more in terms of mystical experience and Buddhism than the 'God of our Fathers' of Judaism). But my time here has really forced me to come to terms with what that 'something' might be . . . I haven't come to this through any blinding moment of illumination or desire to be part of a group—it's been an intellectual process (which I've been fighting emotionally all the way), and I'd like nothing better than to reject it—I just don't think I'll be able to.

"The final shock in this letter is that I may not leave here at the end of July. If I accept this as the truth, I have to take time to learn about it."

The "truth" Mike proposed to accept was Judaism in its most extreme, absolutist form: the God of the Old Testament exists; He has chosen the Jewish people to carry out His will; the Torah (the Five Books of Moses and the Oral Law elaborating on them) is literally the word of God, revealed to the Jews at Mt. Sinai; the creation, the miracles in Egypt, and other biblical events actually happened; the Torah's laws, which are based on 613 mitzvoth (commandments) and govern every aspect of one's existence, must be obeyed in every detail; they are eternal, unchangeable. . . .

A believer could argue that Mike had been drifting because he hadn't found God, that his unhappiness was, in fact, God's way of leading him to the truth. Still, I worried that he was succumbing to an authoritarian illusion in an attempt to solve (or escape from) his problems.

community began to shift its focus from universalism to the cultivation of community and the individual soul, some Jews made conscious decisions to make Judaism more important in—or even the central feature of—their lives and identities. For some, this might mean reclaiming rituals and religious observances that their parents had abandoned. These Jews might send their children to Jewish day schools, which represented a growing movement to increase Jewish learning along with secular studies. For women, it might mean taking up some of the commandments traditionally required only of

The Chabad House Jewish student center on the campus of the State University of New York in Buffalo. Chabad Houses like this one first began to appear on U.S. college campuses in 1967.

men. For others it would mean learning how to make a kitchen kosher or to read Hebrew.

The 1970s saw the beginning of a religious renewal across the spectrum of observance. One of the ways that this became apparent was the growth of the Ba'al Teshuva (BT) movement. Literally meaning "masters of return" or "those who repent," these BTs turned from their secular or less observant upbringings to completely Orthodox lifestyles. The BTs were often well educated and successfully employed, but they found that there was something spiritual missing from their lives. Young women and men found the intellectual engagement and the security of traditional lifestyles and community to be fulfilling. Unlike many other Jewish groups, BTs often brought their message to other Jews and tried to bring them into the fold.

Another group engaging in outreach was the growing Hasidic group Chabad (also called Lubavitch, after the Russian town where it was founded). Chabad sent Jewish emissaries to cities around the globe, hoping to get Jews in those places to come to traditional Jewish lifestyles. Its young men and women also went out in public where they gave Jewish women candles for Sabbath and encouraged Jewish men to put on traditional vestments and pray. In 1967, Chabad sponsored its first center on a college campus, a movement that grew dramatically in number of campuses and influence on Jewish students during the 1970s.

But not all American Jews found that existing religious institutions addressed their goals for living Jewishly. When they wanted more spirituality, but found synagogues incongruous with their religious needs, beginning in the 1970s, some American Jews began to form extra-denominational groups that focused on "spirituality."

HAVUROT

One of the most successful solutions to this want came from a group of individuals who loved Judaism, but sought to explore its meaning with one another outside the bounds of existing institutions. In 1967, a group of young Jewish scholars, rabbis, and political activists formed the first *havurah*, or fellowship. They shunned strict hierarchies, welcomed women, dressed casually, exchanged ideas freely, sang and prayed together, and tried to forge a way to be Jewish that would resonate with their knowledge, ideologies, and emotions. What began as a small group of young adults exploring Judaism on their own terms turned into a nationwide movement. By the early 1970s, people had formed *havurot* in dozens of communities, and they drew many American Jews, some of whom had not been involved in Jewish religious life in years.

Although at first the *havurot* were not consciously feminist, many progressive women joined and became organizers. Judith Plaskow explained the close relationship between feminism and the *havurah* ideologies of personal development through community and human relationship with God: "Certainly, it is no accident that *havurot* have provided a first prayer home for many feminist Jews, at the same time that they have created an intimate space for the experience of God's immanence." These *havurot* brought some women back into Judaism; for others, they provided a more comfortable home within the tradition. But in general they increased the involvement and affirmation of women, as well as traditionally female modes of worship emphasizing spirituality.

In 1973, the *havurah* movement went public: several members compiled *The Jewish Catalog*, a do-it-yourself guide to Jewish practices, lifestyles, recipes, and even arts and crafts. Its witty explanations, amusing illustrations, and inclusive tone charmed Jews across the country. It was the best-selling book, second only to the Bible, ever published by the Jewish Publication Society. It seemed that American Jews were searching for their own personal ways to be Jewish; if they did not find enough support for personal religiosity within their synagogues, they found other resources and other people like them. *Havurot*, unlike many other groups of seekers, did not vanish after the 1970s, although they would slowly become more compatible with existing institutions like synagogues and community centers.

ISRAEL

In the immediate aftermath of Israel's Six Day War in 1967, attachment to Israel had emerged as one of the primary ways of expressing Jewishness in America. But the 1970s would mark a major turning point in American Jews' relationship with Israel. When the 1970s began, American Jews still exuded pride in Israel's decisive victory in 1967. The Yom Kippur War in 1973 continued the overwhelming support from American Jewish groups. But by the end

The First Jewish Catalog

In 1973, the Jewish Publication Society published *The First Jewish Catalog, A Do-it-Yourself Kit.* The amusing and informative book served as a manual for Jews who knew little about Judaism to acquaint themselves with various Jewish traditions, recipes, and even arts and crafts. The three authors used humor and down-to-earth language to make Jewish culture accessible to anyone who was interested. The following sample from the book teaches kosher wine-making and showcases the authors' lively style.

Wine-Making—a little like your zaydeh [grandfather] used to do it:
For everyone wanting to go back to the shtetl in one fashion or another, making sweet kosher wine is a relatively easy way to do it. . . . First of all, you get a shish—preferably a five-gallon size—either a ceramic crock, distilled water bottle, plastic garbage pail, or plastic bottle. Put in two gallons (by volume) of crushed or cut up fruit. . . . Put three gallons of water in the crock with about four pounds of plain old granulated sugar. . . . Stir up the mess and say an appropriate incantation. . . . The wine people recommend that you put a trap on this mess. The trap can be just a tube with a one-hole stopper on one and a glass full of water on the other. The stopper is put into your narrow-necked bottle (where else did you think, dummy) and this has the effect of letting the gases (mostly carbon dioxide) escape from this now foaming mess without letting oxygen in. I suppose that there is a reason for it (I once knew a girl who wrote a Ph.D. thesis on it—no kidding), but I've made wine with bottle trapped and untrapped with no perceptible difference. In fact, if you put enough love into the wine, and HaShem [God] smiles on you, and it comes out good, there is no perceptible difference after a few glasses anyway. The trap also keeps the smell down, which is fine if you don't want your pad to smell like a brewery.

Kosher wine for the sabbath served in a ritual silver goblet, or kiddush cup.

Getting back to the brewery, let it go bloop, bloop, bloop for about a week to ten days. Taste it and add sugar if it's getting sour—otherwise you'll end up with wine vinegar, which is groovy too, but not the name of the game. . . . Whatever you do, don't talk to anyone at wine-making store as they are the biggest bunch of fussbudgets I have ever seen. Good luck in your wine-making, and I'Chaim to all.

President Jimmy Carter met with Israeli Prime Minister Yitzhak Rabin at the White House on March 8, 1977, less than two months after becoming president, as part of a plan to restart peace negotiations for the Middle East.

of the decade, some American Jews began to act a little more circumspect in their support of the Jewish nation.

When the 1970s opened, American Jews almost universally supported Israel. The small nation's very existence had been threatened, and the American Jewish community rallied around its emotional victory. So when Egypt and Syria attacked Israel in 1973 on Yom Kippur, the holiest day in the Jewish calendar, American Jews were outraged and worried. Some 30,000 American Jewish men and women volunteered to go to Israel and fight alongside Israeli forces. Families and organizations sent $675 million to support Israel over the course of the short war. Regardless of their degree of religious and political commitment, Jews united, politically and emotionally, behind the cause of Israel.

American Jews from across the spectrum of observance—secular, Reform, Conservative, and Orthodox—worked together to raise money for Israel and to lobby the U.S. government to support Israel in the conflict. Even if they could not agree on many other aspects of Jewishness, the vast majority of American Jews identified with Israel and wanted to ensure its protection. One Reform temple in New Jersey, upon hearing that there was a shortage of Torah scrolls for Israeli troops, sent several members to present one of its own Torah scrolls to the chief chaplain of Israel's military.

Although wartimes intensified Jewish Americans' rallying around Israel, even during peacetime Israel became a part of many people's Jewish identity.

Egyptian President Anwar Sadat and Israeli Prime Minister Menachem at the Joint Session of Congress on September 18, 1978. During that session, President Jimmy Carter announced the signing of the Camp David Accords the day before; they were the first peace agreement for Israel and an Arab neighbor.

Although fewer than five percent of American Jewish schools had taught Israel as a subject of study in 1959, by 1974 almost all did. Hebrew schools began to teach Sephardi Hebrew, the dialect spoken in Israel, rather than the Ashkenazi Hebrew they had previously taught. Israeli history and the history of Zionism became popular topics for Jewish lectures, schools, and summer camps. American literature and film began to depict more Israelis, and more American Jews began to seriously consider visiting Israel. Especially for cultural Jews living in the United States, Israel could serve as a kind of crystallizing feature of their Jewish identity. For more religious Jews, the return of the Jewish people to the religious Holy Land became a source of pride and identification, even when they had no intention of immigrating.

But at the close of the 1970s, political and social problems in Israel had begun to incite occasional critiques and marked the end of the Jewish-American community's honeymoon with Israel. In 1977, Israel elected a right-wing government, and many of the ensuing policies and events caused some American Jews to reconsider their carte blanche support. For example, some disagreed with hard-line policies toward the West Bank and Palestinians. Despite these few dissenting voices, however, most American Jews remained loathe to criticize Israel publicly. When some American Jews organized Breira in 1973—an organization named after the Hebrew word for "choice" or "alternative"—a large, irate chorus of Jewish voices vehemently objected to their criticisms and calls for Israel to consider giving land to Palestinians.

Although support for Israel reached its high-water mark during the 1970s, the end of the decade marked the beginning of a slow but steady decrease in pro-Israel philanthropy, which accompanied a drop in interest and participation among individual Jews. Sociological studies suggest that Jewish volunteer leaders and groups began to move some of the focus away from Israel during this period. The nature of the change in American attitudes was more a transformation than a simple decrease: Americans saw Israel less through the lens of political and religious Zionism (the ideology of Jewish return to the Holy Land) and more as a modern society with sovereign Jews. As simply another modern, democratic country, rather than a symbol of the fulfillment of religious goals and prophecies, Israel no longer captivated American Jews. Its status as a nation, and not simply an ideal, meant that Israel would be open to diverging opinions and even criticism from Americans. Thus, although the 1970s were generally a period of near-universal American Jewish support for Israel, the end of the decade brought harbingers of change.

FEMINISM

When American women began to establish the second wave of feminism in the 1960s, many were at first uninterested in—or even hostile to—religion. For instance, when Betty Friedan wrote *The Feminine Mystique* in 1963, she did not focus on her Jewishness in either positive or negative ways. She argued that American women had been dealt a set of domestic ideals that women simply could not happily embody. While Friedan was most interested in changing American culture and the way it viewed women's fulfillment in non-domestic realms like employment, she let Jewishness take a back seat. The general feminist movement, however, had a large number of Jewish women leaders and participants. One prominent and public example was Bella Abzug: born of Russian-Jewish immigrants, she was an outspoken supporter of the Equal Rights Amendment and was elected to the U.S. House of Representatives in 1970.

During the 1970s, feminism and Judaism came to interact much more closely, although the interactions were not always positive. Friedan, once quiet on the subject, came to align her motivations for feminism with Judaism. In 1976, she said that her "passion against injustice . . . originated from my feelings of the injustice of anti-Semitism." Other women were not so sanguine about the prospects of Judaism and feminism as similar: many Jewish women who wanted to be involved in feminist organizations found significant anti-Semitism in the feminist movement. Non-Jewish feminists often loudly denounced not only Israel, but also Jews in general as despicable. Other women, a few of whom were Jewish, dismissed Judaism as a hopelessly patriarchal system that only oppressed women. They charged that monotheistic Judaism "killed" the goddesses that were worshipped before its arrival.

Marcia Cohn Spiegel and Jewish Feminism

Author and well-known Jewish-American academic Marcia Cohn Spiegel has written of feeling left out of Jewish life as a girl, and how those feelings came back even more intensely when she became a woman trying to be a leader in the Jewish community. She writes:

I was eager to learn everything, a voracious reader who was never without a book, so starting Hebrew school was anticipated with great excitement—at last I could share the mysteries concealed in the strange letters and words. But eagerness quickly turned to boredom when I found that studying Hebrew was not too different from learning the piano, lots of scales and exercises but no pieces. We learned the alphabet and began reading prayers, prayers with no meaning, with no translation, just reading.

Boredom turned to anger when the boys began to leave the class in a group and returned grinning and smirking and giving the few girls in the class the covert glances of a group who are sharing some kind of secret joke. I knew that they must be doing something magical, mystical, and sexual down in Smoler Hall, but I couldn't imagine what it could be. However, I knew that it was private, and I knew that I was left out. (I was a grandmother before I realized that the boys were learning to put on teffilin preparing for bar mitzvah.) It was hard to be a good Jewish girl after that.

Many years later Cohn Spiegel still found that if she, as a woman, wanted to have a space in the Jewish tradition, she would have to make it for herself:

As Sisterhood president I had the task of preparing the annual Sisterhood Service for Shabbat. I decided to use quotations about women from the sages and found a wonderful source in Famous Jewish Quotations *where I read, "It is better to burn the Torah than to teach it to your daughters." The old feelings of anger and bitterness that my six-year-old self had felt in Hebrew school returned with a vengeance. I determined to use only the words of women, to have a service in which only women participated, only women chanted, only women read from the Torah. In 1976 that was not very easy.*

But many Jewish women, instead of denigrating and abandoning Judaism, sought to change it. One group in the vanguard grew out of a *havurah* in New York: in 1971, women from the group began to meet to discuss interpretations of Jewish law and their implications for women. Eventually, their meetings began to move toward activism, and they named themselves Ezrat Nashim (a clever Hebrew double entendre, meaning both "help of women" and the name of the location where women sat in the synagogue). These particular women were committed to remaining within Conservative Judaism while they called for changes. In 1973, a national movement of Jewish feminists coalesced. The North American Jewish Students' Network organized a conference that attracted feminists from across the nation and thereby helped bring together many smaller, regional groups that had been working toward similar goals. Jewish feminists founded *Lilith*, an independent magazine designed to reach women who struggled to be both women and Jews.

While many Jewish women were pushing to change institutional conditions so that they could experience fulfillment both as women and as Jews, some women had a very particular goal in mind: they wanted to be rabbis. In the Reform movement, 1972 marked the year when the male rabbis finally voted to allow women into the educational track for ordination. The movement's academic institution, Hebrew Union College–Jewish Institute of Religion, confronted the question because a student named Sally Priesand asked to be considered for ordination. She had made her intentions clear many years earlier when she had applied as an undergraduate: Priesand had always wanted to be a rabbi. Although at that time the school had informed her it did "not know what opportunities exist for women in the active rabbinate," by the time she was nearing completion of her classes, the Reform movement decided that women could be rabbis. The Reconstructionist movement, a smaller American-born Jewish group that concentrated on the culture of Judaism, ordained its first woman rabbi in 1974, and the Conservative movement decided to follow suit in 1985.

CONCLUSION

By the close of the 1970s, American culture had begun to move away from its former days of experiment, rebellion, and revolution. American Jews, too, generally began to turn their emphasis from world Jewry to their own families and communities. Synagogue membership that had failed to rebound after the decrease of the early 1960s, increasing intermarriage rates, low birth rates, assimilation, education, and feminism—all on the home front—occupied the thoughts of those concerned about American Jewish communities. American Jews reflected on their own identities when they wondered how to be Jewish and American, when they sought out spiritual practices or eschewed religion in favor of cultural Judaism, when they considered how they felt about Israel, and when they argued for or against allowing women's voices to be heeded. The inward reflection of the 1970s, although divisive at times, would become an opportunity for the growth of the community.

SARAH IMHOFF
UNIVERSITY OF CHICAGO

Further Reading

Allen, Woody. *Four Films of Woody Allen:* Annie Hall, Interiors, Manhattan, Stardust Memories. New York: Random House, 1982.

Cohen, Steven. "Are American and Israeli Jews Drifting Apart?" In *Imagining the Jewish Future.* Ed. by David Teutch. Albany, NY: SUNY Press, 1992.

Diner, Hasia. *The Jews of the United States.* Berkeley, CA: University of California Press, 2004.

Fishman, Sylvia Barack. *A Breath of Life: Feminism in the American Jewish Community.* New York: Free Press, 1993.

Friedan, Betty. *The Feminine Mystique.* New York: W.W. Norton, 1963.

Gal, Allon, ed. *Envisioning Israel: The Changing Ideals and Images of North American Jews.* Jerusalem: Magnes Press, 1996.

Grubin, David. *The Jewish Americans.* PBS (DVD), 2008.

Heilman, Samuel. *Portrait of American Jews: The Last Half of the 20th Century.* Seattle, WA: University of Washington Press, 1995.

Jewish Women's Archives, "Marcia Cohn Spiegel," Available online, URL: http://www.jwa.org. Accessed November 2009.

Kaplan, Dana Evan. "Trends in American Judaism from 1945 to the Present." In *Cambridge Companion to American Judaism.* Cambridge, MA: Cambridge University Press, 2005.

Nadell, Pamela. *Women Who Would Be Rabbis: A History of Women's Ordination 1889–1985.* Boston, MA: Beacon Press, 1998.

Prell, Riv-Ellen. *Fighting to Become American: Jews, Gender, and the Anxiety of Assimilation.* Boston, MA: Beacon Press, 1999.

———. *Prayer & Community: The Havurah in American Judaism.* Detroit, MI: Wayne State University Press, 1989.

Rosenthal, Steven. *Irreconcilable Differences? The Waning of the American Jewish Love Affair with Israel.* Hanover, NH: University Press of New England, 2001.

Sarna, Jonathan. *American Judaism.* New Haven, CT: Yale University Press, 2004.

Seliktar, Ofira. *Divided We Stand: American Jews, Israel, and the Peace Process.* Westport, CT: Praeger, 2002.

Shapiro, Edward. *A Time for Healing: American Judaism since World War II.* Baltimore, MD: Johns Hopkins University Press, 1992.

Siegel, Richard, Michael Strassfeld, and Sharon Strassfeld. *The First Jewish Catalog: A Do-it-Yourself Kit.* New York: Jewish Publication Society, 1973.

Umansky, Ellen and Diane Ashton. *Four Centuries of Jewish Women's Spirituality.* Boston, MA: Beacon Press. 1992.

Wade, Stephen. *Jewish American Literature since 1945: An Introduction.* Chicago, IL: Fitzroy Dearborn, 1999.

Willis, Ellen. "Next Year in Jerusalem." *Rolling Stone* (April 1977).

CHAPTER 10

Jewish Americans Today: 1980 to the Present

THE IMMIGRATION AND Nationality Act of 1965, which essentially abolished the quota systems of the Immigration Act of 1924, continued to have a significant effect on Jewish immigration during the 1980s and beyond. Quotas were no longer based on national origin, opening the doors to non-European emigres, especially Russian and Iranian Jews. The Jackson-Vanik amendment to the 1974 Trade Act, which linked human rights, such as the "freedom to emigrate" to normal trade relations with the United States, had also called attention to the Soviet Union's attempts to deter Russian Jews from emigrating. In the latter part of the 1980s, when President Mikhail Gorbachev established his policies of *perestroika* (political and economic reforms) and *glasnost* (openness and transparency in government), thousands of Soviet Jews were finally able to emigrate. Eventually, some 1.5 million Soviet Jews fled.

After the Iranian Islamic Revolution in 1979, over 35,000 Jews immigrated to the United States in the 1980s, profoundly affecting the makeup of the Jewish communities of Los Angeles. It was estimated that in 2010 over 100,000 Iranian Jews resided in the United States, and some claimed that more than 25 percent of the Beverly Hills population were Iranian Jews.

Another concept that became increasingly relevant in the 1980s was Aliyah, or Jewish immigration to Israel. In the 1980s, over 153,000 Jews immigrated to Israel, with almost 40,000 of them coming from the United States.

Many religious Jews believed that it was part of the 613 commandments for a Jew to eventually return to Israel as a fulfillment of God's promises to the patriarchs Abraham, Isaac, and Jacob. "Making Aliyah" is a recurring part of Jewish prayer and holiday services on Passover and Yom Kippur, which end with "Next year in Jerusalem."

Determining the number of Jewish Americans in the United States is a complex proposition. Judaism is both a religion and an ethnicity, so it is possible to define who is a Jew by either religious practice or by birth, or by a combination of both. It is also possible to convert to Judaism, rather than being born Jewish. The 2006 *American Jewish Yearbook* population survey found that roughly 2.1 percent of the U.S. population were Jewish by birth, that is, 6.4 million Americans had at least one Jewish parent.

Not everyone born into a religion continues to practice that faith, however, so some surveys consider the number of people actively practicing Judaism. According to a 2007 survey taken by the Pew Forum on Religion and Public Life, 1.7 percent of the U.S. population were practicing the Jewish faith. Of that 1.7 percent, 0.7 percent practiced Reform Judaism, 0.5 percent practiced Conservative Judaism, and less than 0.3 percent classified themselves as practicing Orthodox Judaism. The remaining respondents declared themselves "Jewish" without further affiliation.

RUSSIAN JEWS

Arguments surfaced in the 1980s between the American Jewish establishment and the Israelis as to where emigrating Soviet Jews belonged—in the United States or in Israel. Most Soviet Jews wanted to come to the United States, but Israel argued that in order for the nation to survive as a Jewish nation, more immigrants were needed. American Jews, harking back to their lack of action to help desperate Jews during World War II, determined that encouraging Soviet Jews to come to the United States was compensation for having done so little during the start of the war. Jews began to press the government to classify the Soviet Jews as refugees, thus enabling them to receive help with housing, healthcare, and jobs. It became such a rallying cause among synagogue congregations that it increasingly became popular to "twin" with a Soviet Jewish child, one who could not celebrate the coming-of-age ritual for 13-year-old children. Israel countered with claims that it needed the highly educated Russian Jews because it had already absorbed many less-educated Jews from Arab countries.

One solution that worked for a time was the "freedom of choice" concept—Soviet Jews could choose where they wanted to settle. American Jewish organizations compromised with Israel and agreed to a yearly quota of 40,000 Soviet emigres, based on family reunification policies. By the mid-1980s, these concessions were made because of the increased burden of trying to settle so many people into the United States, and also because of what was happening to the Jewish community within the United States. Funds in the 1980s were increasingly directed toward key issues that Jewish Americans faced—intermarriage and assimilation.

JEWISH IDENTITY: RELIGION

Beginning in the 1980s, statistical reports appeared regarding the effects of assimilation (absorption into the cultural tradition of a population) and acculturation (borrowing from the new culture and creating new and blended patterns) of American Jews, the majority of whom were now third generation. The large majority of this cohort came from grandparents who migrated to the United States and who, to a lesser or greater extent, practiced traditionalism. Over time, there was a slow erosion of religious strictures, because Jews increasingly felt safe enough to jettison aspects of their tradition. They were now far more accepted by the larger society than at any time in the history of their presence in the United States. By the 1980s, blatant anti-Semitism was largely absent from American culture.

Jews had become so integrated that they were beginning to exhibit some of the changing family patterns that were emerging in the dominant culture. Men and women were staying single longer, and when they did marry, they were having fewer children. Intermarriage between Jews and Christians continued to increase. Depending upon the study, between 25 and 30 percent of Jews intermarried. A noticeable rise in divorce rates further connected the Jewish minority to the trends in the non-Jewish population. Consequently, Jews increasingly did not maintain a conventional family—a necessary part of Jewish religious and community life.

Higher educational attainment and increasing professionalism helped to erode the traditional practices of Judaism, particularly the Sabbath that required no work. As was typical of many professionals in the late 20th century, Jews were moving to geographic locations as a requirement for their jobs, thus changing the centuries-old tradition of Jews living near each other (for protection and for religious requirements).

It was not surprising, then, that when Jews were surveyed in the 1980s, fewer were affiliated with synagogues and practiced ritual observances than their parents. Second-generation Jews were often affiliated through memberships in such Jewish organizations as B'nai B'rith, Hadassah, and the Organization for Rehabilitation through Training (ORT), whereas 1980s Jews expressed far fewer connections to organizations and to specifically Jewish charitable giving. Their affiliations were often with liberal causes in which they felt they could oppose any latent anti-Semitism by fighting against intolerance and bigotry of any kind, and thus, charitable donations were directed toward helping the downtrodden. This shift from purely Jewish to secular charitable endeavors helped propel Jewish assimilation into liberal and progressive causes, rather than just Jewish causes.

Grand Rabbi Moshe Leib Rabinovich of Borough Park, Brooklyn, New York, in 2006. He was the leader of Munkacs Hasidism, which originated in what is now the city of Mukachevo, Ukraine.

Ethnic and gender diversity in the Jewish-American community increased in the 1990s and 2000s, as more young people who identified as American Jews were foreign born. Waves of immigrants brought their practices and traditions to Jewish communities in the United States. Russian-born young Jews had a relatively high rate of participation in Jewish communal activities such as *yeshiva* study and Jewish religious schooling, creating a resurgence of interest in Judaism within this youth demographic.

Specific cultural celebrations and social experiences have often been mentioned as primary influences on young adults in maintaining a Jewish cultural identity. Participation in camping trips, visits to Israel, and enrollment in Jewish Studies classes in college have helped Generation Y members identify with their faith. Slightly older Generation X members often returned to faith practices at the time of marriage or at the birth of their first child and began or returned to ritual behaviors such as celebrating Hanukkah or participating in Seder dinner.

Alongside the increasing secularization of many Jews came a contradictory trend. A small but growing percentage of Jews decided to return to the traditional observances of their religion in what was known as the *ba'al teshuvah* (returnees) movement. Of the 5.9 million American Jews in the 1980s, approximately 10 percent were Orthodox, and of the Orthodox, 20–25 percent were returnees. This movement flowered in the 1980s but had its roots in the turbulence of the 1960s and 1970s. The Civil Rights Movement, which emphasized the pride of ethnic identity, pushed many involved Jews into a reexamination of their own roots and uniqueness. An anti-establishment ethos was another impetus for the "returnees" as they attempted to promote a life based upon a value system opposed to materialism and acquisitiveness.

The special style of dress—women covering their arms and wearing long skirts, men wearing *tzitzis* (fringes worn on garments), and the unique look (women wearing wigs, men with beards)—offered a way to counter existing fashion dictates. Mysticism, rabbis who could be compared to gurus, extensive rituals, and kosher diets were appealing to those who questioned popular religious trends.

The attraction for women was often similar to the motivation for men to return to conservative orthodox Jewish observance. The second wave of the feminist movement had begun in the 1960s, and by the 1980s, many workplace concerns were being addressed. There was an increasing emphasis on professional education for women and a great influx of females into the workforce. Along with these changes, however, was a growing ambivalence about gender categories and the pros and cons of traditional functions for women. With this upheaval, some women and men were experiencing confusion about family relationships. Returning to a religious tradition that clearly and unambivalently defined roles and promoted marriage and family was a comforting alternative.

The maturing of the second wave of the feminist movement also profoundly influenced other types of Jewish households, and the religion itself. While Sally Priesand had been the first woman to be ordained as a rabbi in Reform Judaism in 1972, it was not until the 1980s that the less-liberal branch of the religion, the Conservatives, ordained their first female rabbi, Amy Eilberg, in 1985. These women were the harbingers of cataclysmic changes in how the large majority of Jews viewed women's spiritual roles. These changes included the notion that women share equally not only in religious practices, but also in the history of the Jewish people. This philosophy led to changes in female prominence not only in the rabbinate, but in lay leadership as well (such as being presidents of congregations). Along with these transformations, prayer books were also examined in an effort to remove gender-biased language. Many liturgical texts were revised accordingly.

Within the broader feminist movement, a small but growing voice of opposition arose against Jews who were feminists, particularly centered on the issue of Israel and its policies. This culminated in the International Women's Conference in 1980 in Copenhagen in which virulent anti-Israel comments were promulgated. Arguably anti-Israel sentiments were not anti-Semitic attitudes, but

A Seder dinner plate with a display of ritual foods. Some of the younger generation of Jewish Americans have been returning to faith practices such as Seder dinners.

Kabbalah

Kabbalah is an esoteric Jewish tradition for contemplating the divine, and for centuries only a privileged few within the religion had access to its secret texts and traditions. For the first 12 centuries of Judaism, the term *kabbalah* referred to the tradition Moses received from God on Mount Sinai. Since the 13th century, there has been little agreement on what precisely constitutes kabbalah, as various rabbis and sects have defined the term in several ways. Commonly, an element of magic is involved, as well as an element of secrecy; kabbalists do not introduce new teachings, but rather claim that they are revealing a part of Jewish tradition long held secret. Early kabbalah texts include the Book Bahir and Sefir Yezira, both of which describe the creation of the world and its divine nature. The Zohar, another early text, appeared in Spain in the 13th century and includes the four stages of knowledge and the 72 names of God.

Key features of kabbalah include an emphasis on personal religious experience, the difficulty of expressing religious truths in language, and in contemporary times, the exploration of the relationship between science and the occult. The Enlightenment in the 18th century drew scholarly attention away from this type of study. By the 19th century, a number of occult societies kept it alive, including the Theosophical Society begun by Madame Helena Blavatsky in the United States in 1875. Blavatsky's writings, inspired in part by kabbalistic texts, influenced esoteric thinking well into the 20th century, and some call her the mother of New Age religion.

A copy of the kabbalah text known as the Zohar published in Italy in 1558.

The form of kabbalah recently popularized by the Kabbalah Centre in the 1990s is based in part on the Zohar, combined with New Age elements such as astrology. Its practices emphasize personal enlightenment and power, rather than service of the divine in the Jewish tradition. Another notable contemporary element is the sale of magical objects, such as the red string or crystals, to ward off danger and to encourage healing. This commodification of esoteric teachings has drawn criticism of kabbalah as "McMysticism," a superficial approach to a tradition that generally requires a deep understanding of fundamental Jewish teachings.

However, celebrity involvement with the Kabbalah Centre has drawn a new generation to discover kabbalah's connections with Judaism and its appeal to seekers of all faith traditions.

some of the prominent Jewish participants such as Congresswoman Bella Abzug and writer Letty Cottin Pogrebin felt very uncomfortable. Participating in a conference in which Zionism was declared a form of racism and Israel was labeled an imperialistic nation relegated the major purpose of the conference—promoting womens' rights—to secondary status behind the dictates of political rhetoric.

By the early 21st century, new opportunities for women's leadership in several Jewish traditions had led to young women's increased participation and commitment. A 2001 survey found that women outnumbered men in Conservative Jewish youth groups and ritual activities, and a 2005 study of Reform Jewish youth yielded similar results.

JEWISH IDENTITY: FAMILY

In the late 20th and early 21st century, the trend toward interfaith marriages continued to affect Jewish family life. More Jews than ever married outside their religion; according to the National Jewish Population Survey in 2001, 47 percent of Jewish marriages in the previous decade had been interfaith marriages.

Jewish denominations have varying attitudes toward intermarriage. Orthodox Judaism considers these marriages "mixed," and Orthodox rabbis will not officiate at a mixed-marriage ceremony. Orthodox young adults are more likely than other Jews to marry early, to marry other Jews, and to claim a strong Jewish identity. Conservative Judaism places heavy emphasis on the conversion of the non-Jewish partner. The Reform tradition is the most open to marriages between Jews and those of different faith backgrounds. In some of these marriages, the non-Jewish partner agrees to convert; in other families, multiple faith traditions are preserved and maintained. Non-Orthodox young Jews reflect the general U.S. trend of marrying at later ages, and are the most likely both to intermarry and to have been raised in an intermarried household. Studies demonstrate that children of intermarriages are less likely to practice Judaism; in 2001, only a third of children in interfaith households were being educated and raised in the Jewish tradition, compared to 96 percent of children in households where both parents were Jewish.

American Jewish families, compared with general U.S. trends, have displayed an increased level of average education and a decreased birth rate. Jewish women tend to be more educated, as over half have received a bachelor's degree. They tend to delay childbearing until their mid- to late 30s, and to have fewer children than the U.S. average (1.38 for Jewish mothers, compared to 1.85 for all U.S. mothers). The relatively low birth rate falls below the rate needed for population replacement, suggesting that the American Jewish population is slowly shrinking over time.

By 2000, 1.5 million people, or roughly 29 percent of the U.S. Jewish population, were between the ages of 18 and 39. Of these members of Generation X and Generation Y, more than half were unmarried, a striking consideration

Grandparents with their grandchildren at Hanukkah. The Jewish-American population is growing increasingly older: by 2001, 19 percent of all Jewish Americans were over 65.

given how many Jewish activities tend to center on married couples and family life.

The aging of the Jewish population in recent years has presented another challenge impacting family life. In 2000, the average age of the American Jew was 42 years old, seven years older than the national average overall. With age have come financial and health worries, including physical challenges that often place caretaking responsibilities on younger members of the family. Many Jewish adults between the ages of 40 and 65 have found themselves in the "sandwich generation," caring for their parents as they raise their children, and bearing the economic burden for both surrounding generations. An increasing number of Jewish community programs have focused on serving the elderly and their caregivers in order to allow people to age with dignity. For example, the Sacred Aging Project has worked with synagogue congregations to develop rituals and assistance for elderly members who need to make long-term healthcare decisions.

The 2000–01 National Jewish Population Survey revealed that 19 percent of the U.S. Jewish population were over 65, and nine percent were over 75.

These percentages were expected to increase as the baby boom generation reached retirement age beginning in 2008. A third of the elderly were widowed, which can create social isolation without a strong community network. The elderly were also most likely to live alone, and to have lived in the same place for 20 years or more. This residential stability, combined with a need for social interaction, can lead to strong involvement for many in Jewish community organizations. The elderly were as likely as any younger generation to participate in adult education and to attend religious services. Compared with younger generations, elderly Jews were more likely to volunteer in their communities and to contribute to Jewish charitable organizations. As the U.S. Jewish population continues to age, it will be essential to elderly people's quality of life for the Jewish community to help their members maintain strong personal networks and encourage contributions to their local communities through philanthropy and volunteerism.

JEWISH IDENTITY: EDUCATION

In part because of the large number of Jewish intermarriages, new importance was placed on Jewish education in the late 20th century. Families with only one Jewish parent needed to find educational resources outside the home to preserve Jewish histories and traditions. In addition to the usual day camps, summer camps, and supplementary schools, Jewish education expanded into new age groups and geographical areas.

Between 1990 and 2002, the number of children enrolled in Jewish preschools doubled to over 100,000 nationwide. This was likely a reflection of both the increased call for Jewish education and the increased need for childcare resulting from educated Jewish women joining the workforce. These younger children brought the religious practices they encountered at preschool back into their homes, and also raised the likelihood of creating new friendships between Jewish parents of children in shared care, thus strengthening Judaism in the communities where such care was available.

For school-age children, a major resurgence of private Jewish day schools provided opportunities for a full state-sanctioned secular education in an environment focused on teaching the Jewish faith. During 1992–2008, enrollment in such schools grew nearly 25 percent across Jewish denominations, and the number of schools increased significantly. Jewish high schools also increased in number and size across the country, expanding beyond the handful of east coast schools that existed prior to 1990.

This increased demand for education worsened a shortage of qualified Jewish teachers. All U.S. Jewish day schools are private, and thus supported by tuition and in some cases by synagogue congregations or foundation funding. They tend to pay below market rates, and thus have problems attracting and retaining qualified teaching personnel. However, teachers' salary increases mean increased tuition, and thus a less affordable religious education for students and their parents. Median tuition at Jewish day schools in 2001 was $11,000 per year, increasing each year since then. In the years ahead, these schools will continue searching for creative ways to make a full Jewish education available to working- and middle-class Jewish families.

At the college level, the number of Jews holding college degrees increased from 40 to 60 percent over these decades. Interestingly, Jewish students were more likely than the average college student to apply to multiple colleges and to choose a college over 500 miles from home. By the time they graduated from college, almost half of these students took at least one Jewish Studies course, indicating an interest in religious self-exploration and identity formation.

DOMESTIC POLITICS

With the Ronald Reagan presidency, right-wing politics returned to the national scene and, concomitantly, conservative Christian evangelicals began to increase their involvement in politics. The alliance of this group with Israel and the Jewish population of the United States during the 1980s appeared to be an untenable relationship, as Jews typically supported liberal causes and, consequently, were the most liberal voting minority group in the country. But one of the tenets of Christian evangelicalism was that in order for the Second Coming of Christ to occur, the Jewish people had to be restored to their land—Israel. Thus, many Jews partnered with the Christian evangelicals because of their support for Israel and their monetary contributions to Jewish efforts to maintain as much of the land in Israel/Palestine as possible. In some studies in the 1980s, four out of five Jewish respondents said the destruction of Israel would be one of the greatest tragedies in their lives. Orthodox Jews in Israel, who determine all personal laws surrounding birth, marriage, divorce, and death, found that the evangelical Christians were not opposed to the Orthodox views on life-cycle issues. Often the two groups were in close agreement.

The rift between Jews and blacks, however, continued unabated in the 1980s. During the Civil Rights Movement many Jews allied themselves with black causes, considering them to be part of a liberal agenda against intolerance and bigotry. However, the union of these two groups, both targets of discrimination during the first part of the 20th century, began to collapse during the second half of the 1960s for many reasons. By this time, black Americans were convinced that they could run their own civil rights struggle without the assistance of whites, particularly Jews.

In 1967, the Conference for a New Politics, a gathering of antiwar and civil rights activists, condemned Israel as an imperialist state against the Palestinians. This gathering was a harbinger of the difficult relations that continued into the 1980s between black Americans and Jews.

In 1984, Jesse Jackson ran for president of the United States for the Democratic Party. Privately he referred to Jews as "Hymies" and to New York City as "Hymietown." He also embraced Yasser Arafat, who was the head of the Palestine Liberation Organization. These acts convinced Jews that Jackson was anti-Semitic. Louis Farrakhan, the national representative of the Nation of Islam, was another black activist in the 1980s who also incited Jews and blacks. After Jackson made his anti-Semitic comment to a reporter, he received death threats, and Farrakhan immediately responded that anyone who harmed Jackson would be harmed as well. This led to the chair of the Anti-Defamation League labeling Farrakhan a "Black Hitler."

In an infamous speech, later censured unanimously by the U.S. Senate, Farrakhan called Hitler "a very great man" who "rose Germany up from the ashes of her defeat." Later, he publicly called Jews "bloodsuckers" and described Judaism as a "gutter religion." Farrakhan denied these allegations by proclaiming that he would never denigrate a religion that includes Abraham, Moses, and other Prophets whom Allah sent to the Jews. But a transcript of his speech, reported by the *New York Times*, revealed his exact words: "lying and deceit and using the name of God to shield your gutter religion . . ." Partially due to the tremendous publicity Farrakhan received because of these comments and to business dealings related to Jews, he proclaimed that "the black man will never be free until we address the relationship between blacks and Jews." Many efforts continue to reconcile the differences between the two groups.

ISRAEL AND AMERICAN JEWS

Jewish Americans have always had a multidimensional relationship with Israel. Israel has long represented to Jews of every nation a place of safety and security, a nation that will always accept them for no other reason than that they are Jews. In 1950, legislation was passed in Israel called the Law of Return that gave Jews of any nation the right to migrate to Israel and to immediately become citizens. In 1970, the law was amended to include the spouse of a Jew, the spouse of a child of a Jew, and the spouse of the grandchild of a Jew. However, another amendment in 1989 proclaimed that Messianic Jews (a group that aligns Jews with Jewry) were not considered eligible for the Law of Return.

In a survey conducted in the 1980s, a sample was taken of 4.3 million American Jews, and in all age categories about 75 percent felt that Jews in the United States and Jews in Israel shared a common destiny. Of Jewishly connected Jews (those who belong to a synagogue, give charity, go to services), 84 percent believed that Israel was the spiritual center of the Jewish people. Of this group, over 88 percent felt that Israel needed the financial support of American Jews, and an equal percent were familiar with the current social and political situation in Israel. Sixty percent of all Jewish respondents felt somewhat or very emotionally attached to Israel.

Two important factors profoundly affected American Jews' feelings about Israel in the 1980s: the Lebanon War in 1982, and the first Intifada that began in 1987. The Lebanon War was controversial and served not only to shake

American Jews' support for Israel, but also to question the direction of Israeli political policies. Prior to the outbreak of the Lebanon War, there were several skirmishes between the Palestine Liberation Organization (PLO) in Lebanon and Israel. In 1982, the Israel Defense Forces (IDF) invaded southern Lebanon in response to an assassination attempt against Israel's ambassador to the United Kingdom. The most egregious outcomes were the killing of hundreds of Palestinians in the refugee camps of Sabra and Shatila by the Lebanese Christian Militia, killings indirectly attributed to Ariel Sharon, Israel's defense minister.

The other horrendous event was the U.S. Marines' barracks bombing in 1983. Some important consequences of this war included the disillusionment of Israelis and American Jews about the competence of the military and its leadership, as well as the impetus for the creation of Hezbollah, an organization that replaced the PLO in southern Lebanon. The first Intifada (resistance to oppression) began in 1987, triggered by the death of four Palestinians in a traffic accident caused by an Israeli. The uprising stemmed from the frustration caused by the Israeli occupation of territories taken in the Six Day War. The result was six years of Palestinian defiance, often including suicide bombings.

Elderly Jews hold a counter-protest against pro-Palestinian demonstrators in 2006. In 2000, as many as 79 percent of Jewish Americans over 60 continued to feel strong ties to Israel.

As the unrest continued, the Palestinians garnered more international recognition, which led to the Oslo Accord, a realization that the Palestinians should have their own state. The Intifada particularly affected the Israeli economy—tourism dropped dramatically, and fewer people were willing to invest in Israeli businesses. During the 1980s, American Jews were inundated by news of atrocities committed by Israeli soldiers, particularly toward children, and were chagrined that the Palestinian destruction was not equally reported. This ambiguity about events eroded the confidence of some Jews in Israel's ethics and invulnerability.

In the 1990s and 2000s, young people in Generation X and Generation Y continued to be less likely to feel strong Israeli ties, indicating what may be an important trend in future relations between the United States and Israel. Studies have indicated that roughly a third of young Jews feel connected to and support the nation of Israel as important to their faith. This contrasts sharply with the responses of older generations, as in a 2000 survey that demonstrated that 79 percent of respondents age 60 and older felt "very close" or "fairly close" to Israel. Impatience with the ongoing failures of the Middle East peace process has led young adults to question the Israeli state's positions, and many do not identify with Israel as the geographic center of Jewish life. This distancing may eventually result in changes in U.S. foreign policy toward Israel if these generations are not as invested in the maintenance of a Jewish state.

THE UNITED STATES AND ISRAEL

During the 1990s and 2000s, U.S.-Israel relations actually strengthened as the political situation in the Middle East grew ever more complicated. In 1991, at the beginning of the Gulf War in Iraq, President George H.W. Bush's administration successfully convinced Israel not to retaliate when it became a target for Iraqi scud missiles. Israel's restraint prevented the breakup of the coalition forces that fought Iraq in order to reestablish the sovereignty of Kuwait. The Bush administration also succeeded in negotiating a partial construction freeze in the occupied territories in 1992 as part of peace negotiations, but further progress waited until the next administration.

Under the Clinton administration, in 1993, the Declaration of Principles was signed in Oslo, Norway. This declaration involved both Israel and the Palestinian Liberation Organization (PLO), and it established a Palestinian Authority with the ability to negotiate on behalf of a future state and to administer Palestinian territories. It also provided guidelines for Israel to withdraw from sections of the Gaza Strip and the West Bank, two long-disputed areas. The Jordan-Israeli peace treaty of 1994 was signed in part due to U.S. pressure on Jordan's King Hussein to normalize relations and negotiate territorial disputes with Israel. The United States rewarded Jordan by forgiving its trade debt. For the first time since 1948, the Israel-Jordanian border was open to commerce and travel. The accords set forth in the Declaration of Principles were slightly expanded and reaffirmed in the Wye River Memorandum of 1998. Violence between the two states continued, however, and the peace process had not succeeded by the end of President Bill Clinton's second term.

President George W. Bush entered office in 2001. During his first term, a Road Map for Peace was created through international efforts. The United Nations joined the United States, the European Union, and Russia in setting forth principles for future peace negotiations, including the creation of an independent state of Palestine. In April 2003, Mahmoud Abbas became the first prime minister of the Palestinian Authority. In spite of the progress toward

The Terrorist Attacks of September 11, 2001

In the wake of the horrific attacks on September 11, 2001, a number of conspiracy theories quickly surfaced as to who was responsible. Osama bin Laden, the leader of Al Qaeda, took responsibility for the World Trade Center and Pentagon attacks in a video discovered in Afghanistan in November 2001.

In spite of Al Qaeda's video message, the rumor persisted that Israeli operatives had carried out the attacks in secret, and that 4,000 Jewish Americans had not come to work at the World Trade Center that day because they had been told in advance of the planned attacks. In order to debunk this particular conspiracy theory, the U.S. State Department released an article on misinformation containing the following statistics:

A total of 2,071 occupants of the World Trade Center died on September 11, among the 2,749 victims of the WTC attacks. According to an article in the October 11, 2001, Wall Street Journal, *roughly 1,700 people had listed the religion of a person missing in the WTC attacks; approximately 10 percent were Jewish. A later article, in the September 5, 2002,* Jewish Week, *states, "based on the list of names, biographical information compiled by the* New York Times, *and information from records at the Medical Examiner's Office, there were at least 400 victims either confirmed or strongly believed to be Jewish." This would be approximately 15 percent of the total victims of the WTC attacks. . . .*

This 10–15 percent estimate of Jewish fatalities tracks closely with the percentage of Jews living in the New York area . . . If 4,000 Jews had not reported for work on September 11, the number of Jewish victims would have been much lower than 10–15 percent.

The anti-Semitism evident in such accusations persists years after the attacks, in spite of media sources from *Scientific American* to PBS's *Nova* to *Popular Mechanics*, which have reviewed the available facts and revealed the impossibilities of an external conspiracy. Only direct confrontation of such conspiracy theories can put to rest the rumors surrounding this American tragedy. The Web site Snopes.com, a resource for debunking urban myths created in 1995, states:

One need only have read newspaper accounts of the thousands of deaths, viewed TV news interviews with the grieving families, and scanned the lists of the dead and missing to know that the terrorist attack on New York City claimed the lives of Christians, Jews, and Muslims; agnostics, atheists, and the non-religious alike. No religion was spared, no denomination singled out. Ordinary people of all nationalities suffered.

the creation of a Palestinian state, neither Israel nor the Palestinian Authority has fulfilled the obligations outlined by the Road Map. In 2006, Hamas became the ruling party in the Palestinian parliament, but both Israel and the United States refused to recognize Hamas's rule as legitimate because it was considered a terrorist group. Armed conflicts between Israel and Palestine, and between Israel and the group Hezbollah in Lebanon, further derailed the peace process.

In the late 2000s, U.S.-Israel relations continued to be key to U.S. foreign policy. In a July 2008 survey of 800 American Jews, 78 percent supported a "two-state solution," including the creation of an independent Palestine and recognition of Israel by all Arab nations. Eighty-seven percent of respondents supported the United States' playing an active role in ending the Israeli-Palestinian conflict.

JEWISH AMERICANS IN POLITICS

The most well-known Jewish Americans in politics in the 1980s were newly elected senators Carl Levin, Arlen Specter, and Joe Lieberman, each of whom already had long and distinguished careers in 2009. Elected in 1979, Carl Levin is the longest-serving senator ever to come from Michigan. Republican turned Democrat Arlen Specter is the influential senator from Pennsylvania, the 16th most senior member of the Senate in 2010.

Joe Lieberman, an Orthodox Jew from Connecticut, was elected to the U.S. Senate in 1988. As Al Gore's running mate for the Democrats in 2000, he was the first Jewish candidate on a major party's presidential ticket. In 2008, he won reelection as an Independent, though liberal on domestic issues such as abortion and gay rights and conservative on foreign policy concerns such as the Iraq War. Senator Lieberman has been a strong supporter of Israel. All three have risen to leadership positions in the Senate.

Michael Bloomberg, who made his fortune in the information industry, expanded his success into the political arena, taking office as the mayor of New York City in 2002. Born in Boston and educated at Johns Hopkins and Harvard, his business sense made him a success in the world of systems development. When he ran for mayor, he used his personal wealth to finance his campaign, arguing that New York needed a mayor with proven business sense after the economic downturn that followed 9/11. His policies as mayor were very popular, particularly in the area of education reform, and he was reelected by a large margin in 2005. In 2009, he again financed his successful reelection campaign, this time winning by a close margin.

Ben Bernanke became chairman of the Federal Reserve in 2006, and his position took on new importance during the sub-prime lending crisis of 2008. During 2002–06, the U.S. housing market grew at an unprecedented rate, especially in urban areas. House values rose by double digits in many markets, and lenders offered no-deposit, low-introductory-interest (sub-prime)

Ruth Bader Ginsberg

Ruth Bader Ginsberg is the first Jewish female (and only the second female) Supreme Court justice. Ginsberg's legal career includes many notable accomplishments. She began her legal studies at Harvard. She was in her second year of classwork when her husband Martin, a third-year law student, was diagnosed with cancer. She took notes in his third-year classes and supported him throughout the treatment process; he recovered and managed to graduate with the rest of his Harvard class. The Ginsbergs then moved to New York, where Martin began work as an associate in a New York law firm. Ruth transferred to Columbia Law School, where she finished her degree work. She was the first woman to be selected for both the Columbia and Harvard law reviews, an indication of her future success. After completing her law coursework at Columbia, she founded the first law journal devoted to women's rights issues, the *Women's Rights Law Reporter*. After teaching at Rutgers Law for nine years, she returned to Columbia in 1972, where she became the first female law professor hired with tenure. In 1980, President Jimmy Carter appointed her a federal appeals judge in the Washington, D.C., circuit court. She served until 1993, when she was appointed to the Supreme Court.

At her nomination ceremony, Ginsberg described the obstacles she faced at the beginning of her law career: "I had three strikes against me. I was Jewish, I was a woman, and I was a mother. So if a door would have been open a crack in either of the first two cases, the third one was too much." She is not an observant Jew, in part because of bouts with sexism in her adolescence. Her mother died the day before her high school graduation, and in a 2004 interview, she reflected: "When my mother died, the house was *filled* with women, but only men could participate in the minyan . . . That time was not a good one for me in terms of organized religion." Yet there is a *mezuzah* (a piece of parchment inscribed with verses from the Torah, often contained in a decorative case) mounted outside her office door in the Supreme Court chambers, and her children and grandchildren have been educated in the Jewish tradition. "The Jews love learning, they're the people of the book. So it's a heritage to be proud of." In her legal decisions, she is generally considered a liberal justice, a champion of women's rights and of civil liberties. Her contributions to the Court will likely shape the nation's legal history for decades to come.

Justice Ruth Bader Ginsberg joined the Supreme Court in 1993.

housing loans to people who would not otherwise have been able to afford to purchase a house. After an initial loan period, when the introductory interest rates adjusted back to normal rates, many people could no longer make their mortgage payments. Wave after wave of property foreclosures followed, and the housing bubble popped in 2008. Property values began to stagnate, and a glut of houses filled the market. Several major banks and international corporations faced bankruptcy and credit issues due to bad debts from these sub-prime loans. Bernanke, working with Treasury Secretary Henry Paulson, coauthored a controversial $700 billion bailout plan that passed into law in October 2008.

JEWISH AMERICANS IN BUSINESS

Jewish Americans, like any other group of Americans, represented some of the most positive and some of the most negative values of the late 20th century. A few notorious businessmen and women became symbols for the excesses of the "me generation" of the 1980s, while the vast number of Jews conducted their business in an ethical fashion. Perhaps no one personified the glorification of the self in the 1980s more than Leona Helmsley, daughter of a Polish-Jewish immigrant hatmaker who later became a billionaire hotel operator and real estate investor. She was indicted for tax evasion, filing false personal, corporate, and partnership tax returns.

Other pivotal figures of the 1980s were Ivan Boesky and Michael Milken, both of whom were models for the character of Gordon Gekko in the 1987 Oliver Stone movie *Wall Street*. Gekko's famous line, "Greed is good," harkened back to Ivan Boesky's comment, "I think greed is healthy. You can be greedy and still feel good about yourself." Boesky was a multimillion-dollar financier who bet on corporate takeovers; but according to Securities and Exchange Commission investigations, these "bets" were based on tips from insiders. As part of his efforts to reduce his prison sentence, Boesky informed on several of his insider contacts, the most well known of whom was Michael Milken. Milken during the 1980s was called the "junk bond king," the man who developed the market for so-called junk bonds. Boesky revealed that Milken had been an insider trader and had committed fraud. Subsequently, Milken was indicted on 98 counts of racketeering, fraud, and tax evasion. He eventually served just 22 months in prison. After release from prison, Milken devoted his life to charitable causes and largely recovered his reputation.

In the economic boom years of the 1990s, the rising importance of information technologies to the U.S. economy brought other Jewish Americans in business into the limelight. Larry Ellison, founder of Oracle Corporation, was among those who profited the most from growth in the information industry. His company, which created relational databases and business intelligence software, gave him a net worth that rose as high as $18 billion. Michael Dell, founder of the Dell Corporation, was best known for his work with personal computers. Dell was the most successful PC company in the world and made its founder a wealthy man, with a net worth that reached more than $17 billion. Both men appeared regularly on the annual *Forbes* list of the world's richest people, and were also well known for the work of their charitable foundations.

JEWISH AMERICANS IN SPORTS, CULTURE, AND ENTERTAINMENT

Jewish-American athletes continued to compete successfully on the world stage, most notably in recent Olympic games. In 1996, gymnast Kerri Strug became a heroine for a generation of girls when she competed in the vault exercise. She completed her final vault in spite of multiple torn ligaments so that the U.S. women's team could take home the first-ever U.S. team Gold medal. In 2002, figure skater Sarah Hughes won Gold after landing seven triple jumps in her long-program skate. In 2008, 41-year-old mother Dara Torres made international headlines when she made the U.S. Olympic swim team in two events, the 50-meter and 100-meter freestyle. As the oldest female swimmer in Olympic history, she inspired women across the country when she brought home two Silver medals, one in the 50-meter and one in the 4x100 relay.

In the world of television, prominent Jewish personalities of recent years have included Barbara Walters, Gilda Radner, and Jerry Seinfeld. Barbara Walters did not have a religious upbringing, despite her parents being Jewish, and she did not emphasize her roots. Gilda Radner, famous for her appearances on *Saturday Night Live*, died of ovarian cancer at age 42 in 1989. Her early death spurred ovarian cancer awareness, especially focusing on high risk women—Ashkenazi (European) Jews.

Jerry Seinfeld, raised in a Jewish household, created *Seinfeld*, a semi-autobiographical television show that became a hit of the late 1980s and early 1990s. Although rarely mentioning Jewishness in his shows, he created characters who were stereotypically Jewish mothers, both in his character's mother and George Costanza's mother. The comic devices he used harkened back to the rich tradition of Jewish Catskill Mountains comedians of previous decades.

Two Jewish film icons of the late 20th century were Woody Allen and Steven Spielberg, both unabashedly Jewish emissaries in their artistic work. Woody Allen was particularly prolific in the 1980s, with such films as *Hannah and Her Sisters*, the recipient of seven Academy Award nominations and winner of the Oscar for Best Writing. In 1986, he received the Golden Globe for Best Screenplay for *The Purple Rose of Cairo* (rated by *Time* magazine as one of the 100 best films ever made). *Radio Days* (1987) depicted the stories of his Jewish-American youth in which the members of his family each relied upon a favorite radio show to allow them to escape the boredom of their own lives. In his darker-than-usual movie *Crimes and Misdemeanors* (1989), his

Seinfeld

Jerry Seinfeld, a stand-up comedian, made television history with his wildly popular sitcom *Seinfeld*, which aired on NBC from 1989 to 1998. In 2002, *TV Guide* named the series the "greatest television program of all time." Its Upper West Side setting and Jewish humor created a backdrop for comedic must-see television for almost a decade. *Seinfeld* was pitched to the networks as a "show about nothing." While Jerry Seinfeld was the lead writer as well as the series' star, Jewish writer Larry David was also a key part of the show's success. The show centered on the daily social lives of four single New Yorkers, played by Seinfeld, Julia Louis-Dreyfus, Michael Richards, and Jason Alexander. Episodes mingled footage of Seinfeld doing a nightclub stand-up routine with the events that supposedly inspired the evening's act. Secondary characters added bizarre humor and plot complications, and guest appearances by celebrities such as David Letterman and Candice Bergen were frequent.

Several features of the series led to its popular success, including unique language, multiple converging plotlines, and use of implausible coincidences. Made-up words and catchphrases from the show entered commonplace usage across the United States, including "Yada yada yada," "re-gifter," and "close talker." Show writers called this coined phrasing "Seinlanguage," and Jerry Seinfeld published a book by that title in 1993. A central rule of the series for the writers in working with the central characters was "no hugging, no learning." Unlike many sitcoms, the characters were not written to gain audience sympathy as they stumbled from outrageous situation to situation without gaining any moral insight.

During its run, *Seinfeld* was rarely discussed in terms of its Jewishness. As series star Jason Alexander remembers, "between Larry and Jerry and their writing staff, and the network guys, it just became a Jewish show . . . they would tell you, if anything, it's a New York show." But since the show's end, many scholars of religious studies and popular culture have critiqued the show's portrayal of Judaism and New York Jewish culture. With humor derived from gender relations, generation gaps, and Jewish cultural archetypes such as the *schlemiel* (fool), *Seinfeld* continues its cultural influence after a decade of syndication.

main protagonist, Judah Rosenthal (played by Martin Landau), turned to his long-forgotten Judaism to reconcile his belief that God was actually watching him after all. Again Allen was nominated for Best Director.

Another prodigious film director and screenwriter doing some of his most important work in the 1980s was Steven Spielberg, named by *Life* magazine as the most influential person of his generation. During this decade, he directed *Raiders of the Lost Ark, E.T. The Extra-Terrestrial* (nominated for Academy

Among the continuing development of memorials to the Holocaust in the late 20th century were the six glass and steel towers of Boston's New England Holocaust Memorial (1995), which was designed by architect Stanley Saitowitz.

Awards for Best Director and Best Picture), and *The Color Purple* (nominated for Best Picture). He also released *Indiana Jones and the Last Crusade.*

Spielberg's biopic about Oskar Schindler, *Schindler's List,* won seven Oscars in 1994, including Best Picture. The film tells the story of a member of the Nazi Party who went from employing Jewish slave labor in his weapons factory to saving the lives of over 1,200 Jews. It was because of this film that Spielberg created The Shoah, a project wherein 50,000 Holocaust victims have been interviewed about their experiences. These interviews are available for research at seven universities around the country.

JEWISH AMERICANS IN LITERATURE

Three particularly well-known Jewish playwrights produced plays in the late 20th century that either had specifically Jewish themes, or wherein Judaism was an important motif of the work: Neil Simon, David Mamet, and Wendy Wasserstein.

Neil Simon returned again and again to explain the closely autobiographical experiences of what it was like to grow up as a Jew in 20th-century America. In the 1980s, Simon presented his "Eugene Trilogy," three plays that focused on the coming-of-age of Eugene Morris, a Russian-Jewish teenager. David Mamet's most famous plays were written in the 1980s, including *Glengarry Glen Ross* and *Speed-the-Plow*, for which he received Tony nominations. His specifically Jewish-themed works, however, date from the 1990s (*The Old Religion*) and 2000s (*Five Cities of Refuge: Weekly Reflections on Genesis, Exodus, Leviticus, Numbers and Deuteronomy*, and *The Wicked Son*).

Wendy Wasserstein's Jewish themes were muted but nonetheless a part of her heritage (a grandfather was a famous Jewish-Polish playwright). Her plays were about how a young Jewish woman, or any career-minded woman, dealt with the treacherous path and often ambiguous messages of the women's liberation movement. Her most famous work, *The Heidi Chronicles*, written in 1988, received the Pulitzer Prize for Drama and the Tony Award for Best Play.

In the early 1990s, the sprawling two-part play *Angels in America: A Gay Fantasia on National Themes* by Tony Kushner focused in part on the struggle for contemporary Jewish identity in the face of the AIDS epidemic. It combined historical Jewish figures such as Ethel Rosenberg and Roy Cohn with fictional characters seeking answers to questions of life, belief, and death. Part One, *Millennium Approaches*, was first performed in 1990; the second part, *Perestroika*, premiered in 1992. Both parts won Tony Awards for Best Play. A television miniseries of the play was produced by HBO Films in 2003, and an opera version premiered in 2004 in Paris.

Of particular renown among Jewish-American writers in the late 20th century were Saul Bellow, Philip Roth, and Bernard Malamud. Each of these writers in their own styles grappled with assimilation of Jews into 20th-century American life. Saul Bellow was of Russian-Jewish origin; he won the Pulitzer Prize in 1975, the Nobel Prize for Literature in 1976, and the National Medal of Arts in 1988.

He often used Jewish characters in Chicago to represent the alienated man of modern America and how he learns to exist in a culture of materialism and aloneness. Frequently, though, he was optimistic about an individual's ability to transcend his own limitations and, at the least, to reach self-awareness.

Unfortunately, Bellow represented to some the mouthpiece of controversies between Jews and blacks during the 1980s. His famous comment about people of color in *The New Yorker*—"Who is the Tolstoy of Zulus? The Proust of the Papuans?"—thrust him into the position of being a proponent of white Western culture.

Bellow's friend and contemporary, Philip Roth, provoked even more debate about Jewishness and acculturation than either Bellow or Malamud. In the 1980s, he continued his ongoing tirade against Jewishness and the religious requirements of special foods (keeping kosher), particular holidays, and the necessity to marry Jewish to carry on the traditions. He created his alter ego, Nathan Zuckerman, in the four novels of that period, *The Ghost Writer, Zuckerman Unbound, The Anatomy Lesson,* and *The Prague Orgy.* As Zuckerman rejected his Jewish heritage, the traditions of the Old World, and the mores of his parents, he learned that freedom from those strictures for secular Jews also brought a sense of alienation and emptiness.

Roth went on to win the Pulitzer Prize for Fiction for his novel *American Pastoral* in 1998. The story focuses on a Jewish-American businessman from New Jersey, Seymour Levov, whose life is turned upside down by the social upheaval of the 1960s. Roth's 2004 work *The Plot Against America* imagines an alternate history in which Charles Lindbergh became president of the United States in 1940, resulting in national anti-Semitism.

Another first-generation Jewish American struggling to determine Jewish identity in a Christian world, Bernard Malamud was the son of Russian-Jewish immigrants. His most famous novel, *The Natural,* was made into a film in 1984 starring Robert Redford.

Chaim Potok, author of The Chosen, *signing books in 1985.*

Other notable Jewish novelists writing in the late 20th century were Joseph Brodsky, Chaim Potok, Leon Uris, and Cynthia Ozick. Their works were informed by their Jewish backgrounds. Joseph Brodsky won the Nobel Prize in Literature in 1987 and became the Poet Laureate of the United States in 1991–92. He was born in Russia and wrote his poems and essays in Russian, but he was a U.S. citizen. After he received the Nobel Prize an interviewer said, "You are an American citizen who is receiving the prize for Russian-language poetry. Who are you, an American or a Russian?" Brodsky replied, "I am Jewish—a Russian poet and an English essayist."

Chaim Potok was predominantly known for his Jewish-themed books in which protagonists who were mainly American-born Orthodox Jews grappled with their Jewishness in a modern America. The struggle was often between father and son as in his most famous novel, *The Chosen,* which came out in 1967. It was popularized by the film version in 1981. The question of maintaining religion and yet adapting to personal and societal demands was the theme of many of his other books. Other works include: *The Book of Lights, Davita's Harp,* and *Theo Tboiasse.*

In the 1980s, Leon Uris, the author of the groundbreaking 1958 novel *Exodus,* continued his Jewish-based themes with *The Haj,* a novel about a Palestinian Arab family and what occurred in their homeland from the 1920s to the 1950s. Cynthia Ozick's essays and short stories were also often about Jewish-American life. In 1986, she received the Rea Award for the Short Story. She published extensively in the 1980s, including *The Shawl* in 1989.

The 2000s were a time of success and critical recognition for several new Jewish-American literary figures, including Jonathan Safran Foer. Foer's debut novel, *Everything is Illuminated,* burst onto best-seller lists in 2002. It used a variety of literary devices including multiple simultaneous story lines, time shifting, and semi-autobiography. Foer's novel details a trip to the Ukraine to search for a woman named Augustine who saved his grandfather's life during the Nazi invasion. The novel was a success and was turned into a film in 2005.

Two of the most prominent Jewish faces in contemporary literary criticism, Harold Bloom and Stephen Greenblatt, published important scholarly and popular works during the 1990s and 2000s. In 1994, Bloom's *The Western Canon* opened a new chapter in the culture wars when he provided a list of meritorious works and insisted that reading should be done for aesthetic rather than political reasons.

That work's popularity and the ensuing controversy over the definition of a literary canon spurred Bloom to write further works for general audiences, including *Shakespeare: The Invention of the Human* (1998) and *How to Read and Why* (2000). Greenblatt coined the term *new historicism* to apply to the techniques of considering literature in its historical context and published *Practicing New Historicism* in 2000. He also added to the Shakespearean canon with his biography *Will in the World* (2004), which stayed on the *New York Times* best-seller list for nine weeks.

JEWISH AMERICANS IN MUSIC AND FINE ART

In the world of music, in 2007, the Klezmatics became the first Jewish band to win a Grammy Award. They won for their album *Wonder Wheel,* which

The Grammy Award–winning Jewish band the Klezmatics in 2006.

includes previously unsung Woody Guthrie lyrics set to klezmer music.

The field of Jewish visual arts received a West Coast boost when the Contemporary Jewish Museum of San Francisco opened a new facility in June 2008, designed by prominent architect Daniel Libeskind. While the Jewish Museum in New York had long been a home for Jewish arts across history, the Contemporary Jewish Museum focused on art created since around 1950, including spaces for performance art as well as traditional visual art forms such as painting and sculpture. Prominent Jewish artists from this time period include *New Yorker* cartoonist William Steig, feminist artist Judy Chicago, puppeteer Alex Kahn, and illustrator Mark Podwal.

CONCLUSION

In 2006, Jewish Americans made up 2.2 percent of the U.S. population. They have seen numerous changes in lifestyle and culture in recent decades, many of which were brought on by assimilation and intermarriage. However, new arrivals from Jewish communities throughout the world, but especially from the former Soviet Union, have changed the nature of the American Jewish community in other ways. New immigrants have sometimes even strengthened the practice of various forms of the Jewish faith in their communities. Jewish Americans were also highly visible in popular culture and the arts in the late 20th century. Despite having to battle discrimination through much of their history in the United States, Jewish Americans have thrived in America and have long been an important part of American culture and society.

Myrna A. Hant
UCLA Center for the Study of Women
Heather A. Beasley
University of Colorado

Further Reading

Address, Richard F., with Andrew Rosencranz. *To Honor and Respect: A Program and Resource Guide for Congregations on Sacred Aging.* New York: Union for Reform Judaism Press, 2005.

Bial, Henry. *Acting Jewish: Negotiating Ethnicity on the American Stage and Screen.* Ann Arbor, MI: University of Michigan Press, 2005.

Blair, Sara and Jonathan Freedman, eds. *Jewish in America.* Ann Arbor, MI: University of Michigan Press, 2004.

Bloom, Lisa. *Jewish Identities in American Feminist Art: Ghosts of Ethnicity.* New York: Routledge, 2006.

Cohen, Steven M. *American Assimilation or Jewish Revival?* Bloomington, IN: Indiana University Press, 1988.

Dan, Joseph. *Kabbalah: A Very Short Introduction.* London: Oxford University Press, 2006.

Danzger, M. Herbert. *Returning to Tradition.* New Haven, CT: Yale University Press, 1989.

Davidson, Lynn. *Tradition in a Rootless World.* Berkeley, CA: University of California Press, 1991.

Dershowitz, Alan M. *The Vanishing American Jew.* New York: Simon and Schuster, 1998.

Diner, Hasia R. *The Jews of the United States.* Berkeley, CA: University of California Press, 2004.

Falk, Avner. *Anti-Semitism: A History and Psychoanalysis of Contemporary Hatred.* Westport, CT: Praeger, 2008.

Friedman, M., M. Kane, and M. Stollman. *URJ Young Men's Project: Young Men and their Presence in the Reform Movement.* A Project of the Union for Reform Judaism Youth Division and the North American Federation of Temple Brotherhoods, 2005.

Gabler, Neal, Frank Rich, and Joyce Antler. *Television's Changing Image of American Jews.* New York: The American Jewish Committee, 2000.

Greenberg, Blu. *On Women and Judaism: A View From Tradition.* Philadelphia, PA: Jewish Publication Society of America, 1998.

Greenberg, Richard H. *Pathways: Jews Who Return.* Northvale, NJ: Jason Aronson Inc., 1997.

Greenspoon, Leonard J. and Ronald A. Simkins, eds. *American Judaism in Popular Culture.* Omaha, NE: Creighton University Press, 2006.

"Identifying Misinformation: The 4,000 Jews Rumor." U.S. State Department, 2005. Available online, URL: http://usinfo.state.gov/media/Archive/2005/Jan/14-260933.html. Accessed October 2008.

"J Street Poll of American Jews." Conducted June 29–July 3, 2008. Available online, URL: http://www.jstreet.org/page/media-advisory-new-survey-american-jewish-community. Accessed October 2009.

Kaplan, Dana Evan. *The Cambridge Companion to American Judaism.* London: Cambridge University Press, 2005.

Mikkelson, Barbara and David. "Absent without Leave." Available online, URL: http://www.snopes.com/rumors/israel.asp. Accessed October 2008.

National Jewish Population Survey, 2000–2001. United Jewish Communities, 2003.

Ochs, Vanessa L. *Words on Fire.* Boulder, CO: Westview Press, 1999.

Pogrebin, Abigail. *Stars of David: Prominent Jews Talk about Being Jewish.* New York: Broadway Books, 2005.

Prell, Riv-Ellen. *Fighting to Become Americans.* Boston, MA: Beacon Press, 1999.

Raphael, Marc Lee, ed. *The Columbia History of Jews and Judaism in America.* New York: Columbia University Press, 2008.

Sarna, Jonathan D. *American Judaism: A History.* New Haven, CT: Yale University Press, 2004.

Schick, Marvin. "A Census of Jewish Day Schools in the United States: 2003–2004." New York: AVI CHAI Foundation, 2005.

Ukeles, Jacob B., et al. "Young Jewish Adults in the United States Today." American Jewish Committee, 2006.

"U.S. Religious Landscape Survey." Pew Forum on Religion and Public Life, 2007. Available online, URL: http://religions.pewforum.org. Accessed October 2009.

Wenger, Beth S. *The Jewish Americans.* New York: Doubleday, 2007.

Wertheimer, Jack, ed. *Imagining the American Jewish Community.* Waltham, MA: Brandeis University Press, 2007.

American Jewish Committee: An organization founded in 1906 with the original intent of stopping harsh pogroms occurring in Russia.

American Jewish Congress: A consortium of Jewish American leaders whose goal is to protect and promote Jewish interests.

anti-semitic: A term meaning "against Jews" that was coined by German Wilhelm Marr in a pamphlet titled, *The Victory of Germandom over Jewry* (1879).

Anti-Defamation League: An organization founded in 1913 following the lynching of Leo Frank, a 31-year-old Jew who was wrongfully accused of having murdered a 13-year-old girl.

Ashkenazim: Jews descended from areas along the Rhine River in Germany.

bar mitzvah: A ceremony honoring a 13-year-old Jewish boy's passage into adulthood.

Bergson Group: The most vocal organization to denounce the plight of Jews in Europe during World War II, the group demanded that a specialized Jewish fighting force should enter the war's actions with the sole intent of rescuing Jews from further persecution.

B'nai Brith: The first Jewish fraternal organization.

blood libel: A centuries-old anti-Semitic myth that claimed that Jews would kidnap prominent people, murder them, and then use their blood in the creation of matzo.

brichah: The process by which post-Holocaust European Jews relocated to Palestine after World War II.

chavurot: Small groups of friends.

Conservative Judaism: A sect of Judaism originating in the United States that differed from Orthodox Judaism in the formality by which people of Jewish faith adhered to commandments in religious texts.

converso: Spanish term for Jews that underwent conversion to Roman Catholicism during the era of the Inquisition in Spain.

Damascus Affair: An incident in 840 in which many Syrian Jews were arrested after being accused of participating in blood libel rituals.

Ezrat Orechun: The first Jewish charitable organization in the United States.

gentile: A non-Jew.

hacham: A rabbi.

Hadassah: The official women's Zionist movement of America, today boasting over 270,000 members.

halakhic: According to Jewish law.

Hanukkah: An eight-day Jewish holiday, also known as the Festival of Lights, commemorating the rededication of the Holy Temple in Jerusalem in the 2nd century B.C.E.

Hasidism: A sect of Judaism that stresses complete and total adherence to Jewish religious texts.

havurah: A fellowship.

hazzan: A Jewish vocal musician who traditionally led Jewish congregations in singing hymns.

Hebrew: The official language of Judaism.

Holocaust: In general, a holocaust means the death of a large number of people, but the term is more often used to refer to the systematic murder of six million Jews during the reign of Nazi Germany.

Immigration Act of 1924: U.S. legislation that nearly halted the wave of Jewish immigration into the United States that had occurred between 1910 and 1920.

Israel's Herold: The first Jewish weekly newspaper.

"Jew Bill" of 1826: A piece of legislation in Maryland that allowed Jews to hold office, practice law, and become officers in the Maryland state militia.

Jewish Question: A centuries-old concept referring to the struggle of Jews to establish equality or found a national homeland.

Jewish Welfare Board: An organization founded in 1917 following the U.S. declaration of war on Germany that sought to train rabbis and other Jewish clergymen for military service.

Jewishness: A milder way of following the Jewish faith that stressed assimilating into American culture, rather than strictly adhering to Jewish religious principles.

Judeo-Christian Tradition: A phrase that promotes commonality and cooperation between followers of Judaism and Christianity. It was instrumental in enabling Jewish and Christian soldiers to fight alongside one another without the distraction of religious conflict.

Kaballah: A set of teachings focusing on God's relationship with mankind.

kaddish: Term that traditionally refers to a prayer that is given to mourn the loss of a loved one.

Kahal Kadosh Beth Elohim: A synagogue that is the second-oldest Jewish place of worship in the United States.

kehillah: A community.

kiddush: A Jewish ritual where a blessing is recited with wine or grape juice.

kibbutz: Term for the planned communities in Israel that are usually fortified against attack and that practice communal socialism.

kosher: Food that has been prepared according to Jewish dietary law.

Kristallnacht: German word referring to anti-Jewish attacks in Germany on November 9 and 10, 1938, literally "night of the broken glass," during which the glass fronts of thousands of Jewish-owned business were broken, Jews were beaten, and some 90 to 100 were killed in mob actions.

Landsmanschaften: A local society that often tried to offer assistance and aid to those in need.

Marrano: A Jew forcibly required to conform to the principles of Christianity, but who would still adhere to the tenets of Judaism under secrecy.

mechitza: A partition designed to separate men and women in public settings.

mennorah: A seven-branched candelabrum that is used to symbolize the burning bush that was seen by Moses.

mikveh: A ritualistic bath similar to what is used in Christian baptism rituals that is designed to immerse oneself in Judaism.

Mitzvot: A word referring to over 600 commandments or rules written in Jewish law.

National Council of Jewish Women: An organization founded in 1893 to assist newly-arrived Jewish immigrants in the assimilation process.

Nationality Act of 1965: An act of Congress that all but abolished the quota systems of 1924, allowing increased freedom for emigrating Jews to enter the United States.

Naturalization Act of 1740: An act eliminating the need for a Christian oath to obtain citizenship in British American colonies, greatly increasing the ease with which Jews could become citizens.

Orthodox Judaism: A sect of Judaism that promoted strict adherence to the laws of Torah and denied most efforts of liberal interpretation of the faith's religious texts.

Pale of Settlement: A region of Russia where Jews were allowed to establish permanent residence.

Paper Wall: Phrase referring to the red tape and bureaucratic resistance that occurred when American Jews concerned about their persecuted brethren in Europe sought and failed to bring them to America for safekeeping.

parnas: A president.

pogrom: A riot instigated by a mob hostile to a particular race, ethnicity, or religion.

Protocols of the Learned Elders of Zion: A forged document supported by influential Americans that increased feelings of anti-Semitism in the United States.

Purple Gang: A criminal organization that arose during the Great Depression and was headed by Jewish gangster Abe Bernstein.

Reconstructionist Judaism: A sect of Judaism originating from the teachings of Rabbi Mordecai Kaplan, who advocated that Judaism should be an ever-evolving faith that should change its rules and obligations with society.

Reform Judaism: A movement that sought to challenge traditional Jewish beliefs and doctrines.

rimonim: Finials that adorn the ends of the bars on the scrolls of the Torah.

Rosh Hashanah: Jewish holiday also known as "The Jewish New Year."

Secular Judaism: A sect of Judaism stressing the embrace of Jewish culture but denying the practice of any theistic religion.

Seder: A ritual feast that marks the beginning of the Jewish holiday of Passover.

Sephardi: A Jew originating from the Iberian Peninsula.

sha: Yiddish word similar to the English grunt "sh," meaning "be quiet."

Shabbat: A Jewish day of rest that is observed from sundown on Friday evening until Saturday night.

shalom: Hebrew word meaning peace.

Shearith Israel: The first synagogue to be built in New York City.
shechita: The ritualistic slaughter of mammals in accordance with traditional Jewish laws of diet.

Shoah: Yiddish term for the Holocaust.

1682 Acts of Trade of Navigation: A series of acts applicable to the British American colonies that some used as a means to disrupt Jewish commerce and trade.

spermaceti: A wax originating from sperm whales that made the 18th century Jewish community in Newport, Rhode Island, a financial success.

Star of David: Named after King David of ancient Israel, the Star of David is oftentimes used as a logo of Judaism.

suburbanization: Assimilating into a suburban area after migrating from a city, a process that many Jews underwent after World War II.

Synagogue: A Jewish place of worship.

talit: Prayer shawls.

teffilin: Boxes with parchment worn by observant Jews during prayer.

terefah: Non-kosher meat.

teshuvah: Repentance.

Torah: The Five Books of Moses, or all of Judaism's religious texts.

Touro: A synagogue in Newport, Rhode Island; that was constructed in 1763 and remains in use to this day.

treif: Food that has not been prepared according to Jewish law.

Virginia Statute for Religious Freedom: Legislation written by Thomas Jefferson that granted myriad rights to people regardless of religion persuasion. It was seen as a declaration of freedom by Jewish communities in Virginia.

Yeshiva: Rabbinical school.

Yiddish: A Jewish language that differs from Hebrew in its level of formality.

Yiddish Art Theatre: A theater founded in 1918 that featured Jewish actors and entertainers.

Yishuv: Hebrew word for Jews living in Palestine during the time of British administration.

Yom Kippur: Jewish holiday also known as "The Day of Atonement."

zakhor: To remember something.

Zionism: A political movement whose goal is to establish a Jewish homeland.

INDEX

Index note: page references in *italics* indicate figures or graphs: page references in **bold** indicate main discussion.

A
Abbas, Mahmoud 183
Abramowitz, Rachel 149
Abzug, Bella 142–143, 177
Academy Awards 87, 188
acculturation. *See* assimilation
Act for Religious Freedom 29
activists 140
   See also Civil Rights Movement
Acts of Trade and Navigation (1682) 10
Adams, John 36
Adventures of Augie March, The (Bellow) 124
African Americans
  Civil Rights Movement 108, 141
  colonial era viii
  discrimination x, xii
  military service 42, 103
  popular music 150
  soldiers 108
  See also slavery
AIDS epidemic 191
Air force. *See* military service

Holiday, Billie 84
Holland
 Dutch colonies 3–4
 Jews in 1, 3, **5**, 6, 9
Hollywood (CA)
 American Jews and 85, **87–88**
 blacklist 126
 The Day of the Locust (West) 87
 filmmakers move to 66
 moguls *88*, 91
 patriotic films 103
Holman, Nat 65
Holocaust
 American Jews and **99**, 113
 confirmation of 96, 99
 death camps 102, 108
 Diary of Anne Frank (film) and 136, 149
 Franklin D. Roosevelt and 105, *106*
 "Never Again" 96, 146
 Night (Wiesel) 136, 137
 Quota system (1924) 82, 92
 Schindler's List and 190
 The Shoah and 190
 Soviet Jews and 148
 survivors 110, 122, 130, 135
 See also Nazi Germany
Holocaust Memorial 190
Holy Land. *See* Israel; Palestine
hometown societies 82
Honky Tonk 85
horse racing 63, 90
Houdini, Harry 66, *66*
House Un-American Activities Committee
  123
How to Read and Why (Bloom) 193
Hughes, Howard 87
Hughes, Sarah 188
Hungarian Satmars 138
"Hymies" 180
"Hymietown" 181

I
"I Got Rhythm" (Gershwin and Gershwin) 84
immigration
 1820-1859 33–34
 1900-1920 ix, 57–58, 62, 65
 1920-1939 75

North Carolina 29–30
Northwest Ordinance 29
Nostra Aetate 137
Nuremburg 102
Nutter, McClennen, and Fish 68

O

occupations
    garment workers xi, xii, 48, 49, 82, 91, 108
    retail merchants 26, 58, 91, 103, 108
    white collar professionals xiii, 58, 62, 95, 108, 173, 175, 186
Oglethorpe, James 15, 16–17
Old Religion, The 191
Oral Law 161, 181
Orbach, William 148
Orechun, Ezrat 32
Organization for Rehabilitation through Training (ORT) 173
Orthodox Judaism 79, 122
    1960s 140
    1970s 155
    Ba'al Teshuva movement 162, 174
    The Chosen (Potok) 193
    Herman Wouk 123
    immigrants 3, 112, 122
    intermarriage 177
    Israel and 165, 180
    National Council of Synagogue Youth 140
    practices of 172
    rabbis march on D.C. 97–98
    yeshiva 146
    Yeshiva University 122
Out of the Shadows (Cohen) 48
Ozick, Cynthia 159, 192

P

Pale of Settlement 49
Palestine 62, 83, 96, 110, 114
    See also Israel; Zionism
Palestine Liberation Organization (PLO) 181, 182
    "Declaration of Principles" 183
Palestinians 96, 110, 180, 182, *182*
"Paper wall" 99
Paramount Studios 66, 87
Paris Peace Conference 70
Parks, Rosa 143
Passenger Traffic of Railways, The (Weyl) 67
Passing of the Great Race, The (Grant) 58

Produced by Golson Media
President and Editor   J. Geoffrey Golson
Layout Editors   Oona Patrick, Mary Jo Scibetta
Author Manager   Susan Moskowitz
Consulting Editor   Michael Feldberg
Copyeditor   Barbara Paris
Proofreader   Mary Le Rouge
Indexer   J S Editorial